Immersive Office 365

Bringing Mixed Reality and HoloLens
into the Digital Workplace

Alexander Meijers

Apress®

Immersive Office 365: Bringing Mixed Reality and HoloLens into the Digital Workplace

Alexander Meijers
RIJSWIJK, The Netherlands

ISBN-13 (pbk): 978-1-4842-5844-6
https://doi.org/10.1007/978-1-4842-5845-3

ISBN-13 (electronic): 978-1-4842-5845-3

Managing Director, Apress Media LLC: Welmoed Spahr
Acquisitions Editor: Jonathan Gennick
Development Editor: Laura Berendson
Coordinating Editor: Jill Balzano

Cover image designed by Freepik (www.freepik.com)

Distributed to the book trade worldwide by Springer Science+Business Media New York, 233 Spring Street, 6th Floor, New York, NY 10013. Phone 1-800-SPRINGER, fax (201) 348-4505, e-mail orders-ny@springer-sbm.com, or visit www.springeronline.com. Apress Media, LLC is a California LLC and the sole member (owner) is Springer Science + Business Media Finance Inc (SSBM Finance Inc). SSBM Finance Inc is a **Delaware** corporation.

For information on translations, please e-mail booktranslations@springernature.com; for reprint, paperback, or audio rights, please e-mail bookpermissions@springernature.com.

Apress titles may be purchased in bulk for academic, corporate, or promotional use. eBook versions and licenses are also available for most titles. For more information, reference our Print and eBook Bulk Sales web page at www.apress.com/bulk-sales.

Any source code or other supplementary material referenced by the author in this book is available to readers on GitHub via the book's product page, located at www.apress.com/9781484258446. For more detailed information, please visit www.apress.com/source-code.

Printed on acid-free paper

Innovation allows us to explore and uncover new ways of doing things. Using the latest technologies like emerging experiences and Microsoft products and services will bridge the gap between mixed reality and Office 365, allowing the future office workspace to innovate.

Table of Contents

About the Author

Alexander Meijers is a professional who inspires, motivates and support others and help them to innovate. His goal is to help organizations achieve more by creating, improving and working smarter. This with the aim of shortening business processes and improving the environment for employees. As a Global XR Tech lead and Microsoft Windows MVP for Mixed Reality, working for Avanade, he understands business issues and translate them into logical solutions using technology. Additionally, he supports companies in applying emerging experiences during their journey in digital transition. He works with technologies such as Virtual, Augmented and Mixed Reality in combination with cloud services like the Mixed Reality services and Azure Digital Twins from the Microsoft Azure platform, Office 365 and Dynamics 365. His primary focus is in manufacturing, utilities and engineering & construction sector. However, he certainly does not stay away from other sectors. He engages in speaking, blogging, and is an organizer of local and global events such as the Mixed Reality User Group in the Netherlands and globally the Global XR Talks and Global XR Bootcamp both part of the GlobalXR.Community.

About the Technical Reviewer

**Jimmy Engstrom** wrote his first line of code when he was 7 years old, and since that day it has been his greatest passion. It is a passion that has made him the developer he is today and has taken him around the world, spreading his knowledge. It has given him awards such as a place in the top ten best developers in Sweden, seven Microsoft MVP awards in Windows development, not to mention becoming Geek of the year. When he is not out spreading his knowledge, he is working as a web developer, trying out the latest tech, or reading up on the latest framework. Jimmy also runs his own company called Azm Dev with his wife, where they focus on "future tech" such as Blazor and holographic computing, but also teaching UX and presentation skills. He is the cohost of a podcast called *Coding After Work* and also a Twitch channel with the same name.

A big thank you to my wife, Jessica, who has been picking up my slack while reviewing this book.

Love you!

Acknowledgments

I want to thank first my family for supporting me during writing my first book ever. They have given me the time and space to start writing on such a new subject. Thank you, my love Tessa, and my children Evy, Quinn, Owen, and Colin for being so patient with me.

I'm privileged, honored, and humbled to be a Windows Developer MVP for Mixed Reality. Being an MVP has brought me an incredible group of good friends in the community and at Microsoft; each of them has been a source of inspiration. Without their knowledge and support, I wouldn't be able to write a book like this.

Introduction

Welcome! You have taken the first step in challenging yourself to combine mixed reality and the Office 365 platform together to create solutions for the office workplace of today. This applies to the developer who wants to expand their knowledge of the Office 365 platform into the world of mixed reality by creating immersive experiences and three-dimensional visualizations using the Microsoft HoloLens 2. This likewise applies to mixed reality developers who are looking for opportunities to extend their repertoire toward serving the everyday business needs of workers in corporate office environments.

Whether you know Office 365 and want to move toward mixed reality, or whether you know the Microsoft HoloLens 2 and want to build functionality around Office 365 data, this book helps you to step up and accomplish your goal of bridging between mixed reality and Office 365.

Imagine being able to sit at your desk and surround yourself with a three-dimensional chart showing your work relationships as mined from your Outlook contact list. Maybe you want to visualize the relationships between users based on their interactions. Or perhaps you want to use mixed reality as an extended platform to maintain your environment by adding users to sites in your SharePoint environment. Reading this book helps you to extend your digital workplace into three-dimensional space. It describes in several chapters the tools and techniques needed to load, save and visualize data from Office 365 on a Microsoft HoloLens 2 device.

Chapter 1: Immersive Experiences

One of the major new ways of interacting with the world around you is using immersive experiences. We explain how immersive experiences can contribute to the modern workplace. We also explain the differences between virtual reality, augmented reality, and mixed reality—specifically, when to use what. All these realities are slowly merging into a new reality called XR. And as we expect in the future, it depends on the person, the situation, and the sort of information you want which type of device is going to be used. One of the most influential mixed reality devices for the last few years has been the Microsoft HoloLens. We go more into detail about the capabilities of the Microsoft HoloLens 2. We finish with some real-life examples how mixed reality can contribute to the modern workplace. We have several use cases defined, which together can create an immersive experience for an end user. The use cases are all part of each other and will be used as a common thread throughout the other parts of the book.

Chapter 2: Controlling Data

This part of the book explains where we get the data from and how we control it. Control means reading from and writing to Office 365 as the modern workplace. Office 365 is the modern digital workplace for workers at a lot of organizations. We explain Office 365 globally and go deeper into the different forms of insights available. A major part of controlling data is knowing which data you can control. This is defined by the authorization levels and roles that users have. We explain thoroughly how this works. The unified graph is a single point of entrance to control data and content from Office 365 and all related systems. It allows you to read data from and read data to. The chapter discusses the benefits of using the unified graph, and the different APIs and tools like the Graph Explorer. To use the APIs, you need to authenticate and get control from your application. We explain how to integrate this in your applications. There are many APIs available for controlling data. We go into the API calls available for insights about social intelligence, users, and their relations to content and insights.

Chapter 3: Environment and Configuration

An important part of developing applications for Microsoft HoloLens is your environment, the tools and how they are configured. In this chapter we go into each of them in detail. We need to use tools like Unity and Visual Studio. We explain the tools, benefits, and how they work together to help you build your app. We discuss how to test and try out your application using the HoloLens emulator and a Microsoft HoloLens 2 device.

Chapter 4: Unity

We help you get started with building and developing HoloLens apps using Unity. This chapter describes the interface of Unity, the different elements of the environment and how you build and deploy an app for Microsoft HoloLens 2. All the important parts are described, how they work, and how you can benefit from them. In your Microsoft HoloLens project, you will be using different elements from Unity. Each of them is explained, how they work and how they act within your application. When you have created an application, you need to build it and deploy it to an emulator or a device. This chapter describes how you do that, which configurations are needed, and what different options you have. It finishes with you running your first app using an emulator or an actual device. It walks you through the different steps to create a first "Hello World!" app using different elements, objects, and scripting.

Chapter 5: Unity Advanced

Now that we have learned to master Unity to develop an application for HoloLens, we get to the more advanced scenarios. In this part we go into threading and the use of dynamic-link libraries (DLLs). One of the most important things to understand with Unity is the fact that the platform is single threaded. For the modern workplace, we need to call different APIs, which could take some time to return their data. Therefor we need to have some means of multithreading to prevent hanging of the application. Unity offers different ways of implementing such techniques. Each of them is explained thoroughly and their disadvantages and advantages are described. You can use external DLLs in your application. This chapter explains how to integrate those DLLs and how to run the application inside Unity using placeholders or precompiler directives. We also explain what the downsides and benefits are of using DLLs.

Chapter 6: HoloLens

In this part we go into more detail of HoloLens-specific elements during development using Unity and Visual Studio. This incorporates tools and available packages, how to interact, the application lifecycle, and debugging. To make your life easier when developing applications for HoloLens, there are several different toolkits, tools, and packages that you can use. We also explain how the Windows Device Portal can help you develop applications. Interacting with the real world using a HoloLens device creates a true immersive experience for an end user. HoloLens offers spatial understanding, implementation of different gestures, gaze, and the use of voice.

Chapter 7: HoloLens Development

In this part we go into more detail of HoloLens development using Unity and Visual Studio. This incorporates the application lifecycle and debugging. One of the most important things to understand when developing HoloLens applications is the application lifecycle. While you can only create scenery (holograms and other) in Unity, you have the ability of coding from Unity after you build you solution. So what happens when you start using things that are not supported in Unity? Or you need to change your assets? What can you do to prevent this or make sure it doesn't bother you? That is what the chapter is all about. Creating applications for HoloLens will not always go as smoothly as you want. We explain how you can debug your application, even when it is running on a Microsoft HoloLens device. We also explain why it is important to watch, for example, your memory usage and the number of framerates of the application. All these things will influence the stability of your app and the battery of the device.

Chapter 8: Visualization

The power of mixed reality allows us to create 3D immersive experiences. This is something that requires a different way of visualizing data, content, and relations. The way you are going to perform actions like adding a user to a specific site depends on this. This part goes into details of data representation, how social networks can be shown, and what kinds of models are available. This chapter contains a global story about how data can be presented in a 3D model to create a true immersive experience for end users. When we talk about immersive experiences with the modern digital workplace, it all comes to the point of correct visualization of data, content, and relationships. One major one is how social networks are presented. Since a social network comes very close to the Office 365 environment, we explain how this works. Depending on the type of data, you will need some way of displaying data in a 3D world. We will discuss some straightforward models for displaying standard structures of the Office 365 environment and some more intelligent models like the force-directed graph, which gives us the ability to visualize data and relationships.

Chapter 9: Building a Social App

This part explains in steps how to build a social app. This social app will incorporate several functionalities, as partly described in the different scenarios in the beginning of the book. We start with the architecture of the application we are going to build. We identify the different building blocks and how they interact with each other. This will allow the reader to understand how to build more complex applications using Unity and Visual Studio. The next step is building in the use of an external DLL that will do asynchronous web requests to the unified graph API to read data from and write data to Office 365.

Chapter 10: Model Implementation

This chapter goes into detail explaining the implementation of the different models in the application. It is a follow-up to the previous part that is all about the models. We explain how to implement different models, transform data, and load it into the model. Several different ways of data presentation and visualization are discussed.

Chapter 11: Interact with the Model

Finally, we implement the interactions with the application based on Microsoft HoloLens 2. We go into more detail on how to create your own global hand menu, use the AppBar as a context menu, and interact with near and far gestures to control and move the 3D objects between different models. The result will be a fully functional application on your Microsoft HoloLens 2 device.

CHAPTER 1

Immersive Experiences

The world is changing. While nowadays most people are using flat screens to view digital information, more and more technologies are made available to us to view that same information in a 3D space. A 3D space can be created in any reality, from virtual reality to augmented reality to mixed reality, by using different devices.

But the true immersive experiences start when the real world is combined with digital information in such a way that it becomes part of your reality. This chapter goes into current available realities, devices, and use cases that will help you to understand mixed reality.

Realities

When I talk about different realities, it is mostly combinations of the real world around me and how I experience digital information in there. To explain this more closely, I will talk about virtual reality, augmented reality, and mixed reality.

Before we start talking about the different realities, Figure 1-1 shows a diagram containing the realities and how they work in the real and digital world. Combining both worlds results in mixed reality.

© Alexander Meijers 2020

A. Meijers, *Immersive Office 365*, https://doi.org/10.1007/978-1-4842-5845-3_1

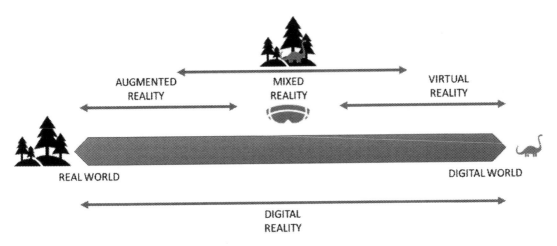

Figure 1-1. *Diagram explaining the differences between virtual reality, augmented reality, mixed reality, and digital reality*

Virtual Reality

Virtual reality (VR) is a way of stepping into a world that is digitally created for you. A VR headset that allows you to experience virtual reality, blocks in principle the real world around you. When using such a headset, you sit down or use a preconfigured area. The preconfigured area is monitored by the headset to make sure that as soon as you leave that area it is visualized in some sort of way in the digital world. As a user, you experience, for example, a visual wall that appears when you move more closely to the edges of the area. One of the biggest issues with VR is that people feel trapped and can experience nausea and lose their balance while walking. It really depends on the quality of the headset. The effects depend heavily on the size of the field of view, refresh rates of the displays, and the level of display resolution. The bigger the size and the higher the refresh rates and resolution, the fewer the issues.

While VR is mostly targeting the consumer market, there are definitely other areas that will benefit from virtual reality. Think of safety and hazard training at nonavailable locations like an operating room. In those cases, immerging into a completely digital world is the only way.

Augmented Reality

Augmented reality means that we enhance the real world around us with digital information. Digital information can be anything from sound to objects like holograms. But the digital information is always presented from a user perspective. Think of a heads-up display like Arnold used as the terminator in the movie *Terminator*. Augmented reality devices are always see-through. In comparison with a VR device, there is almost no case of nausea or losing your balance. As a user you are able to see the real world around you, know where you are, and are able to walk around without hitting objects.

A good example is the Google Glass, which shows step by step information to help a worker to execute work on the factory floor. Another example is providing additional information for an object you are viewing. Think of looking at a house, and financial information like mortgage will appear in your view.

Mixed Reality

Mixed reality is almost the same as augmented reality. It also enhances the real world with digital information. Also, in this case the digital information can be anything from sound to objects like holograms. But it understands your real-world environment. Instead of showing the digital information as a heads-up display, it can tie that digital information to real-world objects–objects like a chair or table in a room, walls and ceilings, and more. Mixed reality devices are just like augmented reality devices; they are see-through and will not cause any discomfort like nausea or instability when walking around. By blending both the real-world and the digital world, mixed reality is creating a true immersive experience.

Mixed reality is one of the new rising technologies from the past few years. It is gaining more and more acceptance from organizations to optimize their business processes. This technology helps companies in successfully managing, supporting, and operating their business processes.

Think of conceptual placement, where mixed reality device will help to configure and design the internal infrastructure of a room before adding the actual equipment. One of the best examples of using mixed reality is support for maintenance, training, and coaching. We are able to show overlays on real-life objects, explaining how to operate a machine or how to dismantle a part. By combining this with information retrieved from sensors or information from back-end systems, the engineer is able to perform tasks that were not be possible to do before. It also helps in training personnel without the continuous presence of a highly skilled engineer.

Mixed reality also provides additional information on real-life objects like, for example, tubes, hoses, valves, and other parts of machinery in plants. Information displayed at the correct locations in space will tell us how fluid is flowing around or what the pressure is. Any information you have can be easily added to the right place to support the work of the engineer.

Another area in which mixed reality can contribute is incident registration or quality control. Mixed reality devices allow us to take pictures, record video, use spoken text and annotations regarding an incident, or find quality issues. The information is registered in a back-end system, and blockchain can be used to keep it secure. Actions taken from the back-end system are pushed back to the mixed reality device to take further steps.

I'm a strong believer in the use of mixed reality to create true immersive experiences for customers.

The Future of Digital Reality

All these realities are encompassed under the term X Reality. X Reality, also called XR or Cross Reality, encompasses a large spectrum of software and hardware that contributes to the creation of content for virtual reality, augmented reality, and mixed reality. The term XR has existed for a long time and could be a more outdated term to use.

Bringing the digital world into the real word and the real world into the digital world

---

Especially when looking at how the future is developing, I'd rather use the term digital reality. For me, digital reality encompasses the tools that allow you to bring the digital world into the real world and the real world into the digital world. In other words, it's a true blend of experiences where it doesn't matter if you are operating from a digital or real world.

Devices

Nowadays, if you look at the consumer market everybody has a smartphone, which has the ability to run augmented reality applications. These applications are built using AR Core for Android and the AR Kit for iPhone. At the early stage of these kits, it was not possible to really use the world around you. But things have changed, and the current versions allow you to understand the real world, in some way, and use it. Hence you could say that both platforms are now actually mixed reality platforms.

What you will see in the nearby future is a shift of all realities to a new single one. The importance of using a specific technique will fade, and totally depends on what you want to accomplish. Instead, you can expect that the choice of device for your experience will become a leading factor in deciding which reality suits you the most.

The choice of a device totally depends on a number of things. It depends on the person executing the work, the process and the location where the work needs to be done, but also the type of information and what the person wants to achieve.

Think of a field worker using a smart glass to install a new engine part because he needs his hands free. Whereas the office worker, sitting in a chair, uses a VR headset to view that same engine part to understand what additional parts need to be ordered to fix the engine the field worker is working on.

It will not stop there. Today we have smart glasses, tablets, smartphones, and computers to create augmented and mixed realities around content and processes. But in the near future contact lenses creating an immersive experience using the processor power of your smartphone will become available.

Modern Workplace

While mixed reality is nowadays mostly used in industry, I find it interesting to explore other areas in which it could be used. One of them is the modern workplace and how we can digitalize this into the 3D world. Tools like Office 365 are used in the modern workplace. It allows people to collaborate and work more closely around content to improve their work processes. The Office 365 suite contains a lot of different applications like Teams, SharePoint, and Office tools. Working together at a distance is easy. You can reach each other via chat, voice calls, and other means. Working together in such an environment creates relationships between the content, based on actions. Think of people who have worked on the same document, like a manager who has approved a presentation before it was sent to the customer; how often you are sending emails to colleagues and customers; and even what those emails are about. All these interactions cause relationships between content.

Visualization

Be careful not to overengineer the design at the expense of usability. If you try to make it too beautiful, it will lose its advantage doing visualization in 3D space. You will need to find a balance between functionality that improves the worker process and beautifying the experience.

HoloLens

HoloLens is a mixed reality device produced by Microsoft. It was the first device that was able to create a true immersive experience by combining the real world together with digital information. Until 2018, the release of the Magic Leap, no other device was able to do the same.

Mixed Reality Device

HoloLens is often reverted to as an augmented reality device. But its cameras and sensors allow you to combine it with the real world, making it a mixed reality device. Still, HoloLens can do both. You could build an application that will not use anything of the surrounding real world. It is even possible to imitate VR on the HoloLens. HoloLens uses the color black (officially not a color) to define where the view is transparent. You can change the way HoloLens uses that color, which causes it to completely overlap the real world with the digital information from the scene in your app. However, an actual VR device works much better in that space.

History

The first version of the device, also called HoloLens 1, was released to the public on March 30, 2016. There were two versions: the Commercial Suite edition and the Development edition. The difference was not in hardware but only in software. The Development edition was sold for $3,000 and had no warranty. It was mostly used for development purposes in teams building mixed reality for customers. The Commercial Suite edition was sold for $5,000 and came with a warranty. This version contained more functionality in the software, allowing the device to be used in, for example, Kiosk mode. MDM (mobile device management) support was part of the product. A Commercial

Suite edition was needed for customers who wanted to use the device and its software in production. Updating a Development edition to a Commercial Suite edition is nothing more than installing another key during setup. This key was provided by Microsoft during an upgrade process.

Next Generation Device

Today we have the second generation of the device called HoloLens 2. HoloLens 2 has been incredibly improved at the hardware and software level, starting with putting on the device. It is perfectly balanced in weight across the head, which makes it more comfortable than the previous version. Putting the device on your head is so much easier; it only requires rotating the knob at the back and putting the device on your head like a hat.

In Figure 1-2 shows the Microsoft HoloLens 2 device.

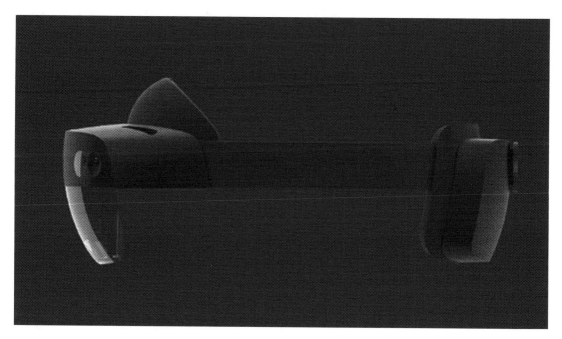

Figure 1-2. *An example of the Microsoft HoloLens 2 device*

You normally took the device off your head when programming it. Now, HoloLens 2 allows you to flip the front screen up. This makes it easier to watch your computer screen or talk with someone without looking through the glasses. The application(s) are still running on the device when the display is flipped up. The device will show the output of your application as soon as you flip the display down again. When the display of the device is flipped up, no gestures, voice commands, or other means are registered by the device.

Eye Tracking

Eye tracking is one of the new features of HoloLens 2. Each new user is recognized by the device and requires calibrating their eyes to use eye tracking. During calibration, the user needs to stay still and look at a diamond, which moves to different locations. The whole process takes just a couple of minutes. What I really like about this is that when you are showing an application and a new user puts on the device, it is asked to calibrate their eyes. After calibration, the HoloLens 2 brings the user back to the application at the state where it left.

As soon as the device is started you need to log in. The same iris scan is now used to log in the user. The device recognizes the user and logs on with their account. By default, it is bound to the Active Directory of your organization. But it is also possible to use a custom role-based security provider. The advantage of having iris scan is that the user does not have to type in a username and password every time they want to log in. This is a convenient function, especially for workers on a factory floor.

Field of View

The field of view has been improved. It is more than two times bigger in all directions. My first experience gave me a better immersive experience than HoloLens 1. With HoloLens 2 you notice the edges less, and it feels as if it flows more to the outer sides you can't see with your own eyes, which gives you a more relaxing view. Even flipping the display up and down again is not distracting from the digital information you are viewing.

Gestures

While there were just a few simple gestures with HoloLens 1, you have full hand gesture control with HoloLens 2. Hands are tracked on 25 joints per hand. This allows the device to create a digital representation of both your hands. It does not matter if you move or rotate your hands or even swap them. The device will register each hand separately and allows you to control their movements. It also allows you to implement from simple to incredibly complex hand gestures. That creates endless possibilities.

On the first HoloLens we had the tap, tap and hold, and bloom gestures. The tap gesture allowed you to select something. The tap and hold allowed to select, hold, and release something. The bloom gesture allowed you to open or close the start menu. It also allowed you to bring up a menu during the run of your application to return to the start menu, to start or stop a recording, and Miracast your output to another screen to allow people watch with you together. While the tap gesture can still be used with HoloLens 2, the bloom gesture is not being used anymore. To open the start menu, you simply turn your hand up and you will see a start menu button on your wrist. By selecting it with one of the fingers of your other hand, you can show the start menu or hide it. For me that experience is almost science fiction.

When you build interactions for HoloLens apps, you can divide your interactions into two different categories:

- Gestures

- Manipulation

Gestures allow you to control, for example, menus and buttons or allow you to start a specific action, while manipulation is all about, for example, controlling an object's size or position. Gestures and manipulation support the use of both hands, both eyes, and the voice. You can see in Figure 1-3 an example of a person using gestures to manipulate a hologram in midair.

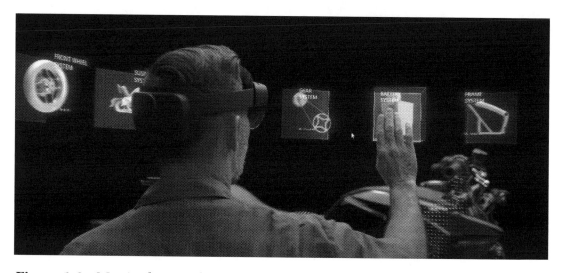

Figure 1-3. *Manipulation of a hologram by using gestures with the HoloLens 2*

Even the device can perform a kind of gesture. Think of the gaze, which is an invisible line from the center of the device in the direction you (or actually the device) was pointed. That functionality is still there. But it gets even cooler. With the new gestures of HoloLens 2, you can point with your index finger to an object, button, or other 3D object. As soon as you do that, it replaces the gaze. You get a line from the tip of your index finger to the pointed object. When you stop, the gaze from the device is active again.

Because you can now use all parts of your hand, you will be able to implement gestures that allow you to press a button or touch a 3D object in your view. Think of picking up an object and passing it to your other hand. Even though you will not have any haptic feedback, for me those gestures felt almost as if I touched the objects in the real world. In Figure 1-4 you will see some examples of near interaction states with hologram objects using your finger or hand.

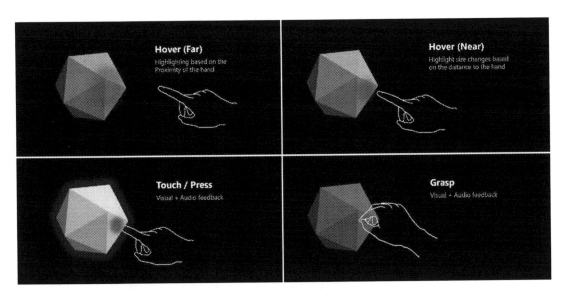

Figure 1-4. *An example of near interaction states*

When you have calibrated your eyes on the HoloLens 2, you are able to select, indicate, and even control something by looking at it. The device will track the direction in which your eyes are looking. Controlling the difference between selecting or taking control over a 3D object can be reached by implementing the duration in time you are looking at that object.

Voice commands offer additional ways of implementing gestures or manipulation. Voice is mainly used as a support on hand and eye track gestures. Instead of pressing the button you are looking at or gazing at, use a voice command to press it. Or you can use sentences that will control different functions in your app.

All these gestures and manipulations give you endless possibilities.

Think of controlling the search for a city on a map by using only your eyes looking at some part of the map. While your eyes move to the border of the map, the map scrolls further. Zooming in or out the map can be accomplished by pinching with your hands from and to the map. By looking straight at the same city or location, the map will select it.

Reading text on a 2D board in the air by using only eye tracking can give you some interesting effects. When you reach the lowest rows of the visible text, the text automatically starts to scroll up, allowing you to read further. Even the reading speed can be determined and can be used to speed up or down the scrolling of the text. And looking more in the middle of the visible text will pause the scrolling.

Combining gestures makes it even better. Let's say you have some objects on a table and you want to have control over them by using gestures. For example, you want to move them to another spot on that table. By looking at an object it becomes selected. Using voice commands and looking at another spot at the table will move the object to that position. Another way of picking up the object is by walking to it and picking it up by hand and placing it somewhere else on the table; because you can hold onto the object, you can walk with it to another side of the table. If you don't want to walk to the object, pick it up from a distance. Combine looking at it and grabbing it in the air; that allows you to pick up that same object and place it somewhere else. Combining gestures can make this action feel more natural.

MEM Display Technology

Microsoft has completely developed the device in-house. When they started developing the displays for the HoloLens 2, there was nothing there yet. They had to create them from scratch.

To achieve this, they used state-of-the-art custom silicon in combination with advanced laser technology for superior brightness and color. The HoloLens 2 features the world's lowest power high-definition MEMS display.

MEMS are micro-electro-mechanical systems that contain tiny mirrors that move back and forward in a very fast way to render the image. One mirror, called the fast scan, moves horizontally and one mirror, called the slow scan, movies vertically. In Figure 1-5 you can see how both mirrors work together to display the image.

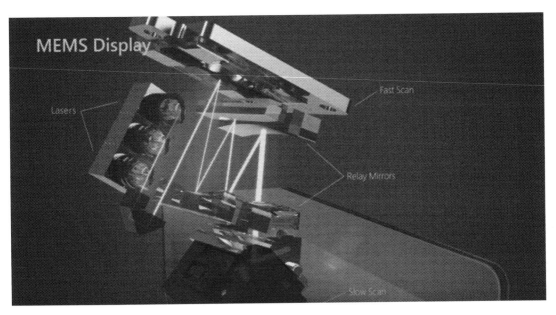

Figure 1-5. *MEMS display using slow and fast scan with mirrors to draw an image*

When using MEMS, you don't have to have a bigger sensor to get a wider field of view. By changing the angle of the mirror with MEMS you can achieve the same thing. By using this technology, Microsoft was able to go from the initial 36 degrees to 51 degrees, which brought the field of view two times bigger.

The photons produced in the laser travel all the way through the light engine through the waveguide into your eyeball. Algorithms are used to determine where the head is moving to, to allow the device to display the image at the right position. Due to the larger eye relief used in the device, HoloLens can even support wearing glasses using this technology.

The device delivers a much higher contrast than the first HoloLens, due to the use of laser technology. The lasers will only be active when showing the pixels that are part of the image. The laser shuts off and does no projection when there are no pixels to draw. This creates a better view and see-through of the whole field of view area. Using this high-contrast technique will allow to HoloLens 2 to be used more easily outside, even when the visible brightness of the light is higher than 1,000 light nits.

The device can render millions of pixels per second, with a resolution matching the human eye. This quality even allows developers to render 8pt font that is still readable.

HoloLens Emulator

Microsoft has released a HoloLens emulator since the first HoloLens was produced. The emulator for HoloLens 2 was already available since April 2019, while HoloLens 2 was still not released. This emulator has been optimized and improved based on developers' testing in the field. The emulator allows you as a developer to build and test applications without the actual device. But the functions of the emulator are of course more limited. One of those big limitations is not having the camera and sensors allowing you to build up a spatial map of the environment. It is still possible to load static rooms, which can be used to test your scene and functions. Controlling hands and virtual devices within the emulator can be done through the keyboard or by using an Xbox controller. More about the HoloLens 2 emulator and HoloLens 2 implementations will follow further on in this book.

Use Cases

This section of the chapter discusses how mixed reality can be a benefit for the office worker, and describes a few use cases of using the HoloLens as a mixed reality device in the modern workplace.

Data Visualization

While HoloLens is a mixed reality device mostly is used in industry, it does not exclude other areas in the field. Extending the modern workplace is one of them. Imagine the office worker viewing and handling data from a different perspective. But be careful with this. I see a lot of implementations where the experience in mixed reality is almost or the same as on the screen of your computer. Think of presenting a bar chart from Excel in the same way on a real-world table in 3D space. It allows you to view that bar chart from a different angle, but that can also be accomplished by rotating the bar chart on your screen.

To enable the office worker to do more with their data, you need to think about the following:

- How can the office worker benefit from it?

- Are there means to visualize the data differently?

- Can we enrich the data by using the surrounding?

- Is it possible to target the current situation of the office worker?

- Can we interpret the data differently from where we are standing or viewing the data?

- How does the office worker interact with the data?

- Are we using the surroundings to create a true immersive experience?

- Is the data shared across other office workers?

- Is there a need for collaboration with other office workers?

- How does the data stay secured and safe while bringing it into the 3D space?

Combining the answers to all these questions will result in data visualization apps in the mixed reality world that will give office workers a step forward.

Collaboration

Collaboration is an important part of the life of an office worker. Working together with others in a team for a project or similar interest area is essential. In such a team, the members have a common cause. Being part of such a team means doing things like having discussions, creating and reviewing documents together, and finishing tasks.

Normally if we look at a team operating in the Microsoft space, the team is using products like SharePoint, Teams, Planner, and Skype. Subsequently, other tools are used for maintaining additional content or share content to people who are not able to join the team through that Microsoft space. These tools are powerful and can combine and link different content to support the work of the office worker.

One of the key factors of success is working together in the same room. If these office workers work at the same location, it is easy to have meetings and share and collaborate by using projection screens and smart boards. But this is not always the case. Nowadays, office workers work from home. And a lot of companies have multiple locations, sometimes worldwide, causing office workers in the same team to split up. Doing a Skype call is not always enough. It is just not the same experience as being in the same room.

You want to have a solution that brings office workers and their content together using mixed reality. Mixed reality allows us to create digital virtual content in our real-world environment. This allows us to still be in our own safe environment together with others and the content we are collaborating around. So how does that work? Let's say you have a meeting planned with other members of your team. The first step is putting on a HoloLens and logging in with iris scan, which logs you on to the Azure Active Directory. The next step is identifying which meeting you have. That could be done in several different ways:

- Opening the meeting in Outlook on your device and clicking a link or button as part of the invitation

- If the meeting requires you to have access to a certain workspace like Teams, you could use a tag containing a unique identifier identifying that Teams site.

- Getting a list of available meetings and/or spaces in your device where you can choose from. Naturally, the meeting that is closest to the current date and time is shown on top.

Certainly there are more ways, but keep in mind that you need to identify a certain meeting or workspace. The others need that too, to be part of the same experience.

Mixed reality used as a collaboration tool will help office workers to achieve more!

The next step is the experience together. For that, we need a spot in the room that indicates the middle of the room in which we are all standing or the table at which we are all sitting. Each team member joining the meeting is created as an avatar at the location of the other team members. An avatar consists of a head and hands. The reason for this is that we can track both head and hands of a user wearing a HoloLens. Moving the different parts of the avatar as the original team member creates an experience that lets you believe that you are in the same room interacting with them. The identified workspace can be shown at the nearest wall or put on a table. All team members can control the content and view it simultaneously. Since we can generate virtual content and bind it against real-life objects, you can create digital content from that workspace and place it around you. And there you go! Using mixed reality allows you to collaborate with other office workers. Is this currently possible with today's technology? Yes, it is. Currently, there is a mixed reality app called "Spatial" that does something similar.

Extending Your View

Another interesting use case is extending your view of your screen. Normally, as a developer, you use at least two screens at your desk. I at least do when I'm debugging source code or I need to have the technical documentation visible when programming. But imagine you are not working at your home or the office. Nowadays it is rather normal to work anyplace anywhere, like me now working at a holiday location with only my laptop at the table. Imagine putting on a HoloLens and getting different kinds of information based on the context you are working on. See it like additional screens that show the data you need. And because we do not have the limitations of a regular screen, we can immerse the user in the data in a 3D space. There are different ways in how you could approach this use case.

The simplest solution would be opening additional applications on the HoloLens. The issue with that is not all Windows 10 applications on your PC will run on a HoloLens device. It is, however, possible to open a browser on a HoloLens. When the application is web based, it can be opened. HoloLens allows you to open multiple web browser instances showing those applications around you. However, only one web browser can be active. Meaning that if data in a web browser is changing a lot, the change of data is only reflected when you make that particular web browser active.

Another one could be using a sharing tool that allows extending your current PC desktop to other screens. In this case, the HoloLens will provide a 360-degree screen for you. Since the tool is not yet there, it needs to be built for HoloLens. Such a solution would require a very good WIFI link between the PC and the HoloLens, since you are sharing a video signal. Second, you need to transform gestures to actual mouse interactions for controlling the shared view.

Both solutions are not that bad. But are they really creating an immersive experience for the user? In both solutions, there is no real interaction between the PC and the HoloLens. Let's think a little bit further. What if the link between both PC and HoloLens is not the connection but the account you used to log on? Consider that most applications used by the office worker are Microsoft based, part of the Office 365 application landscape, or connected in some way through the use of a Microsoft work or school account or a Microsoft account. Now picture the office worker, working in Excel on some data that needs to be changed frequently. That office worker wants to see what other sets of data are influenced. The office worker could open several different data sets and visualize those in 3D. Changing values in Excel would automatically reflect the data sets and the connected visualizations in the HoloLens 3D space. Now imagine you are working together with others on the same data. They could also put on a HoloLens device and experience it.

Analyzing Data

As a former SharePoint guy, I'm interested in how the Microsoft space like Office 365 and all its applications can be extended to 3D space. Office 365 is a collection of tools that are available through the Microsoft Cloud and are extended by Office tools installed on your computer. While the last part is not necessary, since all Office tools are available online, the experience of those online versions is of course with less functionality but still enough to work with. Even this book is written using the online variant of Microsoft Word.

There are so many different things you could do when Office 365 is extended to your real-life world. Think of one or more of the following:

- View data using different 3D presentations

- Understand the complexity of SharePoint site structures

- Have a "walkthrough" through your data

- Manipulate data using gestures, location, and eyes

- View relationships based on different contributions and actions

- View only data that contributes to the data you're looking at

- Use the environment of the room to place, sort, and control the data

- Determine the importance of data based on your location in the room

There are more uses you can think of. But this gives you an idea of how you can work with Office 365 data in 3D space.

Just like the previous use cases, you need to log in as a user. Depending on your rights and permission within the Office 365 environment, different data can be accessed. Data retrieved is viewable in different formats and models. The model that is used depends heavily on how various data is related to each other. Here are some examples to explain what I mean:

- Child-parent relationships like site structures or team members belonging to a specific Teams site are mostly viewed in a somewhat structured way. Think of a plane, cube, or another known form.

- Relationships based on probability can use more complex viewing models. An example is the force-directed graph—a model that more dynamically displays the relationships between data by using probability to determine its position in 3D. We will go deeper into this model further in the book.

- Many-to-many relationships: data that is related to other data based on different metadata. Based on the metadata, your model—which uses plane, cube, or other form—is transformed by clicking different segments.

- Data without relationships: data that has no really significant reason to be related to other data is placed in different segments of your environment to be viewable and/or editable.

It gets even more interesting when you take your own location in the room into account to determine the importance. If you have a relationship based on probability, the model is most likely presented in the room in 3D, allowing you to walk around it. Depending on the location of the device and the direction it's looking, you could determine which part of the data is most important at that time.

With the new HoloLens, by using eye tracking you can go even further. This can be used to determine which part of the model you have looked at the most to determine its importance. But it also allows you to have an idea what the person is looking for and use that to deliver more related data to the data that is viewed.

When it comes to manipulating data in 3D space, it gets just incredible. Because you have gestures that allow you to pick up data and do all kinds of interactions with it, you move into the future. An example is picking up a SharePoint site object and folding it open to view its lists and libraries. Deleting an object could be like throwing it away into a real-world basket in the room.

This last use case will be used in this book to explain further how mixed reality can create a true immersive experience using HoloLens.

CHAPTER 2

Controlling Data

This chapter explains where we get the data from and how we control it. Control means reading from and writing to Office 365 as the modern workplace. I will explain how data is part of the different services in Office 365 and how you can access your data by using the Microsoft Graph API.

Office 365

Office 365 is the modern digital workplace for workers at a lot of organizations. This chapter describes Office 365 globally and goes deeper into the different forms of insights available. A major part of controlling data is which data you can control. This is defined by the authorization levels and roles that users have. This chapter will explain thoroughly how that works.

Teams in the Modern Digital Workplace

The modern workplace consists of several productivity services in Office 365. While in the early days SharePoint as a product was the center of productivity, nowadays Teams has taken over that role. Teams is a platform that brings the power of different Office 365 productivity services together in one interface to provide the ultimate collaboration experience for users. For that reason, we will be focusing on Teams, users, relationships, and insights for our mixed reality application.

Teams is sometimes referred to as a hub for teamwork. Teams can be accessed through a web interface or via an app on Windows, iOS, and Android.

In Teams it is possible to work with people inside your own organization as well with people outside your organization. The modern digital workplace is a place where people cocreate content like documents, wiki pages, and other information. But it is also a place where people can communicate which each other through chat, calls, and organized

© Alexander Meijers 2020
A. Meijers, *Immersive Office 365*, https://doi.org/10.1007/978-1-4842-5845-3_2

meetings. Teams even allows you to connect with third-party applications, which become part of the Teams you are in. In Figure 2-1 you will see an example of a Teams workplace.

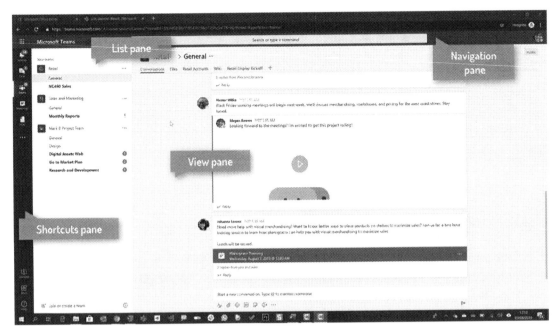

Figure 2-1. *An example of the Teams web interface*

Microsoft Teams can be divided into several panes. There are not really names for those panes, so I have named them in Figure 2-1 as I see them myself.

Microsoft Teams is so named because users are grouped in teams based upon the work that each team needs to accomplish together. Depending upon your job role, you could be a member of many teams.

Teams Channels

Each team consists of one or more channels. These channels can be private or available to every other member. A channel has, by default, the Conversations and Files tabs. Additional tabs can be added. Channels allow you to create connectors to third-party applications and services. In Figure 2-2 you see a list of possible connectors.

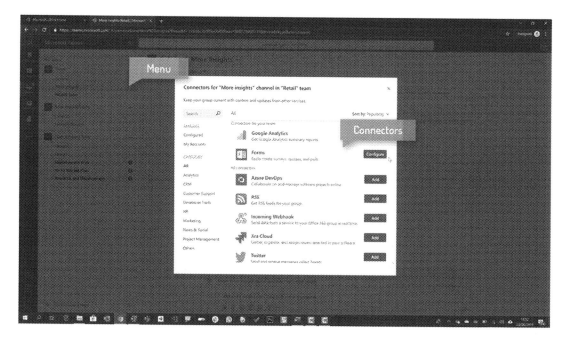

Figure 2-2. *Adding a connector to a channel in Teams*

When such an application or service is installed and configured, it can appear in the Conversations tab as content or as an additional tab in the channel. The output and functionality are determined by the manufacturer of the application or service. Channels allow the user to set notifications on new posts and mentions.

Additional Apps in Teams

Teams allows you to extend your environment with many available Microsoft and third-party apps and services, as you can see in Figure 2-3.

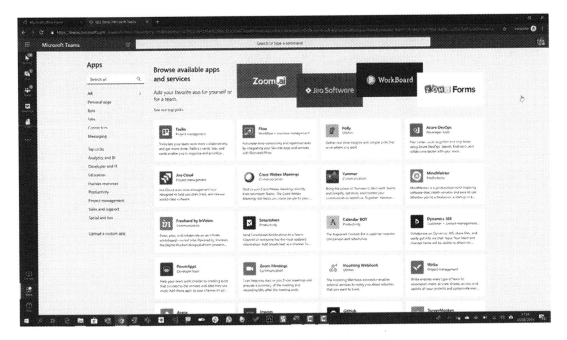

Figure 2-3. *Available apps that can be combined with Teams*

It is possible to combine information depending on the needs of your collaboration in the teams of which you are a member. Let's say you work together with another company that uses Trello—a project management tool. Teams allows you now to simply integrate Trello through a view in your collaboration environment.

Users and Roles

You can work together with people from your organization and with people from external organizations. People from external organizations must be invited to join a team. An external user does not need to have their own Office 365 tenant. In that case, you are inviting someone with a Microsoft account. Keep in mind that a user with a Microsoft account has less functionality in Teams because the account is not bound to any license within Office 365. In Figure 2-4 you will see an overview of the users who are members or owners inside a workspace in Teams.

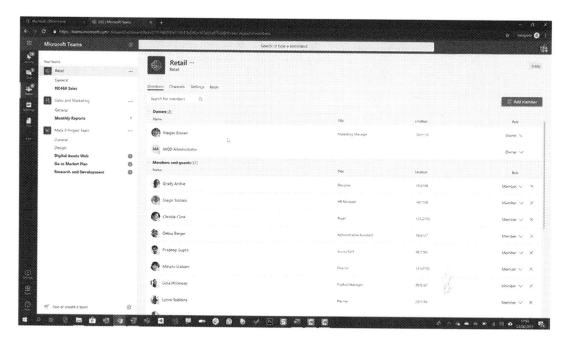

Figure 2-4. *An overview of members and owners inside Microsoft Teams*

Teams only specify two roles, named Team Member or Team Owner. A Team Owner can do anything within the workspace of Microsoft Teams. *Anything* means actions like creating or deleting a team, adding or deleting a channel, adding members, adding tabs, adding connectors, and adding bots. A team member has, by default, most of the same rights except for creating and deleting a team and adding members. A Team Owner can turn off some of the actions for Team Members. Think of removing the ability to add a tab by a Team Member.

A team can have up to a hundred owners. But keep this number lower to have the team more manageable. Also, orphaned owners—people who have left the company—will not dilute the system, because they are removed from it.

Content and People

Another interesting part is the relationship between people to people and people to content. In Office 365 we have something called Office Delve. Office Delve manages your Office 365 profile and organizes information like documents and people around you, based on intelligent analytics. Figure 2-5 shows an example of an Office Delve page inside Office 365.

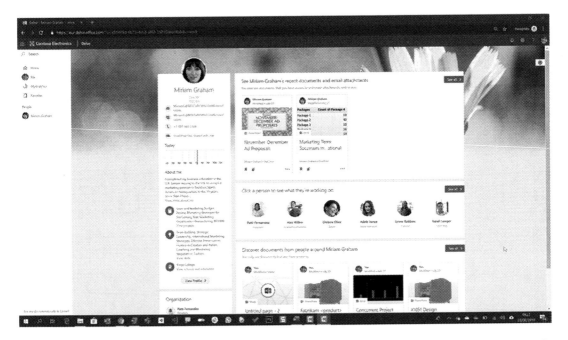

Figure 2-5. *An example of an Office Delve page, which shows related content and people*

Office Delve is a great example showing how everything is connected based upon interactions between people and interactions with content.

People are related to other people based on social intelligence. Social intelligence is mostly based on how people communicate with each other. Insights allow you to retrieve information such as documents trending around you based on those social interactions between people and content.

You can imagine what possibilities insights will bring into the 3D space.

Microsoft Graph

Microsoft Graph allows you to build solutions that target consumers and enterprise users in Azure and Office 365. This broad reach gives you as a developer a broad set of API calls behind a single point of entry. It allows you to read and write data. We will start with the benefits of using Microsoft Graph, how you authenticate to get access, and what it takes to integrate and use the Microsoft Graph API inside your solution for mixed reality.

Overview of Microsoft Graph

Microsoft Graph is a single and still growing platform that allows you to build rich solutions for a broad set of different platforms. Microsoft Graph provides a RESTful web API that allows you to access a variety of cloud service resources from Azure and Office 365. By using Microsoft Graph, you can add value to your own build solutions and applications.

Microsoft Graph is a user-centric environment. This means the different sets of endpoints are mostly from a user's perspective. Think of getting content for a specific user, determining relationships with other users, and more.

Separately, there are several endpoints allowing you to get specific content. Examples are getting SharePoint sites, lists, and list items. But there are also some seriously cool endpoints that give you more intelligent results and deep insights. Examples are returning the documents that are trending around you, and social intelligence by returning people who are related to you based on interactions you have with them. Another example is determining what the best team meeting times are. All these results are based on usage patterns and give you data back based on internal artificial intelligence running in the system from which the data is coming.

All data coming from the endpoints in Microsoft Graph are in real time. That means when your solution is saving changes in content or a meeting is rescheduled through an endpoint, that change directly reflects the data read from Microsoft Graph.

Microsoft Graph currently supports two versions, called v1.0 and beta:

- v1.0 is the generally available API and needs to be used when you create production applications.

- beta includes the next planned API functionality that is still in preview. It is recommended to use this version only in development and not for production applications.

That said, the beta version contains a lot of new and interesting endpoints, which allows you to do more than ever. Just keep in mind that endpoints can change during the preview. If you still decide to use it in a production application, make sure that you keep track of the documentation until it becomes part of the v1.0 version.

Microsoft has comprehensive documentation of the Microsoft Graph API. That documentation contains a very good description of authentication and how to use the API. Also, each endpoint and the properties in both versions are described in detail, with resulting JSON examples.

Since Microsoft Graph is a RESTful web API, you can access it from any platform. Microsoft has the Microsoft Graph SDK released for several different platforms. SDKs consist of two components: a service library and a core library. The service library consists of models and request builders to access the many datasets available in Microsoft Graph. The core library contains the more basic overall functionality for handling the data from and to Microsoft Graph. The core library consists of retry handling, authentication, payload compression, and secure redirects.

The Microsoft Graph SDKs allow you to build solutions fast and easily. They are wrappers built in rich and strongly typed languages around the endpoints, allowing you to be less busy accessing the endpoints and more focused on building your solutions. Keep in mind that in most cases the endpoints from the beta version are not available in the Microsoft Graph SDK.

Currently supported platforms are Android, Angular, ASP.NET & MVC, iOS Swift, iOS Objective-C, Node.js, PHP, Python, React, Ruby, Universal Windows Platform (.NET), and Xamarin. This book only focuses on the Universal Windows Platform. This is the platform used for building mixed reality applications for Microsoft HoloLens.

Microsoft provides a Microsoft Graph Quick Start system, which allows you to quickly build an app that connects to Office 365 by calling the Microsoft Graph API. This quick start would normally generate a Universal Windows App that can authenticate and connect to Office 365 through the Microsoft Graph API. But in our case, we are not able to use that generated application. When building mixed reality apps, we use Unity and Visual Studio. These tools will automatically generate a Universal Windows App for us. We can use the generated code inside the quick start project in our own Universal Windows App project. But to fully understand the process behind the quick start we are going to explain each part step by step in the following subchapters.

App Registration

Before we can start building an application that uses the Microsoft Graph API, we need to register that application. Registering is done through an app registration in the Azure portal.

App registration allows you to integrate the application or service with Azure Active Directory (Azure AD). App registration is needed to use the Azure AD capabilities. First of all, you need to log on to the Azure portal using your Azure account. Open a browser of your choice and type the following link:

```
https://portal.azure.com
```

Log in using a valid tenant account that has enough rights to add a new app registration in Azure AD. If everything went well, you will see the portal of your Azure environment as shown in Figure 2-6.

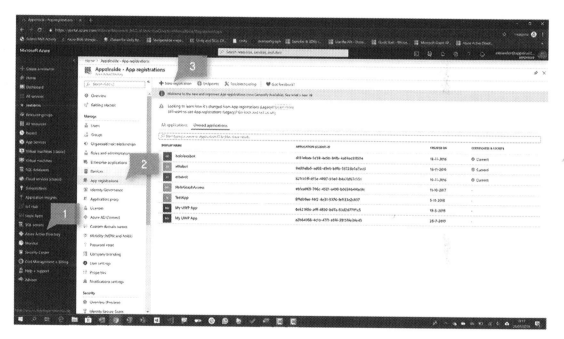

Figure 2-6. *The Azure portal and the steps to add a new app registration*

Select *Azure Active Directory* on the left side column and select *App registrations* in the second column. At the top of the middle screen a menu bar with the menu option *New registration* appears. Select that menu option. A new window appears to register a new application, which you can see in Figure 2-7.

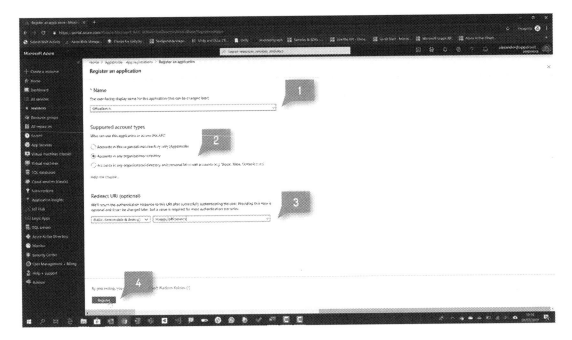

Figure 2-7. *Registration of a new application in Azure*

The app registration form consists of three initial fields that need to be filled in. Give the app registration a *name*. The name does not have to be the same as your application but can help to identify its registration in Azure. Then there are different *supported account types*:

- **Accounts in this organizational directory** means that the application that you register can be used only in this specific tenant. This is the best choice if you want to create an app that will only be used inside your organization.

- **Accounts in any organizational directory** means that the application can be used across any tenant. This option is more suitable for applications to be used by many organizations.

- **Accounts in any organizational directory and personal Microsoft accounts** is the same as the preceding, with the addition that it also allows being used with personal accounts outside any organization. This option is more suitable for organizations that work together with external people who do not always have an account in a tenant.

For our purpose, we have selected accounts in any organization. You can see that selection in Figure 2-7.

The last setting is the redirect URI, which is returned as a response by a successful authentication from your application. It is optional and mostly used to redirect to a specific location within a web application. We are building an application for Microsoft HoloLens 2. This application is a native application. Therefor we require the use of a redirect URI. This redirect URI, assigned by the Microsoft identity platform, can be used for validation. No application secret is required, since we are registering for a native application.

Press the Register button to finalize the registration. Select the just-created app registration to view more information and to set other settings. More settings will be explained in the next chapters.

Authentication

This section goes into more detail about how you need to authenticate from your application against the Microsoft Graph API using the created app registration.

The best method of authentication is using the `Microsoft.Identity.Client` NuGet package. This package contains the Microsoft Authentication Library for .NET based on MSAL.NET. The MSAL.NET library allows you to easily obtain tokens from the Microsoft identity platform. These tokens allow you as a developer to sign in users to their work and school accounts, personal accounts, and other social identities.

Create a Blank Universal Windows application that allows you to authenticate. Open Visual Studio 2019. A dialog will appear for creating a new project, as shown in Figure 2-8.

1. Use this search field to search for a UWP project template.

2. Select the Blank App (Universal Windows) project.

3. Press the Next button.

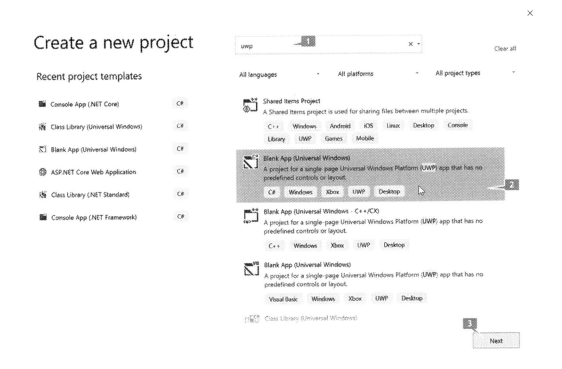

Figure 2-8. *Creating a new project in Visual Studio 2019*

In the next step you'll configure the name, solution, and folder of the new project, as shown in Figure 2-9.

1. Enter the name Office365ConsoleApp for the project.

2. Select the folder location.

3. Press the Create button to create the console application project.

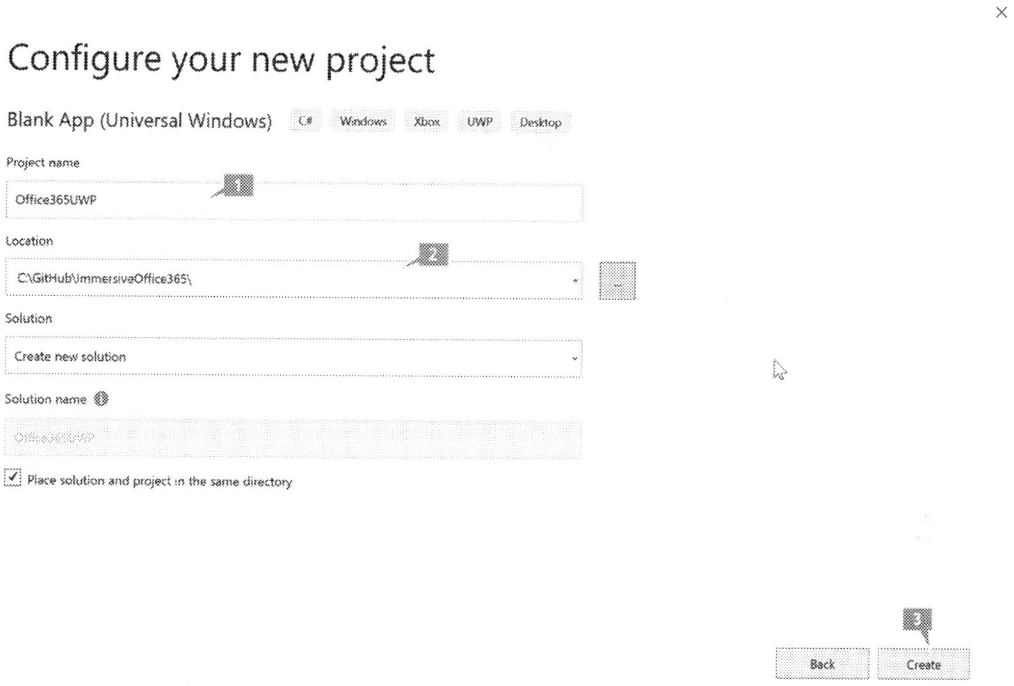

Figure 2-9. *Configuring your new project in Visual Studo 2019*

The `Microsoft.Identity.Client` NuGet package can be used for .NET core UWP applications. This NuGet package has been heavily in development for the last year. Currently the package is on a stable version `3.0.9` and higher.

We need to add the `Microsoft.Identity.Client` NuGet package to the project. Right-click the project in the solution explorer and select *Manage NuGet packages* from the menu. Browse for the required package by name and add it to the project.

Using this latest version of the package will install a conflicting dependency. That dependency is named `System.Runtime.Serialization.Formatters`. This package conflicts due to some references that are also part of the `WinRTLegacy` reference. The `WinRTLegacy` reference is necessary for the UWP project. To prevent this conflict, you will need to make sure that the version of the `Microsoft.NetCore.UniversalWindowsPlatform` Nuget package is at least on version `6.2.9`.

Create a new C# class with the name AuthenticationProperties. Add the following code to that class:

```csharp
public class AuthenticationProperties
{
    public string ClientId;
    public string ClientSecret;
    public string TenantId;

    public string[] Scopes;
}
```

These properties are required to authenticate against the app registration. Create another class called AuthenticationHelper. Add the following code to that class:

```csharp
public class AuthenticationHelper
{
    public string TokenForUser = null;
    public string RedirectUri { get; set; }
    public AuthenticationProperties Authentication { get; set; }

    public AuthenticationHelper()
    {
        Authentication = new AuthenticationProperties();
    }
}
```

We require one more method: GetTokenForUserAsync. This method will return a user token based on the user that logged on with its credentials. Add the following code to the class AuthenticationHelper:

```csharp
public async Task<string> GetTokenForUserAsync()
{
    var app = PublicClientApplicationBuilder.Create(Authentication.
    ClientId).WithRedirectUri(RedirectUri).Build();

    var accounts = await app.GetAccountsAsync();
    AuthenticationResult result;
    try
```

```
{
    result = await app.AcquireTokenSilent(Authentication.Scopes,
    accounts.FirstOrDefault()).ExecuteAsync();
    TokenForUser = result.AccessToken;
}
catch (MsalUiRequiredException)
{
    result = await app.AcquireTokenInteractive(Authentication.Scopes).
    ExecuteAsync();
    TokenForUser = result.AccessToken;
}

    return TokenForUser;
}
```

The preceding code requires having several properties set to get it to work. These properties are as follows:

- Application (client) ID

- Permissions

- Redirect URI

The first value is called the client ID. The client ID can be found in the overview page of your app registration, as can be seen in Figure 2-10.

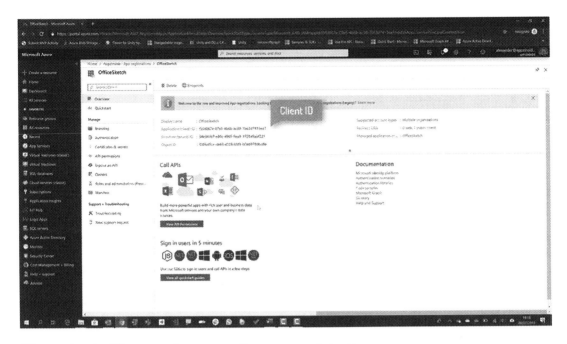

Figure 2-10. *The overview page of an app registration*

The client ID needs to be passed into the `PublicClientApplicationBuilder` method or into the `PublicClientApplication` method.

The second value is the list of delegated permissions and scopes. At the moment we will be using `User.Read` and `User.Read.All`. Permissions and scopes are more extensively discussed in the next section.

The third value is the redirect URI. During the authentication process this URI is checked with the list of URIs defined in the app registration. If it is not found, you will not get a user token.

Add the following code to the MainPage class in the MainPage.xaml.cs file:

```
public MainPage()
{
    this.InitializeComponent();

    Execute();
}

async void Execute()
{
    AuthenticationHelper helper = new AuthenticationHelper();
```

```
    helper.Authentication.ClientId = "<your client id>";
    helper.Authentication.Scopes = new string[] { "User.Read", "User.Read.
    All" };
    helper.RedirectUri = "<your redirect uri>";

    string token = await helper.GetTokenForUserAsync();
}
```

Set a breakpoint on the row with `string token = await helper.`
`GetTokenForUserAsync()`. Build and run the application from Visual Studio. The first time your username and password are requested, a dialog will appear requesting your consent for the required delegated permissions. The dialog will not appear if you already have given consent. If everything went well, the user token is returned.

Permissions and Scopes

Microsoft uses the OAuth 2.0 authorization model to implement its identity platform. This allows third-party apps to access resources from the Web on behalf of a user. A resource identifier is used to identify the type of resource you try to get access to. To access the Microsoft Graph API, you need to use `https://graph.microsoft.com` as the resource identifier.

Each resource on the Web, like Microsoft Graph API, has a set of permissions defined that determines if your application can access that particular part of the API. For example, getting access to SharePoint sites in the Office 365 tenant reveals the following permissions:

- Sites.Read.All

- Sites.ReadWrite.All

- Sites.Manage.All

- Sites.FullControll.All

These permissions, like the preceding list, are divided into small chunks of the API. This allows your application to request specific parts of that API. Your application needs to request these permissions from an administrator or a user. They need to approve the request before your application can access data or act on behalf of the logged-on user. Only request those permissions your application needs. That will give more confidence to the user of the application, which will let them consent much easier.

These types of permissions in OAuth 2.0 are called *scopes* but are also often referred to as *permissions*.

The Microsoft identity platform has two types of permissions: delegated permissions and application permissions. Each permission type defines how consent is arranged and if a user is needed. We also have something we call effective permissions. Effective permissions are the permissions that your app will have when making the actual request to the resource. Effective permissions differ between the types of permissions. The permission types, consent and effective permissions, are shown in Table 2-1.

Table 2-1. *Permission Types and Effective Permissions*

	Delegated permissions	Application permissions
Purpose	Application that needs a user context to access content and data	A background service or daemon that does not need any user
Signed-in user	Present	Not present
Consent	[1]User or an administrator	Only by an administrator through the Azure Portal
Consent dialog	The user or administrator will get a dialog with the requested permissions and allows it to grant or deny it. This will be shown during the first time the application is used by the user. The dialog will reappear when the consent is denied in a later state.	No consent dialog is shown.
Effective permissions	The intersection of the least privileged of the permissions and the privileges of the signed-in user. Your application can never have more privileges than the signed-in user. Privileges of the user within an organization can be determined by policies or memberships of roles.	The full level of privileges as stated by the requested permissions

[1]Some higher-privileged permissions can only be given consent by an administrator.

Permissions in Our Application

In our application, we want to use delegated permissions. Doing so allows us to get data and content on behalf of the signed-in user. This means we need to define which permissions our application wants to use. These permissions are shown to the user during the consent process. This process allows the user to view the permissions requested. It also allows the user to grant/deny access.

Note   Keep in mind that while the application has granted permissions, the user rights of the signed-in user supersede these permissions as defined in the effective permissions. For example, when the application has the permission *Sites.Read.All* to read sites from SharePoint, only sites that the logged-on user has access to are returned, hence context security.

There are two methods to define the permissions for an application. The first method is defining them in the app registration. There are two places in the Azure portal where you can add permissions. This can be done through **Expose an API** and **API permissions**. The latter is the recommended way, since it allows you to select easily from different sets of delegated or application permissions, while the other option expects you to add them manually. In Figure 2-11 you can see how to add a permission via **API permissions**.

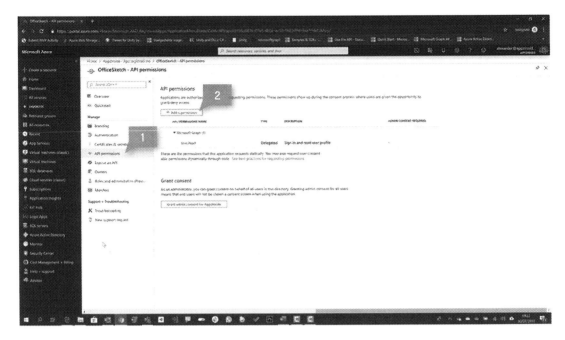

Figure 2-11. _Changing the permissions for an app registration_

Press the Add a permission button. This will lead you to a page where you can select one of the available APIs. Select the Microsoft Graph API. This is shown in Figure 2-12.

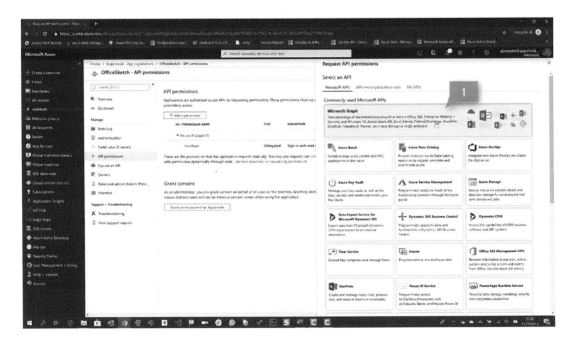

Figure 2-12. _Selecting the Microsoft Graph API to add permissions_

The final screen as shown in Figure 2-13 allows you to select from a list of delegated permissions or application permissions.

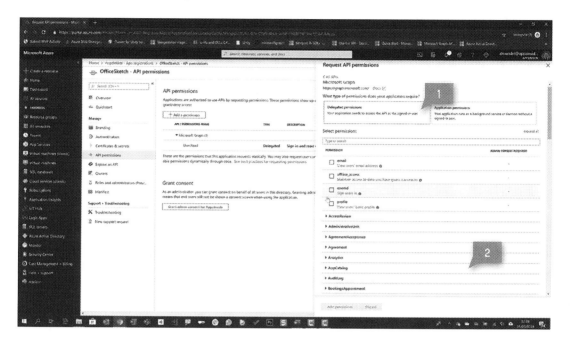

Figure 2-13. *Adding or removing one or more permissions*

Select delegated permissions and select the following permissions to add to your app registration:

- **User.Read and User.Read.All** – Allows us to access and read the properties of registered users

- **People.Read and People.Read.All** – Allows us to access relationships between people based on content

- **Group.Read.All and Group.ReadWrite.All** – Both used for reading and writing to Teams. Team sites are basically groups under the hood.

- **Sites.FullControl.All** – Allows us to read from and write to sites

The result can be viewed in Figure 2-14. All permissions selected are added to the app registration. You will notice that one of the added permissions, *Sites.FullControl.All*, is not granted. That permission requires administrator consent.

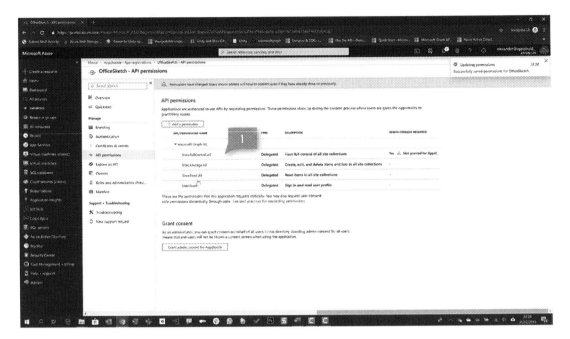

Figure 2-14. *View of the added permissions to your app registration*

It is also possible to add permissions through code, as you have seen in the two source code examples, when the `AcquireToken` methods are called. In both cases, you need to use a string collection like `string[]` containing the permissions you want to use with the application. The following source code is an example where some permissions are set through code:

```
AuthenticationHelper.Instance.Authentication.Permissions = new string[] {
"User.Read.All", "Sites.Read.All", "Sites.Manage.All", "Sites.FullControl.
All" };
```

This technique allows you to dynamically add and remove permissions whenever your application authenticates using OAuth 2.0. It allows developers to more easily add additional permissions during the development of the application without the need for access to the Azure portal environment. But keep in mind that changing the permissions will initiate a request for consent again.

Content Retrieval

There are many APIs available for controlling data. This section goes into the API calls available for insights around social intelligence, users, and their relations to content and insights. That means that we are also retrieving information about Teams, SharePoint sites, documents, and more. Some of these APIs are still in beta and can change over time. Something you need to take into consideration: APIs that are in beta are not recommended by Microsoft to use in a production-ready application.

Microsoft Graph API

Using the Microsoft Graph API requires understanding how to use the various API calls and the underlaying functionality like querying, throttling, and batch processing.

Each request made to the Microsoft Graph API is constructed as follows:

```
https://graph.microsoft.com/{version}/{resource}?{query-parameters}
```

Microsoft Graph has two versions of their API: v1.0 and beta. You will need to fill in {version} the values v1.0 or beta, depending on which resource you want to access.

The {resource} field refers to the resource you want to access. Resources are, for example, users, groups, drives, and sites. There is also a special resource called me. me represents the currently signed-in user and allows you to access content around that user. An example of getting information from the current user is as follows:

```
https://graph.microsoft.com/v1.0/me
```

Some resources require specifying an id property. An example would be getting information for a specific user in Office 365, based on the id of that user.

```
https://graph.microsoft.com/v1.0/users/24fcbca3-c3e2-48bf-9ffc-c7f81b81483d
```

It is also possible to access additional resources. The earlier named resources like users are called top-level resources. Let's say you want to get all the emails from the current user.

```
https://graph.microsoft.com/v1.0/me/messages
```

Query parameters can be used to customize the response from a request. These query parameters can be used for several different actions, as shown in Table 2-2.

Table 2-2. *Query Parameter Action Examples*

Action	Parameter	Description
Run method	$count, $expand, $metadata	Getting the total count of events `/me/calendar/events?$count=true` Expand the result with related members for groups `/groups?$expand=members` Return an overview of the Microsoft Graph Data model `/v1.0/$metadata`
Filter	$filter	Get all events by Lorenz `/me/calendar/events?$filter=surname -eq 'Lorenz'`
Format	$format, $orderby	It is possible to specify the format of the result `/me/calendar/events?$format=xml` Current known formats are json, atom, and xml.
Search	$search	Retrieve all events where the body contains the text mixedreality `/me/calendar/events?$search= "bodyPreview:mixedreality"`
Select	$select	Select allows you to retrieve specific columns `/me/calendar/events?$select=start,end, attendees`
Paging	$skip, $top	These two parameters can be used to create paging. Return the second page of a ten-page results `/me/calendar/events?$skip=10&top=10`

It is also possible to combine the different actions in query parameters to get even more specific data. The following is an example that shows getting the top ten search results in messages and sorting them on the displayName field.

```
https://graph.microsoft.com/v1.0/me/messages?$search=mixedreality&top=10&or
derby=displayName
```

Keep in mind that accessing the resource requires your application to request that permission.

Throttling

Throttling is an important part of any API. Throttling is to prevent overuse of resources. While the Microsoft Graph API can handle a large number of requests simultaneously, when the number of requests gets too high that will downgrade the reliability, quality, and performance of the service. That's where throttling comes into play. As soon as you exceed the throttling threshold, the number of requests allowed by that session is limited for some time.

When your requests are throttled, you will get an HTTP 429 Too Many Requests message. The response header will, depending on the resource, contain a suggested wait time for your application to implement and respect. Current resources providing a wait time are user, photo, mail, calendar, contact, attachment, group, people, and drive. Throttling happens quicker with write actions than with read requests.

Throttling is not tenant bound. Throttling in your application can happen when accessing data across multiple tenants or in a single tenant.

If throttling in your application takes place, you are mostly doing one of the following:

- Making a large number of requests or writes

- Requesting or writing too frequently

- Not waiting at least the given wait time for retries

It can also be possible for throttling to happen when the number of requests is too large across multiple applications in a single tenant.

It is important to think about what your application is doing and really needs. Think of breaking up the data you are writing or retrieving from the resource. Only get data that you need at that point in time, and don't try to retrieve everything before you need it. Let user interactions drive when you write to or retrieve from the resource. Doing so will create natural pauses between the calls made to Microsoft Graph and will tend to prevent you from exceeding the threshold.

Batch Processing

Batch processing allows your application to combine multiple requests into a single call. The results of all requests are combined into a single JSON payload. This can be very useful when your view of data contains information from different parts of the Office 365 tenant. Instead of doing each request separately, you are now able to combine them in a single request.

Due to that, all are in one request executed instead of multiples, meaning that you have fewer network latency issues.

Often you exceed the URL length limit when building complex queries. Using batch requests allows you to bypass those URL length limitations because the query becomes part of the request payload.

Batch processing requests always use the POST method. The following request URL is used:

```
https://graph.microsoft.com/v1.0/$batch
```

The JSON body of the request specifies each request as part of the batch processing. There is a required property requests, which is an array of the individual requests.

```
{
  "requests": [
    {
      "id": "1",
      "method": "GET",
      "url": "/me/events"
    },
    {
      "id": "2",
      "method": "GET",
      "url": "/me/calendars"
    }
  ]
}
```

Each individual request contains three required properties named id, method, and url. The id property is used to correlate the request. You will find the id property again by the result of the batch processing. The method specifies what kind of request is executed. method can be GET, POST, and other. The url property contains the request path to the resource.

44

The result of the call is completely random. Due to the `id` property that correlates to the initial request, you will be able to identify each result to one of the initial requests.

It is possible to control the order in which the individual requests are executed. This can be helpful in certain scenarios. An example would be adding a new event to the default calendar before retrieving the current schedule of that calendar. In the following example, we use two POST requests. The first request adds a new event on a certain day to the default calendar. The second post retrieves the calendar around that day. If we run the batch processing normally, it could be that the newly created event does not appear due to the order in which the requests are executed. You can specify a dependency with `dependsOn` between two requests. The `dependsOn` property is an array of ids of the individual requests. In the following example the second request has a dependency on the first one. The batch processing will therefore first execute the request with `id=1` and then with `id=2`.

```
{
  "requests": [
    {
      "id": "1",
      "method": "POST",
      "url": "/me/events",
      "body": {
        "subject": "Mixed Reality Workshop",
        "body": {
          "contentType": "HTML",
          "content": "Let's have a mixed reality workshop together"
        },
        "start": {
          "dateTime": "2019-08-02T12:00:00",
          "timeZone": "Pacific Standard Time"
        },
        "end": {
          "dateTime": "2019-08-02T14:00:00",
          "timeZone": "Pacific Standard Time"
        },
```

```
      "location": {
        "displayName": "Innovation lounge"
      }
    },
    "headers": {
      "Content-type": "application/json"
    }
  },
  {
    "id": "2",
    "dependsOn": [ "1" ],
    "method": "POST",
    "url": "/me/calendar/getschedule",
    "body": {
      "schedules": [ "admin@M365x165852.OnMicrosoft.com" ],
      "startTime": {
        "dateTime": "2019-08-01T09:00:00",
        "timeZone": "Pacific Standard Time"
      },
      "endTime": {
        "dateTime": "2019-08-03T18:00:00",
        "timeZone": "Pacific Standard Time"
      },
      "availabilityViewInterval": "60"
    },
    "headers": {
      "Content-type": "application/json"
    }
  }
 ]
}
```

The POST method used in this example requires having a body and headers property specified. The body property contains the required configuration for the request. The headers property needs to at least have the content type specified.

Graph Explorer

The Graph Explorer allows us to test the Microsoft Graph API in its fullest. It is a web-based environment that is accessed by the URL `https://developer.microsoft.com/en-us/graph/graph-explorer` and allows you to try out all the different requests in the `v1.0` or `beta` version without writing any line of code. You can use the Graph Explorer with a demo tenant from Microsoft when you are not logged in, as you can see in Figure 2-15.

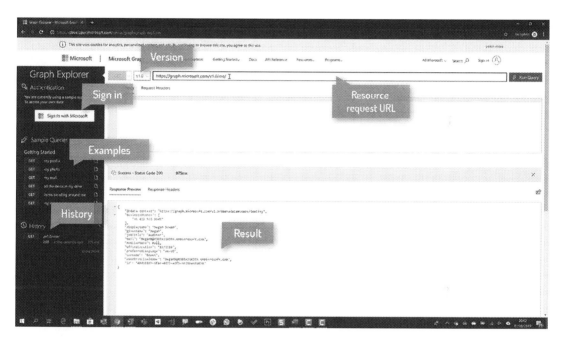

Figure 2-15. *Microsoft Graph Explorer explained*

Graph Explorer's initial state is signed in with a sample account for accessing content. The sample account is part of a demo tenant of Microsoft: the same type of demo tenant that you can request through the demo environment of Microsoft. This allows you to experiment with all the resources in the Microsoft Graph to its fullest.

You can sign in with your own account. But keep in mind that it needs enough rights to access the different parts of the Microsoft Graph API. If you do not have enough rights, it is possible to add additional permissions. But you need to log in again to get consent.

The left bar contains examples of different sets of functionalities. These match the permission sets. By clicking an example, it is requested and shown on the right part.

The right part of the explorer allows you to select several things. It allows you to select the method. By default, it is set to GET. If you are not signed in with an account, no other methods are available. You have the option to use either of the versions: *v1.0* or *beta*. Finally, you can enter a request URL to request a resource. Keep in mind that the result shown in the bottom part can differ based on the selected version. The result is shown in Figure 2-16 in JSON format. It allows you to see easily what to expect from a request to a specific resource.

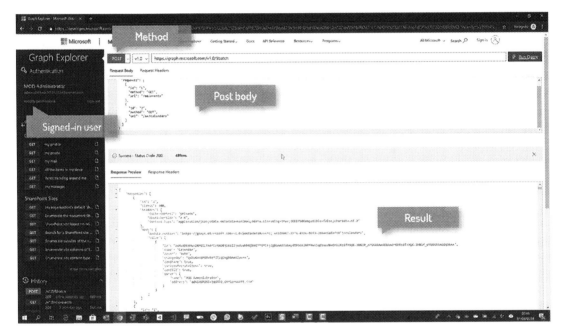

Figure 2-16. *Microsoft Graph Explorer with the POST method*

In Figure 2-16 you see when a user has signed-in to the Microsoft Graph Explorer. We have now signed in with a user. This allows us to select, for example, the POST method. In this scenario we are executing a simple batch process using the Graph Explorer. Just below the request URL we can enter the Request body and Request headers. Running the query will give the result again in the right part below.

Microsoft Graph Client Library

In the previous sections we learned how to authenticate, and use the Microsoft Graph API and the Graph Explorer to do requests on the API. Implementing such into an application can become complex and exhausting because of all the pieces you have to build yourself. Why not use an existing library? Microsoft has created the Microsoft Graph .NET client library.

The Microsoft Graph .NET client library targets *.NETStandard 1.1* and *.NET Framework 4.5*. It can be used directly in a UWP project generated by Unity or from a separate UWP DLL.

This library can be added in your solution by using a NuGet package called *Microsoft.Graph*. It works together with the Microsoft identity provider (MSAL) to create a `GraphServiceClient` object. This object handles all requests to the Microsoft Graph from building queries, sending to, processing, and getting results back as a response for you. Each API call in version v1.0 of the Microsoft Graph is represented as a building object in this library. The following is an example of getting the tasks of the current user:

```
var user = await graphClient.Me.Planner.Tasks.Request().GetAsync();
```

This call will return a collection list of `PlannerTask` objects, which can be iterated due to the `IEnumerator`. The `PlannerTask` object is derived from the base class `Entity` and contains several properties describing the information of the task—for example, `PercentComplete`, `OrderHint`, `Title`, `PlanId`, `CreatedBy`, and many more.

The following code is an example that retrieves the `GraphServiceClient` based on an `accesstoken` from the authentication provider and the URL to the Microsoft Graph API:

```
public GraphServiceClient GetGraphService(string accessToken)
{
    GraphServiceClient graphClient = new GraphServiceClient(
        "https://graph.microsoft.com/v1.0",
        new DelegateAuthenticationProvider(
            async (requestMessage) =>
            {
                token = accessToken;
                requestMessage.Headers.Authorization = new AuthenticationHe
                aderValue("bearer", token);

    }));
```

```
    return graphClient;

}
```

After you have retrieved a valid GraphServiceClient, you can start using different methods that correspond with the Microsoft Graph API. In the following example, we are retrieving the Teams you have joined as user, based on the userId property of the method:

```
public async void GetJoinedTeams(string userId, string accessToken)
{
    GraphServiceClient graphClient = AuthenticationHelper.Instance.
    GetGraphService(accessToken);

    if (graphClient != null)
    {
        var teams = await graphClient.Users[userId].JoinedTeams.Request().
        GetAsync();

        foreach (var team in teams)
        {
            // list through retrieved teams
        }
    }
}
```

Using this library gives you an advantage. You don't have to implement complex code to retrieve JSON payloads based on calling URLs and transform them into readable properties in a class. Instead, you have a library containing objects of each of the parts of the Microsoft Graph API and an engine doing everything for you. This includes also handling errors.

The library only contains the objects that are part of version *v1.0* of the Microsoft Graph API. In case you want to use the *beta* version, you will need to implement yourself some code for getting the information of that object.

The next chapters will go into more detail of some of the resources of the Microsoft Graph API. These are the resources we will be using in our final application to visualize and control content from an Office 365 tenant.

User

The most important resource type within the Microsoft Graph API is the user. Almost any call is from a user's perspective. Users have relationships with other users and groups based on their mail, files, and events in calendars. The user resource type represents an Azure AD account. Each user in the Office 365 tenant is therefore represented by a user resource. There are several methods available that allow you to retrieve and control user resources.

To get a list of available users, you can use the following request:

```
GET
https://graph.microsoft.com/v1.0/users
```

The equivalent for this request using the Microsoft Graph library is as follows:

```
var users = await graphClient.Users.Request().GetAsync();
```

The call returns a collection of users.

To retrieve a single user, you will need the id or the userPrincipalName of that user using the following request:

```
GET
https://graph.microsoft.com/v1.0/users/{id | userPrincipalName}
```

The equivalent for this request using the Microsoft Graph library is as follows:

```
var users = await graphClient.Users[userId].Request().GetAsync();
```

If you want to retrieve the signed-in user, you can use the /users/me request without any parameters. Each of these calls returns a single user or in case of a list, a collection of users. The JSON payload of a user is like the following:

```
{
  "@odata.context": "https://graph.microsoft.com/
  v1.0/$metadata#users/$entity",
  "businessPhones": [
    "+1 412 555 0109"
  ],
  "displayName": "Megan Bowen",
  "givenName": "Megan",
  "jobTitle": "Auditor",
```

```
  "mail": "MeganB@M365x214355.onmicrosoft.com",
  "mobilePhone": null,
  "officeLocation": "12/1110",
  "preferredLanguage": "en-US",
  "surname": "Bowen",
  "userPrincipalName": "MeganB@M365x214355.onmicrosoft.com",
  "id": "48d31887-5fad-4d73-a9f5-3c356e68a038"
}
```

The Microsoft Graph library returns an object User containing the same properties as the JSON payload from the request.

It is also possible to have more control over users. You can create, update, or delete a user via the Microsoft Graph API. Those requests are as follows:

POST
https://graph.microsoft.com/v1.0/users

PATCH
https://graph.microsoft.com/v1.0/users/{id | userPrincipalName}

DELETE
https://graph.microsoft.com/v1.0/users/{id | userPrincipalName}

It is also possible to control users by adding or removing them as members from within a SharePoint site or a Teams site.

Teams

Retrieving teams via the Microsoft Graph API requires using the group resource type. In principal, a group is a collection of users or principals who share the access to a set of resources in your Office 365 tenant. The group resource represents an Azure AD group. This can be an Office 365 group, also called a team, or a security group. Office 365 Groups have a groupType = "Unified" defined.

Groups are resources that can only be used in scenarios with work or school accounts. To execute operations related to groups needs administrator consent.

To retrieve a list of Office 365 groups, you can execute the following request containing a filter:

```
GET
https://graph.microsoft.com/v1.0/groups?$filter=groupTypes/
any(c:c+eq+'Unified')
```

The equivalent of this request in the Microsoft Graph library is as follows:

```
var groups = await graphClient.Groups.Request().Filter("groupTypes/
any(c:c+eq+'Unified')").GetAsync();
```

The JSON payload of a list of groups is as follows:

```
{
    "@odata.context": "https://graph.microsoft.com/v1.0/$metadata#groups/
    $entity",
    "id": "02bd9fd6-8f93-4758-87c3-1fb73740a315",
    "deletedDateTime": null,
    "classification": null,
    "createdDateTime": "2017-07-31T18:56:16Z",
    "creationOptions": [
        "ExchangeProvisioningFlags:481"
    ],
    "description": "Welcome to the HR Taskforce team.",
    "displayName": "HR Taskforce",
    "groupTypes": [
        "Unified"
    ],
    "mail": "HRTaskforce@M365x214355.onmicrosoft.com",
    "mailEnabled": true,
    "mailNickname": "HRTaskforce",
    "onPremisesLastSyncDateTime": null,
    "onPremisesSecurityIdentifier": null,
    "onPremisesSyncEnabled": null,
    "preferredDataLocation": null,
    "proxyAddresses": [
```

```
        "SPO:SPO_896cf652-b200-4b74-8111-c013f64406cf@SPO_dcd219dd-bc68-
        4b9b-bf0b-4a33a796be35",
        "SMTP:HRTaskforce@M365x214355.onmicrosoft.com"
    ],
    "renewedDateTime": "2017-07-31T18:56:16Z",
    "resourceBehaviorOptions": [],
    "resourceProvisioningOptions": [
        "Team"
    ],
    "securityEnabled": false,
    "visibility": "Private",
    "onPremisesProvisioningErrors": []
}
```

Normally you wouldn't request all the groups in the system. From a user-centric point of view, it is more logical to get the groups representing the teams for a specific user. And that can be achieved by executing the following request:

```
GET
https://graph.microsoft.com/v1.0/me/joinedTeams
https://graph.microsoft.com/v1.0/users/{id | userPrincipalName/joinedTeams
```

The equivalent in the Microsoft Graph library is as follows:

```
var teams = await graphClient.Users[userId].JoinedTeams.Request().
GetAsync();
var teams = await graphClient.Me.JoinedTeams.Request().GetAsync();
```

The JSON payload of the result is as follows:

```
{
    "@odata.context": "https://graph.microsoft.com/v1.0/$metadata#groups",
    "value": [
        {
            "id": "02bd9fd6-8f93-4758-87c3-1fb73740a315",
            "displayName": "HR Taskforce",
            "description": "Welcome to the HR Taskforce team.",
            "isArchived": false
```

```
        },
        {
            "id": "13be6971-79db-4f33-9d41-b25589ca25af",
            "displayName": "Business Development",
            "description": "Welcome to the BizDev team.",
            "isArchived": false
        },
        {

            "id": "8090c93e-ba7c-433e-9f39-08c7ba07c0b3",
            "displayName": "X1050 Launch Team",
            "description": "Welcome to the team that we've assembled to
            launch our product.",
            "isArchived": false
        }
    ]
}
```

This JSON payload does not contain the actual group resource. But it contains main properties like displayName, description, and isArchived. The id corresponds to the id of the group. That allows you to retrieve the *group* resource through the following request:

```
GET
https://graph.microsoft.com/v1.0/groups/02bd9fd6-8f93-4758-87c3-
1fb73740a315
```

The equivalent in the Microsoft Graph library is as follows:

```
var group = await graphClient.Groups["02bd9fd6-8f93-4758-87c3-
1fb73740a315"].Request().GetAsync();
```

People

The people entity is part of social intelligence in Microsoft Graph. It allows you to aggregate people around a user based on information. The information is a collection of mail, contacts, and information gathered from social networks. The result is ordered based on relevance. Relevance is based on several things:

- Collaboration patterns
- Business relationships
- Communication with others

Execute the following request to find the people who are related to the current user:

```
GET
https://graph.microsoft.com/v1.0/users/{id | userPrincipalName}/people
```

The equivalent in the Microsoft Graph library is as follows:

```
var people = await graphClient.Users[userId].People.Request().GetAsync();
```

These requests will return a JSON payload containing a collection of person resources. For example:

```
{
    "@odata.context": "https://graph.microsoft.com/
    v1.0/$metadata#users('48d31887-5fad-4d73-a9f5-3c356e68a038')/people",
    "@odata.nextLink": "https://graph.microsoft.com/v1.0/me/people?$skip=10",
    "value": [
        {
            "id": "33b43a5b-87d6-41ec-91f8-a2610048105f",
            "displayName": "Marketing",
            "givenName": null,
            "surname": null,
            "birthday": "",
            "personNotes": "",
            "isFavorite": false,
            "jobTitle": null,
            "companyName": null,
            "yomiCompany": "",
```

```
        "department": null,
        "officeLocation": null,
        "profession": "",
        "userPrincipalName": "",
        "imAddress": null,
        "scoredEmailAddresses": [
            {
                "address": "Marketing@M365x214355.onmicrosoft.com",
                "relevanceScore": 30,
                "selectionLikelihood": "notSpecified"
            }
        ],
        "phones": [],
        "postalAddresses": [],
        "websites": [],
        "personType": {
            "class": "Group",
            "subclass": "UnifiedGroup"
        }
    },
    { ...
  }]
}
```

Each item in the result is defined by the property personType. This contains two child properties, which describe the item. Property class defines if it is of type *Person*, *Group*, or *Other*. The property subclass contains additional information based on the type class. Some examples of subclass per class are listed in Table 2-3.

Table 2-3. *A List of Possible Subclasses per Class*

Class	Subclass
Person	OrganizationUser
Group	UnifiedGroup, PublicDistributionList
Other	Room, Unknown

Another interesting part of the item is the property `scoredEmailAddresses`. This property contains the property `relevanceScore`. The value is somewhat difficult to explain. It is not really a value in a scale but just a score given by the social intelligence mechanism to imply how relevant it is against the user.

This method/people get more interesting when you start doing this cascaded. Initially you retrieve all people around you. Then for each person you find, you get the people around that person—and so on. This will give you a network of people based on their relevance, which would be interesting to view in a 3D space.

Insights

Another interesting part of the Microsoft Graph API is a feature known as Insights. Insights allow you to retrieve information such as documents trending around you.

These documents can be found on OneDrive, SharePoint sites, email attachments, and even linked attachments from external sources like Google Drive, Dropbox, and Box.

These relationships are calculated based on advanced analytics and machine learning. In principle these relationships work the same as your personal profile page (Office Delve) in Office 365.

There are several lists of documents you can retrieve using the Insights feature. These are given in Table 2-4.

Table 2-4. *Available Document Types*

Insights	Information	Sources
Trending	Documents	OneDrive, SharePoint sites
Used	Viewed and modified documents	OneDrive for Business; SharePoint; email attachments; linked attachments from sources like Google Drive, Dropbox, and Box
Shared	Shared documents with another user(s)	Email attachments, OneDrive for Business links in emails

To get a collection of `trending`, `used`, or `shared` documents, issue the following request:

```
GET
https://graph.microsoft.com/beta/users/{id | userPrincipalName}/insights/trending
GET
https://graph.microsoft.com/beta/users/{id | userPrincipalName}/insights/used
```

GET
https://graph.microsoft.com/beta/users/{id | userPrincipalName}/insights/shared

The equivalent in the Microsoft Graph library is as follows:

```
var trending = graphClient.Users[userId].Insights.Trending.Request().
GetAsync();
var used = graphClient.Users[userId].Insights.Used.Request().GetAsync();
var shared = graphClient.Users[userId].Insights.Shared.Request().GetAsync();
```

It is important to notice that Insights, during the writing of this book, is part of the beta version. The beta version in Microsoft Graph is subject to change, and is discouraged and not supported to use in production applications.

The most interesting Insights request for our application is for trending documents. This returns documents that are interesting to the user based on his behavior and connections with others in the organization. The JSON payload of the trending insights request is as follows:

```
{
    "@odata.context": "https://graph.microsoft.com/
    beta/$metadata#users('48d31887-5fad-4d73-a9f5-3c356e68a038')/insights/
    trending",
    "value": [
        {
            "id": "AQm7WFq6H8FBgSVp2iZDcKBI3WhyDnIVQaNSNdsYiRi-AAAAAAAAAAA
            AAAAAAAAAAAAAAAAAAAAAAAAAAAAAAAJu1hauh_BQYEladomQ3CgAQ",
            "weight": 743614.6241886764,
            "resourceVisualization": {
                "title": "Engineering Excellence",
                "type": "spsite",
                "mediaType": "application/octet-stream",
                "previewImageUrl": "https://m365x214355.sharepoint.com/_
                api/v2.0/drives/b!CbtYWrofwUGBJWnaJkNwoEjdaHIOchVBo1I12xiJG
                L4AAAAAAAAAAAAAAAAAAAAA/items/01ZKFJJWIAAAAAAAAAAAAAAAAAAAA
                AAAAA/thumbnails/0/small/thumbnailContent",
                "previewText": "\t\r\n\t  Engineering Excellence\r\n\t\
                r\n    \r\n  \r\n\r\n\r\n\r\n\r\n\r\n\t\tHome\r\n\t \r\n\
```

```
            r\n\r\n\r\n\r\n\r\n\r\n Documents\r\n\r\nType \r\n  \r\
            nName \r\n  \r\n\r\nThere are no items to show in this view
            of the \"Documents\" document library. \r\n\r\nFollow\r\
            njavascript: SP.SOD.executeFunc('followingc",
            "containerWebUrl": "https://m365x214355.sharepoint.com",
            "containerDisplayName": "Engineering Excellence",
            "containerType": "Site"
        },
        "resourceReference": {
            "webUrl": "https://m365x214355.sharepoint.com/ee",
            "id": "sites/m365x214355.sharepoint.com,5a58bb09-1fba-41c1-
            8125-69da264370a0,7268dd48-720e-4115-a352-35db188918be",
            "type": "microsoft.graph.siteItem"
        }
    },
    {...}]
}
```

Each Insights request result contains a property resourceVizualization and resourceReference. Depending on the type of request, additional properties are added with more information.

The property resourceVizualization contains fields that can be used to visualize the content. Think of properties like title, mediaType, previewImageUrl, and previewText. It also contains information about the container where the document is stored, like its containerWebUrl as location, containerDisplayName as container name, and containerType specifying what the source is.

The property resourceReference contains the reference to the document. It contains the properties webUrl and id, which can be concatenated to get access to the document.

CHAPTER 3

Environment and Configuration

An important part of developing applications for HoloLens is your environment, the tools and how they are configured. This chapter goes into detail about each of them.

Visual Studio

Visual Studio is a suite of several applications that are best-in-class tools used by developers: tools like Visual Studio IDE, Visual Studio Code, Azure DevOps, and Visual Studio App Center. Visual Studio IDE is a rich IDE that allows you to build applications from start to finish. It contains IntelliSense, testing functionality, Git management, and support for several common emulators.

The Microsoft HoloLens 2 emulator is one of those emulators that is supported by Visual Studio IDE. Visual Studio is currently available in one free version called the Visual Studio Community 2019 and in two paid versions called Visual Studio Professional 2019 and Visual Studio Enterprise 2019. The versions differ mainly in functionalities, but all can be used for Microsoft HoloLens development. All versions can be downloaded from the following URL:

```
https://visualstudio.microsoft.com/vs/
```

In the case of a paid version, after installation you are requested to add one or more work, school, or personal accounts. These accounts need to have the license of the selected version.

The following steps show you how to install the Visual Studio Community 2019 version and which workloads need to be selected to start developing for Microsoft

© Alexander Meijers 2020
A. Meijers, *Immersive Office 365*, https://doi.org/10.1007/978-1-4842-5845-3_3

HoloLens. Open a browser and go to the preceding URL. You will see a page similar to Figure 3-1.

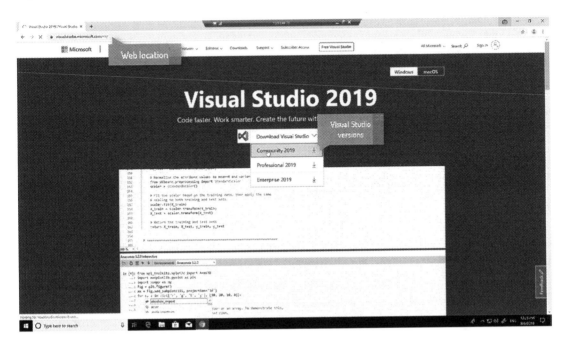

Figure 3-1. *The web page where Visual Studio 2019 can be downloaded*

Select the right version from the dropdown to start the download. An installer file is downloaded to your downloads folder. Run the file, as administrator, to start the installation.

The Visual Studio Installer must be installed first, as you can see in Figure 3-2. This installer can be used anytime to install, uninstall, or modify your installation of tools. This installer will be frequently updated with new options and tools.

Figure 3-2. *Visual Studio Installer must be installed first*

Since we do not yet have anything installed from Visual Studio, the installer will go directly to the workloads page of Visual Studio Community 2019, as seen in Figures 3-3 and 3-4.

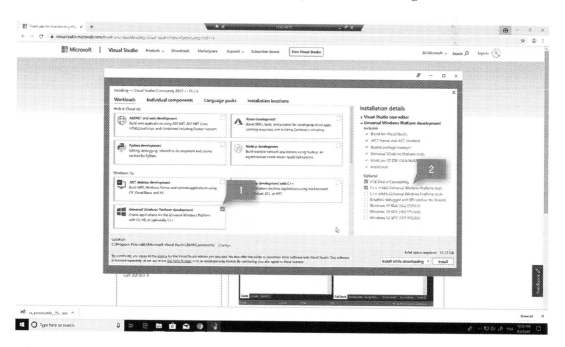

Figure 3-3. *Selection of workload Universal Windows Platform development*

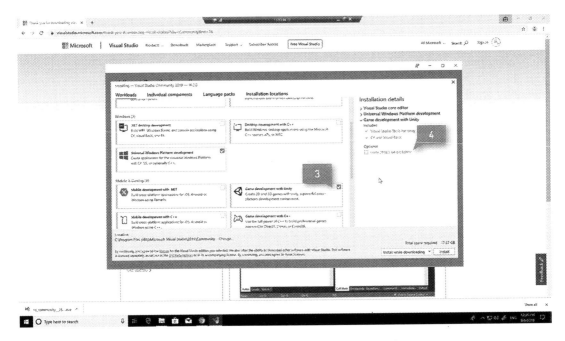

Figure 3-4. *Selection of workload Game development with Unity*

The selected workloads for developing are in all available versions of Visual Studio. You will need to install at least the workloads shown in Table 3-1.

Table 3-1. *Required Workloads*

Workload	Options
Universal Windows platform development	USB Device Connectivity C++ (v142) Universal Windows Platform tools
Game development with Unity	Deselect all options

The workloads in Table 3-1 are needed to start developing for Microsoft HoloLens and for Microsoft Immersive headsets. The second workload, Game development with Unity, has no options selected. We don't want to install the Unity version that is part of the Visual Studio Installer. Instead we will be installing the correct version of Unity later. The version depends on several things, which will be explained in the next chapter.

After the workloads are selected, press the Install button to install Visual Studio. In some cases this can take considerable time, since the installer needs to download the selected workloads.

Unity Hub

The Unity Hub is a tool from Unity that allows you to manage all your Unity installations and projects. Unity Hub should always be your starting point when building applications with Unity. It allows you to install and control different Unity versions on the same machine. Also, it makes sure that when you start your project from Unity Hub, the project is started with the correct Unity version. The Unity Hub can be downloaded from

https://unity3d.com/get-unity/download

A Unity Developer Network (UDN) account is needed to use this tool. Run the tool when it is installed. The tool requires you to sign in the first time with the same account you used on the Unity website. After this, you will have several options on the left side called *Projects*, *Learn*, and *Installs*.

It is possible to add a new installation by selecting from a list of the latest official releases or to locate an existing installed version on your disk, as can be seen in Figure 3-5. A new installation allows you to additionally select the modules you want to install together with the Unity version.

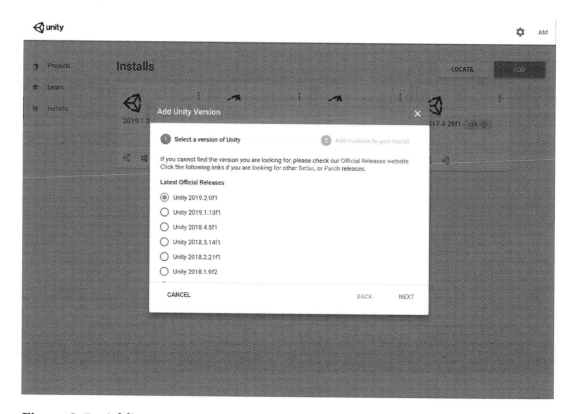

Figure 3-5. *Adding a new Unity version with the Unity Hub*

Adding an existing Unity installation is done through locating the installation on disk. A file explorer is opened when the Locate button is pressed. Browse to the `editor` folder under the Unity installation folder and select the `Unity.exe` file.

Project management allows you to add existing projects from disk or create new ones based on the installed versions of Unity. Creating a new project allows you to select from several templates, as you can see in Figure 3-6.

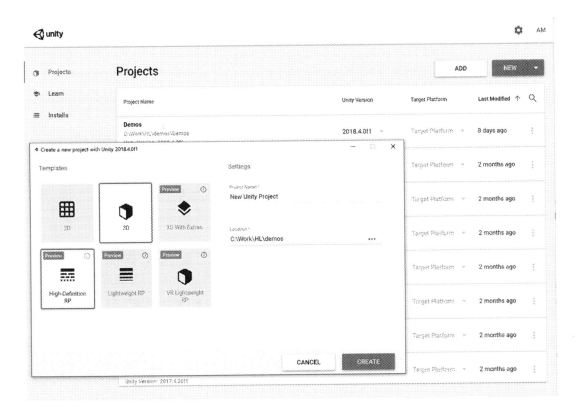

Figure 3-6. *Creating a new 3D project with Unity Hub*

The Unity Hub also contains a learning entry where you will find getting started, tutorial projects, resources, and interesting links that will help you further with Unity development.

While the Unity Hub allows you to select from a variety of Unity versions to be installed on your computer, the version we need depends on the tools we use for developing for Microsoft HoloLens.

Unity

You will need to determine which version of Unity you need to use. Since we will be using the Mixed Reality Toolkit version 2, also called MRTK v2, we need to determine against which version the release of MRTK v2 is built. Initially, you can check in the documentation provided by Microsoft. There is a Getting started with MRTK v2 available on

`https://docs.microsoft.com/en-us/windows/mixed-reality/mrtk-getting-started`

The minimum requirements for MRTK v2 can be found on that page. But if you want to be exact, there is another way. You will need to go to the actual source code of the MRTK v2 on GitHub. The project can be found at the following GitHub URL:

`https://www.github.com/Microsoft/MixedRealityToolkit-Unity`

Select the < > *Code* tab and make sure that you are viewing the latest released branch. Now go into the folder `ProjectSettings` and look for the file called `ProjectVersion.txt`. That file contains the version used by the build team.

There are a lot of different Unity versions available via the download page of Unity. Several versions are released every year, making choosing the right version somewhat difficult. While writing this book, the version used by the team is 2018.4.20f1. This version is a Long Term Support (LTS) version.

It is recommended to use LTS versions of Unity when developing applications for production. These versions are stable for an extended period of two years. LTS versions will not have new features or other improvements, but deliver a stable way for production applications.

The Unity version LTS release 2018.4.20f1 is available via the Unity Hub. Not every LTS release is available via the Unity Hub. In that case, you can download the LTS release via the following URL:

`https://unity3d.com/unity/qa/lts-releases`

Run the installation file when it has downloaded. Follow the instructions during the installation. Accept the terms of the license agreement. As soon as you reach the components step, which is shown in Figure 3-7, you need to specify two specific components.

1. Select the component *Unity 2018.4.20f1*.

2. Make sure that *UWP Build Support (IL2CPP)* is selected.

3. Then press the Next button to finish the configuration and install
    Unity.

Figure 3-7. *Components selection during a Unity installation*

Finally, you need to add this newly installed version of Unity into the Unity Hub, as
shown in Figure 3-8.

1. Start Unity Hub and open the *Installs*. Select the Locate button.

2. Browse to the installation folder of the previously installed Unity
    version.

3. Select the Unity.exe application from the Editor folder.

4. Press the Select Folder button. The installed version is now
    available in Unity Hub.

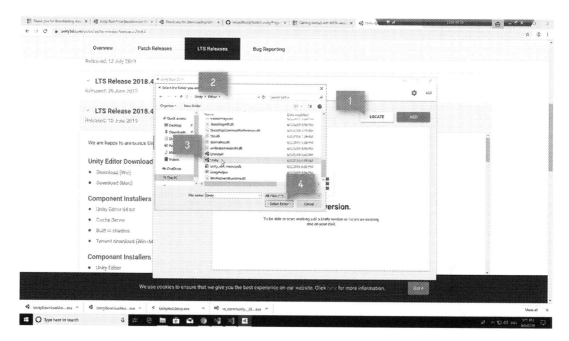

Figure 3-8. *Adding an existing installation to the Unity Hub*

Mixed Reality Toolkit

The Mixed Reality Toolkit (MRTK) is an open source cross-platform development kit for building mixed reality applications. The MRTK v2 targets Microsoft HoloLens, Windows Mixed Reality immersive headsets, and OpenVR. The development kit mainly focuses on the Microsoft HoloLens 2, although it still can be used for Microsoft HoloLens 1. MRTK v2 in combination with Unity creates a powerful combination that accelerates development. The Unity project examples in this book will be using MRTK v2. The reason for this is that MRTK v2 supports hand tracking and eye tracking for Microsoft HoloLens 2.

The minimal requirements for using MRTK v2 are as follows:

- Unity 2018.4.x or higher (it is recommended to use an LTS version)

- Microsoft Visual Studio 2019 or higher

- Windows 10 version 1803 or later

- Windows SDK 18362 or higher

Keep in mind that the Windows SDK is a separate installation from the Windows 10 update. The latest version can be downloaded here:

```
https://developer.microsoft.com/en-us/windows/downloads/windows-10-sdk
```

Make sure that you close the Visual Studio 2019 application before you install the SDK.

Windows Device Portal

The Windows Device Portal allows you to manage and configure a device via a network or USB connection. It is available on each device family such as HoloLens, IoT, and Xbox. The available functionality and features differ per device type. Extensive and advanced diagnostic tools for troubleshooting your app are available for HoloLens. This includes real-time performance of several hardware parts of your device.

The Windows Device Portal is built on top of RESTfull APIs. These allow you to directly access data and control your device from a custom application via the APIs.

You will need to configure two settings on your Microsoft HoloLens 2 to connect through the Windows Device Portal. These settings do not need to be configured when you connect to the Microsoft HoloLens 2 emulator.

Both settings can be found at *Settings* ➤ *Update Security* ➤ *For Developers*.

- Enable the setting *Use developer features*. This option is intended for development use only.

- Enable the setting *Enable Device Portal*. This option turns on remote diagnostics, which allows the Windows Device Portal to control the device. The *User developer features* need to be enabled up front.

Connect the Microsoft HoloLens 2 via a USB connector to your PC. Make sure the preceding settings are met, and the HoloLens is turned on. The Windows Device Portal runs as a web server on the device and can be reached by connecting through a web browser. Open a browser and use the following URL:

```
https://127.0.0.1:10080
```

The device needs to be paired to the PC for the first time. The Windows Device Portal shows you a screen that asks you to reset the credentials. This can be seen in Figure 3-9.

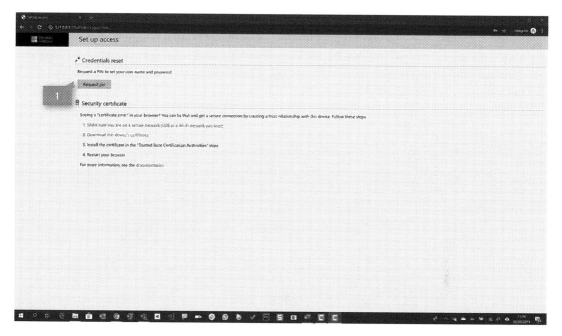

Figure 3-9. *Windows Device Portal—resetting the credentials*

Click the Request pin button. This will show a Request pin number in the HoloLens device.

You need to fill in several values in the Windows Device Portal in Figure 3-10.

1. Fill in the pin that is shown within the Microsoft HoloLens 2 device.

2. Fill in the username.

3. Fill in a password.

4. Press the Pair button to pair the environment with the device.

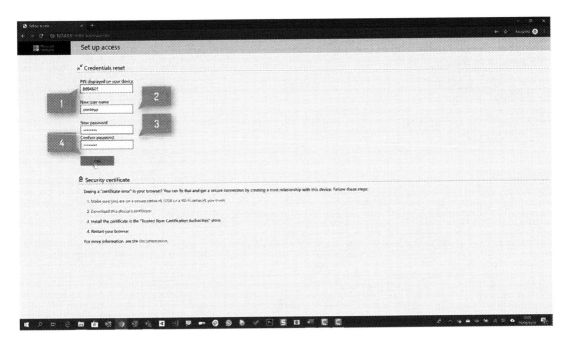

Figure 3-10. *Windows Device Portal—setting up access to the device*

The username and password are requested whenever you start the Windows Device Portal.

It is possible to reset the credentials if you don't know what the username and/or password was. This can be achieved by opening the URL and filling in blanks in both credential fields four times. That will return you to the reset credentials screen again.

The Windows Device Portal for HoloLens shows on the main page the device status and installed Windows version. At the top of the page temperature, battery, and WIFI status are shown. At the left, a menu is shown with all the different functionalities divided into *Views*, *Performance*, and *System* (Figure 3-11).

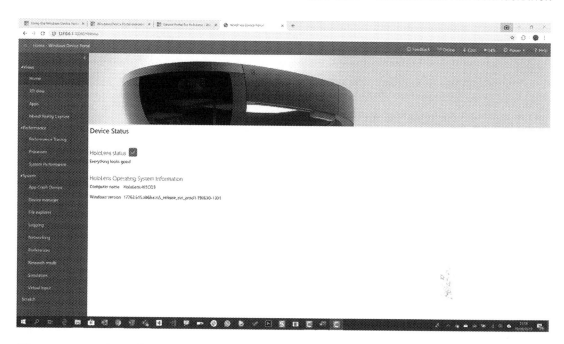

Figure 3-11. *Windows Device Portal connected to HoloLens device*

After the pairing of the device with your PC, you can access the Windows Device Portal via a web browser any time using a USB cable or the WIFI network. Table 3-2 provides the connection URLs to use.

Table 3-2. *Connection URLs for the Windows Device Portal*

Connected via	Connection URL
USB cable	`https://127.0.0.1:10080`
WIFI network	`https://{IP address of HoloLens}`

If connecting to the Device Portal via WiFi, you'll need to specify the IP address of the HoloLens without a port number. That address can be found on the device in *Settings* ➤ *Network & Internet* ➤ *Wi-Fi* ➤ *{connected WIFI}* ➤ *Advanced Options*.

There are some interesting functionalities available in the Windows Device Portal for developers. The 3D view, under *views* ➤ *3D view*, allows you to view in real time what the HoloLens device is experiencing. A snapshot from the continuous flow of spatial mapping can be shown in the view, as can be seen in Figure 3-12.

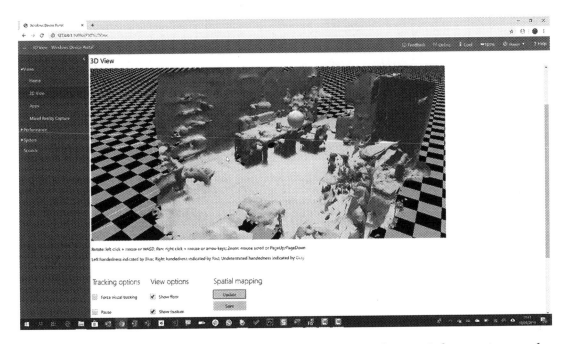

Figure 3-12. Windows Device Portal 3D view showing the spatial mapping mesh

Different options allow you to show the floor, the mesh, and other details. One of those other details is the stabilization plane. This is the area that has the focus of the user and is rendered at high quality; while moving away from that plane, the device uses less calculation and shows lower quality.

The 3D view also shows the current location of the device itself. The HoloLens does not have a GPS but uses the internal, and continuously updated, spatial mapping, which is compared to what the device sees to define its location. It is also possible to show the spatial anchors when used with holograms. Spatial anchors allow you to virtually (invisibly) pinpoint a hologram against the real world. The spatial mapping can also be stored as an object file of type obj.

A developer can deploy applications via Visual Studio. But it is also possible to deploy and manage your applications via the Windows Device Portal. This functionality is found under *Views* ➤ *Apps*. Deploying applications allows you to deploy from a local storage or network. During deployment you can add additional packages and framework packages. Installed applications can be removed or started. Running applications can be viewed, paused, or their process killed.

There are several important functionalities under *Performance*. Let's start with Performance tracing. This allows you to use an available profile or create a custom profile for tracing the device its parts: for example, *First Level Triage, Computation, I/O,* and *Memory.* This allows you to see what happens on the device when running services or applications. It is even possible to trace from starting up the device.

The second functionality, called *Processes*, allows you to view all the running processes in the device. You can see which account the process is running and how much CPU and working set of memory is used.

The third functionality is *System Performance*. This allows you to real-time monitor a lot of different things. For example, you can monitor any of the following:

- CPU Utilization

- I/O read and written

- Memory utilization like total, in use, available, committed, paged, and nonpaged memory

- Network received and sent packages

- Instantaneous system-on-chip (SoC) power utilization

- Instantaneous system power utilization

- GPU engine utilization up to eight engines

- Application frames per second

In Figure 3-13 you can see System Performance in action.

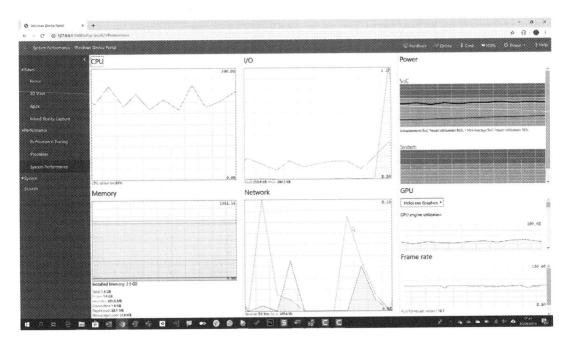

Figure 3-13. *Windows Device Portal system performance*

Why are these values in Figure 3-13 important? They are important because your HoloLens 2 device has, at its best, an uptime of around 3 hours. When building applications, you want to prevent those applications from draining your batteries due to heavy processor and graphics load. This means that building applications for HoloLens requires more than just building an application. You need to think of what you really need to utilize from the device to carefully and thoughtfully manage your power draw.

You also need to keep track of the temperature of the device. Imagine you are building an application that is used in a climate with high temperatures. Such high temperatures could eventually result in automatic shutting down of the device, since the device is self-protected.

Dropping framerates is also something to watch out for. Your application performs its best with a framerate of 60fps. Your application can become less stable when the framerate drops. For example, a dropping frame rate can lead to drifting, slow buildup, and other not preferable behavior. Dropping framerates are caused by several things, such as too many things going on in the update() method of a GameObject. (That particular case is explained in the next chapter). Other possible causes are overly complex objects, lighting, or rendering. Quality output settings for your applications may also be too high and can lead toward reduced framerates.

There are also some functionalities under *System* that can be very useful for developers. These are summed up in Table 3-3.

Table 3-3. *Useful System Functionalities*

Functionality	Description
App Crash dumps	Here you collect crash dumps of your side-loaded applications. The dump files can be opened using Visual Studio for debugging.
File explorer	This functionality allows you to browse through the file structure on the HoloLens. It also allows you to upload and download files. This can be very handy when your application is using storage on the device.
Logging	Logging is real-time event tracing for Windows (ETW). There are several tracing levels available to choose from, like *Abnormal exit or termination*, *severe errors*, *warnings*, and *non-error warnings*.
Research mode	This mode allows your application to access low-level HoloLens sensor streams in addition to the default environmental data you already can access. But keep in mind that this is only for research purposes. You shouldn't use this in a production application. This functionality is not available for applications in the Windows Store.
Simulation	This allows you to record and play back the input data for testing scenarios. *Capture room* will download a simulation room that contains the spatial mapping mesh of the surrounding, head position, hand movements, and environment into a captured file. This captured file, a .xef file, can be loaded into the HoloLens emulator or the Microsoft HoloLens. The latter can be accomplished to set the *Control mode* to Simulation. This disables the sensors on the device and uses the uploaded simulation.
Virtual Input	This is one of the best functionalities in the Windows Device Portal. Instead of using the keyboard in 3D space, you can send over-long and complex texts into text fields. Think of logging in as a user.

The Windows Device Portal is a powerful tool that developers can use to debug their applications, run simulations, and monitor device-specific settings. The Windows Device Portal is available for Microsoft HoloLens as for the Microsoft HoloLens 2 emulator.

Microsoft HoloLens 2

We extensively talked about Microsoft HoloLens 2 in Chapter 1. In principle, not many things need to be configured on a HoloLens device to start developing with it. When the device is initially set up, you will have to go through a setup procedure that explains how to use the device. This helps you to determine the interpupillary distance (IPD) of your eyes and helps you to select a work or school account, or a Microsoft account. You will see the startup menu of the HoloLens device when you have set up the device, as shown in Figure 3-14. You may also open and close the startup menu by pressing the Windows button displayed on your wrist.

Figure 3-14. *Microsoft HoloLens startup menu*

Like any other Windows device, you have settings available. You will find the *Settings* icon in the menu. There are some settings that are important for developers. Let's start with the developer settings. These can be found under *Settings* ➤ *Update & Security* ➤ *For developers*, as can be seen in Figure 3-15.

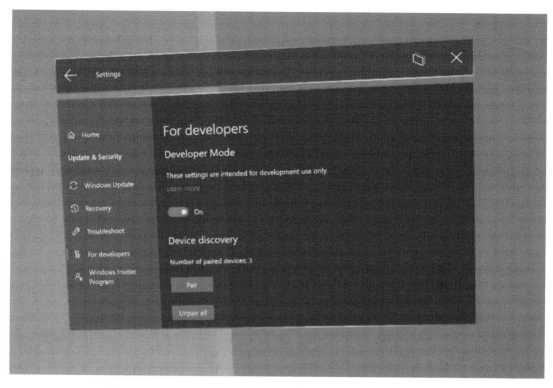

Figure 3-15. *Microsoft HoloLens developer settings*

Use developer features allow you to deploy applications from Visual Studio to your device. Without this option, you can't develop. The second option, *Enable Device Portal*, which can be found by scrolling down, allows you to connect from the Windows Device Portal URL on a local network. This option can't be turned on without the *Use developer features* option.

Another useful setting, which you can see in Figure 3-16, is found under *Settings* ➤ *System* and is called *Holograms*. *Holograms* has two buttons, which allow you to remove nearby holograms or to remove all holograms. This will clear up your 3D space and removes any running applications. If you want to be sure that an application is not running anymore, it is wise to use the Windows Device Portal.

Figure 3-16. *Microsoft HoloLens hologram settings*

You can temporarily leave your running application. Doing so will display the start menu again with an additional home button, as shown in Figure 3-17. This home button allows you to leave the application.

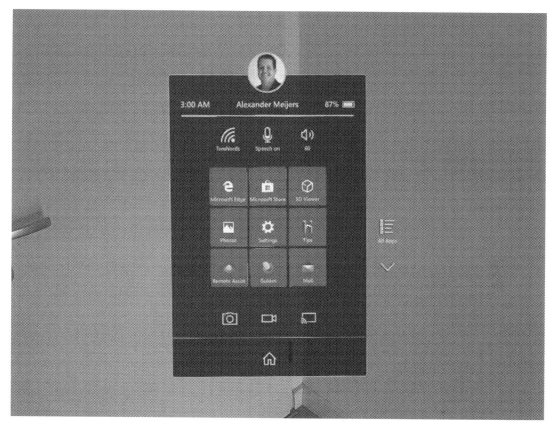

Figure 3-17. *Microsoft HoloLens application menu*

There are two multimedia buttons available at the bottom on the left for starting a video recording or taking a picture. The button on the right allows you to select a presenter for Miracast. Miracast allows you to cast the video signal of the HoloLens device to any other PC. This can be helpful for demonstrations or to have someone else looking over your shoulders and helping you out—for example, finding an issue.

Miracast uses your video camera on the Microsoft HoloLens. Only one application or service can use the video camera. If your application uses the camera, for example with cognitive services, the video signal is not available. This is also the other way around. If you are casting, your application is not able to get control over the video camera.

Microsoft HoloLens 2 Emulator

There is a HoloLens Emulator around if you do not possess a Microsoft HoloLens device. The emulator runs within a virtual machine based on Hyper-V. The emulator allows you to test your mixed reality applications on a PC without a physical Microsoft HoloLens. An application does not have to be altered to run on the emulator. The mixed reality application doesn't even know it is running inside an emulator instead of an actual HoloLens device.

Running the HoloLens emulator has several hardware requirements:

- 64-bit Windows 10 Pro, Enterprise, or Education

- CPU with 4 cores

- 8 GB of RAM or more

- GPU that supports DirectX 11.0 or later and WDDM 2.5 graphics driver or later

You will need to enable the following features in the BIOS of your computer:

- Hardware-assisted virtualization

- Second Level Address Translation (SLAT)

- Hardware-based Data Execution Prevention (DEP)

The performance of the emulator is heavily influenced by the capabilities of your GPU. The Microsoft HoloLens 2 emulator requires you to have the Windows 10 October 2018 update or later installed.

The Microsoft HoloLens 2 emulator and the holographic project templates can be downloaded from the Microsoft website. You will find the download links at the following page:

```
https://docs.microsoft.com/en-us/windows/mixed-reality/using-the-
hololens-emulator
```

Install and start the emulator. Starting the emulator can take some time, since it is spinning up a virtual machine. Just like the HoloLens device, you get a HoloLens startup screen. In Figure 3-18 you see an example of the emulator. A part of the right hand is shown, and the gaze is pointing to the All Apps button. The main difference is the black background, since there is no real world viewed through the emulator.

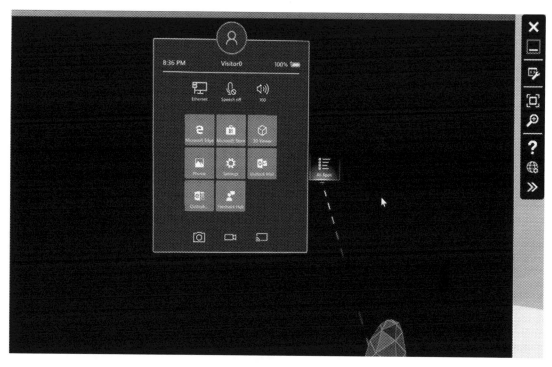

Figure 3-18. *Microsoft HoloLens 2 emulator*

The emulator supports the same tools and functionality when building mixed reality applications for Microsoft HoloLens. You can still use the Windows Device Portal and debug your application using Visual Studio. It is also possible to configure the sign-in with a Microsoft account, which can be used by your application or specific APIs that require a user to be signed in.

The emulator has a toolbar on the right. That toolbar contains several standard buttons that allow you to control the emulator. These buttons allow you to close the emulator, minimize the emulator windows, and request emulator help.

The toolbar also contains two buttons called *Zoom* and *Fit to Screen*. *Zoom* allows you to make the emulator smaller or larger. But if you have a large screen resolution, you will not able to maximize it to the screen. *Fit to Scree*n brings the emulator back to the maximum zoom size or the size of your screen.

The toolbar also contains a button called Perception Simulation Control Panel. That opens a configuration panel, as can be seen in Figure 3-19. This panel allows you to view the current position and the simulated input of the body, head, and hands.

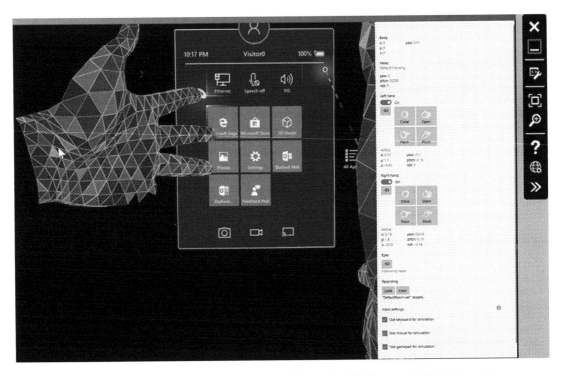

Figure 3-19. *Perception simulation control panel of Microsoft HoloLens 2 emulator*

You can define if the left and/or right hands are shown in the emulator. Even if one of the hands is not shown, you can still control that hand. It will appear as soon as you start controlling it and disappear when you stop. There is a pin that allows you to direct all the input control to one or both hands. For each of the hands, you can control their state. There are currently four hand poses present: Close, Open, Point, and Pinch. These hand poses allow you to simulate any action in an actual Microsoft HoloLens 2. A pin button is available to control the eye gaze direction. This allows you to simulate the eye look direction.

It is also possible to define which input settings, keyboard, mouse, and/or Xbox controller are allowed. A separate settings icon allows you to control for each of them the speed. Input and sensor controls, which are normally done with hands, eyes, and movement of the device, are now simulated via the keyboard, mouse, or an Xbox controller.

Table 3-4 shows the available input options for each input device type.

Table 3-4. *Input Options by Input Device Type*

Input	Mouse	Keyboard	Xbox controller
Walk around	n/a	W = forward A = left S = right D = back	Left stick
Look around	Left-click and drag	Arrow keys	Right stick
Air tap gesture	Right-click	Enter or space key	A button
Bloom gesture	n/a	Windows key or F2	B button
Hand movement for scrolling	Hold Alt key together with right-click and drag mouse up and down. Left Alt key for left hand and right Alt key for right hand		Hold right trigger and A button and move right stick up and down
Hand movement and orientation	Hold Alt key together with left-click and drag mouse. Rotate by using the arrow keys or Q and E key.		Hold left or right bumper and move left stick. Use the right stick to rotate.
Eye gazing	n/a	Hold down the Y key	n/a
Head hazing	n/a	Hold down the H key	n/a
Use keyboard input	n/a	Toggle the F4 key	n/a
Show or hide the main menu	n/a	Windows key	n/a
Reset	n/a	Escape key	Start button
Tracking	n/a	T or F3 key	X button
Hand poses	n/a	Key 7 = Close Key 8 = Open Key 9 = Point Key 0 = Pinch	n/a

The emulator also contains a button called Tools. This pops up a dialog with several tabs. It allows you configure sign-in with a Microsoft account. You will need to restart to log in with a Microsoft account. You will get the same dialogs for logging in with an account as you have on the HoloLens device itself. The second option allows you to enable or disable hardware-accelerated graphics. It depends on the hardware configuration of your PC. If it supports virtualized GPU (GPU-PV) it is enabled. The diagnostics tab gives you the IP address, which you can use to reach out to the emulated device. This is used for the Windows Device Portal. But it is also useful when you are building a service that connects to the Microsoft HoloLens.

The emulator is not able to show the real world in combination with holograms. Therefore, several rooms are available to create test scenarios. These rooms can be found in the following folder:

`C:\Program Files (x86)\Windows Kits\10\Microsoft XDE\10.0.18362.0\Plugins\Rooms`

This folder contains a set of HoloLens XEF format files, which are simulated rooms specifically created for the emulator by Microsoft. These are useful for testing your app in multiple environments. The following rooms are available:

- **DefaultRoom.xef** - A small living room with a TV, coffee table, and two sofas. Loaded by default when you start the emulator

- **Bedroom1.xef** - A small bedroom with a desk

- **Bedroom2.xef** - A bedroom with a queen size bed, dresser, nightstands, and walk-in closet

- **GreatRoom.xef** - A large open space great room with living room, dining table, and kitchen

- **LivingRoom.xef** - A living room with a fireplace, sofa, armchairs, and a coffee table with a vase

It is also possible to create your own simulated rooms through the Windows Device Portal of an actual Microsoft HoloLens device. These recordings are stored as HoloLens XEF format files.

The loaded simulated room in the emulator is not shown by default. Clicking somewhere in the 3D space of the emulator will show a flowing pattern over the spatial mesh temporarily. The only way of showing the room is by deploying an application to the emulator, which draws the spatial mesh.

CHAPTER 4

Unity

Unity is the world's leading real-time creation platform, and is used with building over more than half of the world's games. It has an incredible set of tools, which allows you to build for almost any platform. And the fun part is that nowadays it is not only for building games, but also for creating applications across different industries.

The Unity Editor is the most common and known tool of the Unity suite. It is available on the Mac, Linux, and Windows platforms. It is built up from many strong developer tools, which allows you to create immersive experiences using game elements, game logic, and gameplay. The Unity Editor has a large list of different platforms that you build for, like Android, iOS, Xbox One, Facebook, WebGL, and Universal Windows Platform. Universal Windows Platform is used for building mixed reality applications for Microsoft HoloLens.

This chapter goes into the various interface parts of Unity in this chapter. It explains how to build and deploy your application to a device. For a quick start, let's begin with a Hello world! application.

Interface and Environment

The best Unity version to start with is the latest Long Term Support (LTS) version. During the writing of this book, that version is 2018.4.6f1.

The interface consists of several areas that are used to build your scene and application. The scene is your working area when building an application. It is nothing more than a 3D space in which one or more objects are placed and where all the magic of your application is happening. An application can have one or more scenes. One scene is always defined as the active scene, as shown in Figure 4-1.

© Alexander Meijers 2020
A. Meijers, *Immersive Office 365*, https://doi.org/10.1007/978-1-4842-5845-3_4

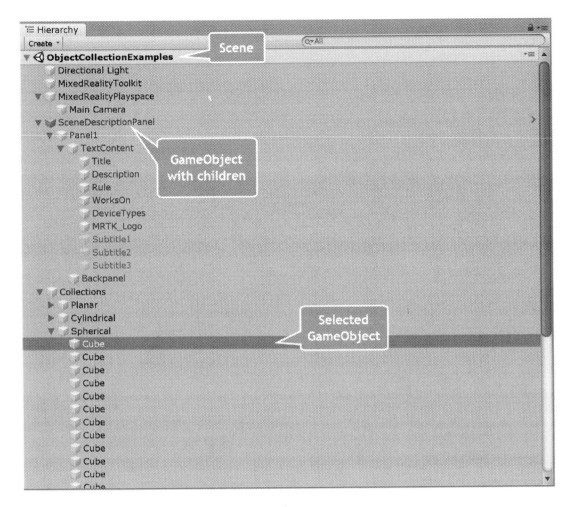

Figure 4-1. *Hierarchy in the Unity interface*

The active scene shown in the hierarchy does not necessarily have to be the start scene in your application. You will need to specify the start scene in the build settings dialog found under *File* ➤ *Build settings.* The scene at the top of the *Scenes in Build* will be the start scene.

The active scene is shown in bold in the hierarchy. A scene contains a hierarchy of different objects like game objects, camera, directional light, and many more. While the hierarchy seen in Figure 4-1 shows a more complex scene, starting scenes are less complex and mostly contain a few GameObjects.

Each scene is saved separately to disk. It is possible to remove a scene, add an existing scene, add a new scene, or unload a scene in your project. Removing a scene will remove the scene from the hierarchy and the Scene overview. Unloading a scene will only remove the scene from the Scene overview. The hierarchy allows you to add or remove objects as a parent or child of another object. It is also possible to move objects to rearrange your scene. Moving objects from parent objects can influence some of their settings. That is explained later.

The scene part of the interface is also called the view area, and contains several tabs that allow you to control the scene or the application. The two main views are *Scene* and *Game*, which are used to visualize a scene from your application. The *Scene* view gives you an overview of what is happening in your scene(s). When you run the application, the *Game* view shows you the result as you would see it in the device. You can see an example of the *Scene* view in Figure 4-2.

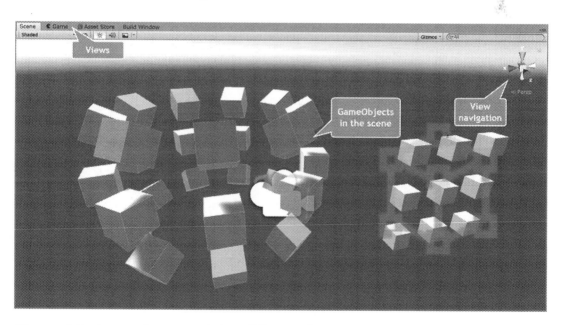

Figure 4-2. *Scene view containing different objects*

Although it is not recommended, it is possible to visualize multiple scenes together. With complex scenes, visualizing them together can cause some confusion because they all show their content through each other.

One other tab is called *Asset Store*. This tab allows you to access an extensive store containing a lot of assets. In some cases these assets are free or available for a reasonable price. If you have bought some assets from the store, the Asset Store tab allows you to access those assets and download them into your project.

Some tabs are generated due to importing specific packages like the MRTK v2. In Figure 4-2 we have a tab called *Build Window*. The *Build Window* tab is generated by MRTK v2 and gives you several options to predefine a Microsoft HoloLens 2 build of your project in Visual Studio. This allows you to preconfigure some settings, which you normally must do manually. This allows suppliers to make your life building applications a lot easier.

The next part of the interface is called the *Projects* window. This window has a hierarchical view of all available assets in your project. Figure 4-3 shows on the left the assets divided into different folders. In this example we have imported the MRTK v2 packages; they appear on the left as `MixedRealityToolkit` and `MixedRealityToolkit.Examples`.

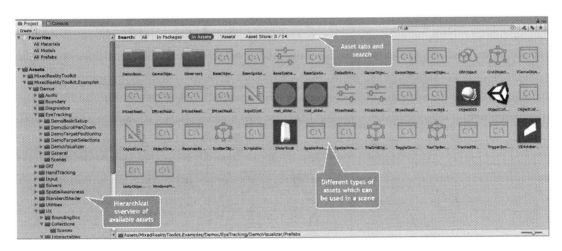

Figure 4-3. *Project overview, which contains all available assets*

When you use the right-click one of the items in the hierarchy, you will be able to do several actions. These actions are shown in Table 4-1.

Table 4-1. *Asset-Related Actions*

Action	Description
Import new asset	This allows you to select an exported asset from another project into this project.
Import package	This allows you to import a package that you have downloaded or created yourself by exporting several assets.
Export package	This function allows you to export a selected part of assets and related assets of the hierarchy as a package to reuse in another solution.
Selected dependencies	This will show you all assets in the project that are dependent in some way to the selected object in the hierarchy.
Find references in scene	This is a useful function that allows you to see where the asset is used in the scene.
Create ➤ …	Allows you to create an asset in your project. Think of camera, game object, script, shader, material, etc.

Unity also allows you to drag different content into the project environment. When the item is dragged in, Unity will convert/transform it to a known format allowing it to be used in your project.

Unity will convert any asset and make it part of the project when you drag an asset into the project space or a part of the project folder on disk. Whenever you start Unity or set the focus on the active Unity application, it will convert added assets.

At the right of the window, the assets are shown as part of the folder that is selected on the left side in the hierarchy. It is also possible to search for a specific asset by typing in a part or the whole name of the asset in the search box. The results can vary depending on which folder is selected in the hierarchy of the *Project* window. It is possible to search by type or label. You can even save a search you have performed.

The *Inspector* window is one of the most important parts of Unity. Based on the location you are in, additional information is shown on the selected part. An example is searching for a specific asset, which will give you some narrowing of the selection possibilities in the *Inspector* window. But the most interesting one is when you select an object in the hierarchy window of a scene. The *Inspector* window will show you all the components used for that specific object, as shown in Figure 4-4. Components describe the behavior for the object and can operate within the context of that object. Each object has at least the `Transform` component, which describes the position, rotation, and scale of the object. Components like the `Transform` are explained later. You will notice that some objects have a lot more components attached, which define behavior, rendering, and many other functions.

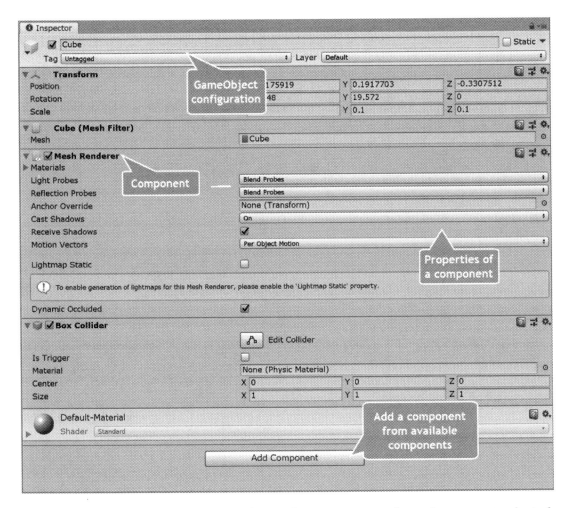

Figure 4-4. *Inspector view, which shows the components from the current selected object in the scene*

Components can be added easily by pressing the *Add Component* button. This will give a popup that allows you to browse through all available components in the project.

Each object selected will have some object-level settings shown at the top of the *Inspector* window. There are a few interesting functions that allow you to control the object.

The checkbox in front of the name of the object allows you to disable or enable the object. Disabling the object will not fire any messages like Start() or Update() to one of its components. Be careful to use this from the Unity configuration or through code.

At the right you will find a checkbox called *Static*. This checkbox will tell the background systems in Unity that this object will not move. You can specify this per system. Using this function wisely can result in a more optimized application.

You can select one of the existing tags or use your own created tag to label your object. Tags can be used to identify a certain GameObject for scripting purposes. An example is using tags for triggers in the Collider script, where you want to identify the group to which your GameObject belongs to. It is also possible to find a GameObject by its tag, using the method GameObject.FindWithTag(). Unity also has some predefined tags like Untagged, Respawn, Finish, EditorOnly, MainCamera, Player, and GameController. You notice that these tags are mostly used in games. But they can be used by your application too if needed.

You can set the layer for an object. These things are incredible! Layers can be used for selective rendering from cameras and to selectively hit objects that have a collider attached. Let's say you have multiple menus or actions in your scene, and you want the user to only be able to select a set of them at a specific moment in your application flow. Specify layers on objects in each of those sets. Your application will use Physics. Raycast() to identify if some object with a collider is hit. This method casts a ray from your finger or from the device itself to a direction with a specific length to see if you are hitting any of the objects. In that method, you can specify which layer(s) needs to be hit and which not by using a layerMask property.

The last part of the user interface is the toolbar, as shown in Figure 4-5. At the far left are the transform tools. These tools allow you to control the *Scene* view and its content. The hand tool is used for panning around the scene. The other tools allow you to edit individual objects in your scene with a move, rotate, scale, rect transform, and transform.

Figure 4-5. *Toolbar containing scene tools, play mode, and other settings*

The two buttons next to the transform tools are called the Gizmo handle position toggles. Gizmos are used in Unity to visualize certain parts, areas or other. They are mostly used for debugging purposes or some form of aid in your Scene. The first button is used for positioning the Gizmo. The first option, *Pivot*, allows you to position the Gizmo to the actual pivot point of the mesh of the object. The second option, *Center*, positions the Gizmo at the center of the GameObject within its rendered bounds. The second button is used for rotating Gizmos. The first option, *Local*, keeps the Gizmo rotation relative to all the GameObjects in the scene. The second option, *Global*, will rotate the Gizmo attached to world space orientation.

The three buttons—*Play*, *Pause*, and *Step*—are used with the *Game* view. By pressing the *Play* button, the application is running the scene. The *Pause* button will pause the gameplay, and the *Step* button allows you to go step by step through the running application.

The collaboration button allows you to share and control your project into Unity cloud. This enables you to work together with the team in the same project. The cloud button opens the Unity Services window. Pressing the account dropdown will give you access to your Unity account.

The layers dropdown will allow you to control which objects, based on their specified layer, are displayed in the *Scene* view. This allows you to quickly review if you have the correct objects in the same layer.

The layout dropdown allows you to control the arrangement of views in Unity. There are already some predefined arrangements available. But it is also possible to create and save your own arrangements.

Mixed Reality Project

The previous section explained the interface and environment of Unity by using some content from one of the examples of the MRTK v2 package. Let's start creating our own mixed reality project for HoloLens.

Start Unity Hub for creating a new project. Click *projects* and click *new*. Make sure you have selected the latest Unity LTS version supported by the MRTK v2. Use the project name *ImmersiveOffice365*, as shown in Figure 4-6.

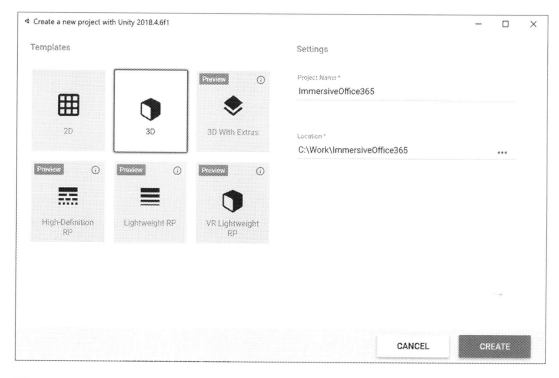

Figure 4-6. *Creating a new mixed reality project for HoloLens*

Start the project by clicking the project in the Unity Hub. This will start the correct Unity version and opens your project. Make sure that you save the current scene by using the main menu *File ➤ Save as* and fill in the name *ImmersiveOffice365*. Preferably, save the scene in a subfolder called scenes, which allows you to store more scenes at the same place in your project.

Normally you can do a lot of settings manually to make your project suitable for Microsoft HoloLens. But instead, we will be using the MRTK v2 to help us out.

Download the latest release version of MRTK v2 at the following location:

`https://github.com/Microsoft/MixedRealityToolkit-Unity/releases`

Currently the MRTK v2 is divided into several packages for download. You will need to download the following packages:

- `Microsoft.MixedReality.Toolkit.Unity.Foundation`

- `Microsoft.MixedReality.Toolkit.Unity.Extensions`

The other packages include tools and examples that we currently do not need in our mixed reality project.

After the download, go back to the ImmersiveOffice365 project in the Unity Hub. From there, you need to import the packages. Importing can be done via the main menu *Assets ➤ Import package ➤ Custom package*. A popup dialog can be seen in Figure 4-7, showing you all the assets contained in the package. Press the *Import* button to import everything into your project.

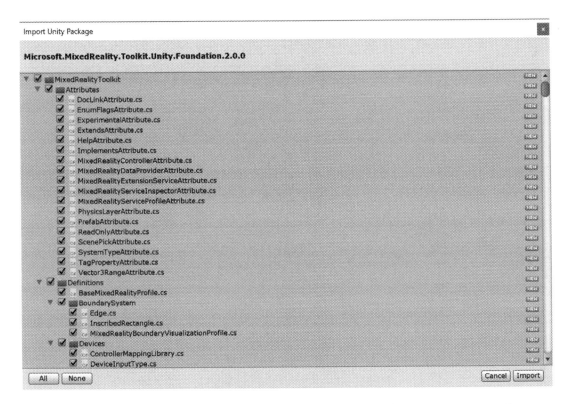

Figure 4-7. *Importing the MRTK v2 foundation as a package into your project*

The MRTK v2 toolkit contains a default profile for Microsoft HoloLens 2. This profile includes several recommendations for configuration to get the best performance for your application.

The next step will update the scene with the MRTK v2 configuration, as shown in Figure 4-8. Open *Mixed Reality Toolkit ➤ Add to scene and configure...* from the main menu. This will add the *MixedRealityToolkit* and the *MixedRealityPlacespace* as GameObjects in your scene. Under the *MixedRealityToolkit* GameObject you will find a configuration component. Select *DefaultHoloLens2ConfigurationProfile*. This will set several configurations for you to have the scene ready to run on a Microsoft HoloLens 2 device.

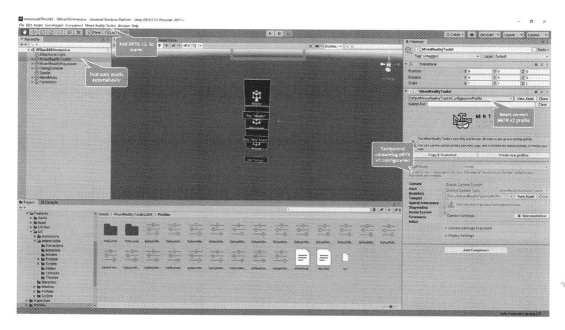

Figure 4-8. *Adding HoloLens 2 configurations to the project by using a profile from the MRTK v2*

Although this tool already helps a lot, several other environmental settings need to be adjusted to get even better performance for a mixed reality application. The following list contains settings that need to be done manually and are recommended:

- **Unity quality settings** – While we all want to have the best graphics and resolution, this can downgrade the performance of your application. You need to think about what quality you really need. Quality is not that important in most cases when we talk about mixed reality solutions for business. The quality also influences the framerate of the application. The lower the framerate, the more unstable your application becomes. Quality level is in most cases set to *Very Low,* which is enough for many applications. This setting can be found under *Edit ➤ Project Settings ➤ Quality.* Start from there and work your way up until the ratio between quality and performance is as you want it.

- **Lighting settings** – Another setting that influences the performance of your application is lighting settings. Lighting, shadows, and light reflection are important parts within the calculation of 3D models in your scene. There is a setting called *Realtime Global Illumination,* which can be turned off to get better performance. You will find this under *Window* ➤ *Rendering* ➤ *Lighting Settings* ➤ *Realtime Global Illumination.* Just as with the quality, you need to think about what you really need in your scene. In most applications being built for businesses, the lighting is even turned off or not present in the scene.

- **Single pass instanced** – Normally a mixed reality application build in Unity is rendered twice. Rendering is done for each eye separately. This effect doubles the amount of work requested from the CPU and GPU, and will influence the performance of your application. By setting this to single pass, Unity is optimizing its rendering pipeline for mixed reality applications. It is recommended to always have this setting enabled. The setting can be found at *Edit* ➤ *Project Settings* ➤ *Player* ➤ *XR Settings.* Make sure that *Stereo Rendering modes* is set to *Single Pass Instanced* and the *Virtual Reality Supported* checkbox is checked. Keep in mind that some custom shaders written for Unity do not support this setting. By selecting those shaders, the scene would be rendered in only one eye.

- **Enable depth buffering**– This option can be beneficial for more hologram stability. Unity will share the depth map with the Windows Mixed Reality platform, allowing the platform to optimize the stability of holograms for your scene. This option can be enabled via *Edit* ➤ *Project Settings* ➤ *Player* ➤ *XR Settings.* Select the *Enable Depth Buffer Sharing* expansion. Also make sure that you keep the bit depth to *16-bit depth* under the *Depth Format* setting. This setting is only available when you have selected the Universal Windows Platform as the build target. This is explained at the end of this chapter.

The MRTK v2 toolkit contains a lot more assets and other items to make your life much easier when developing a mixed reality application for HoloLens. Those are discussed in the next chapter.

We will be using different assets in our Unity project for building a HoloLens application. Some of them are standard within Unity, while others are assets provided by third-party packages. One of those packages is the MRTK v2 package, which simplifies development for HoloLens.

GameObject

A *GameObject* is the base class for any entity found in scenes. That means that, for example, a hologram in your scene is built up from one or more *GameObjects*.

GameObjects can be hierarchical. This allows us to great somewhat more complex assets or place parts that belong together under the same parent *GameObject*. The parent of a *GameObject* is retrieved by the following code:

```
GameObject parent = myGameObject.transform.parent.gameObject;
```

There is no method available for retrieving the child GameObjects of a *GameObject*. This will be explained further in this chapter by using components.

A *GameObject* has an active state, which can be set by the method gameObject. SetActive(true) or gameObject.SetActive(false). The property activeSelf on a *GameObject* will return the state of that *GameObject*. A *GameObject* may be inactive because any of its hierarchical parents are inactive. In that case, the property activeSelf still returns true while the *GameObject* is not visible. If you want to check if the *GameObject* is visible in the hierarchy, you need to use the property activeInHierarchy.

Playing around with the active state of a GameObject can cause strange behaviors. You need to be careful using the active state functionality. As soon as a *GameObject* is inactive, it will not receive any updates anymore through the messaging system. If you only want the *GameObject* to be not visible, it is better to disable the Renderer component. This can be achieved by running the code gameObject.GetComponent<Renderer>().enabled = false.

Unity allows you to easily instantiate a *GameObject* within code. This can be used, for example, to clone an existing *GameObject* or create a prefabricated *GameObject*. The method allows you to assign the parent or to set a specific position and rotation. The following code creates a clone from the *GameObject*:

```
GameObject go = GameObject.Instantiate(gameObject, parent);
```

The following code creates a *GameObject* based on the specific type of MyGameObject:

```
MyGameObject go = GameObject.Instantiate<MyGameObject>() as MyGameObject;
```

Components

A *GameObject* is a visual object in your scene. Each *GameObject* contains components. Components are always attached to a *GameObject* and describe some part of the behavior of that *GameObject*. A component can be a lot of different things. It could be the rendering of the object, the collider that determines how the object is hit, or, for example, a custom C# script attached to it. Each component is derived from a class called MonoBehaviour. Each component has a property called gameObject, referring to the *GameObject* to which it is attached to.

Every object in the scene has a *Transform* component. This *Transform* component is used to store and manipulate the position, rotation, and scale of the object. Several methods are available to control access to the components. The remainder of this section describes the different methods to retrieve a single component or multiple components at once. These methods are based on generic functions.

Let's start with the method for retrieving a single component from a *GameObject* named gameObject. Following is an example of the GetComponent method:

```
[class name] component = gameObject.GetComponent<[class name]>();
```

Following is an example of retrieving a Renderer component from a GameObject:

```
Renderer render = gameObject.GetComponent<Renderer>();
```

A *GameObject* can have several components of the same class. Invoke the GetComponents method to retrieve one or more components at once from a specific type by its class name from the *GameObject* referred to by the property gameObject. For example:

```
[class name][] components = gameObject.GetComponents<[class name]>();
```

Following is an example of retrieving all the DescriptionProperty components from a GameObject:

```
DescriptionProperty[] properties = gameObject.GetCompents<DescriptionProperty>();
```

As we know, *GameObjects* can have children. The following method allows you to retrieve a single component from one of the children of the *GameObject* referred to by the property gameObject:

```
[class name] component = gameObject.GetComponentInChildren<[class
name]>(includeInactive);
```

The following example retrieves the first Collider component, which is found in the children of the GameObject and the children of the children. It works recursively.

```
Collider collider = gameObject.GetComponentInChildren<Collider>(true);
```

The property includeInactive = true allows you to retrieve components from inactive *GameObjects*. To retrieve one or more components of the same class name of the GameObject—its children—you can use the following method:

```
[class name][] components = gameObject. GetComponentInChildren <[class name]>(
includeInactive);
```

The following example retrieves all the Collider components that are found in the children of the GameObject and the children of the children. It works recursively.

```
Collider[] colliders = gameObject.GetComponentsInChildren<Collider>(false);
```

It is also possible to search through the parents of a *GameObject* to retrieve a specific component. The following method will get the component from the *GameObject* itself or any of its hierarchical parents:

```
[class name] component = gameObject.GetComponentInParent<[class name]>();
```

The following example shows how to find a MainStage component:

```
MainStage stage = gameObject.GetComponentInParent<MainStage>();
```

There is also a method to retrieve one or more components from the *GameObject* itself or any of its hierarchical parents:

```
[class name][] components =
gameObject.GetComponentsInParent<[class name]>();
```

The following example shows how to find all the State components:

```
State[] states = gameObject.GetComponentsInParent<State>();
```

It is also possible to add a new component to an existing *GameObject*. The following code shows how:

```
gameObject.AddComponent<[class name]>() as [class name];
```

The following example adds a `Collider` component to the *GameObject* referred to by gameObject:

```
Collider addedCollider = gameObject.AddComponent<Collider>() as Collider;
```

There is no specific method for removing a component. You will need to use the static methods for destroying objects. To remove a component from a *GameObject* gameObject, execute the Destroy method as follows:

```
Component.Destroy([class name]);
```

In this example we get the Collider component from the GameObject and destroy it:

```
Collider collider = gameObject.GetComponent< Collider >();
Component.Destroy(collider);
```

Using the Destroy method will destroy the object at a convenient time by the Unity messages system. An additional method called `DestroyImmediate` is available. This will destroy the object immediately, but this method is not recommended to be used. Use the `DestroyImmediate` method only when you are working and writing in editor code.

Be very careful when destroying objects. Make sure that the objects are not part anymore of an iteration you are going through or are being used by some other part of the application.

As said earlier, there is not really a method available for getting the child GameObjects of a *GameObject*. But since we know that each *GameObject* has a Transform component and we have methods to retrieve those, we can create a collection of children. The following code shows how:

```
Transform[] children = gameObject.GetComponentsInChildren<Transform>(true);
foreach(Transform child in children)
{
    GameObject goChild = child.gameObject;

    // some code
}
```

Behaviors

This chapter has been using some script examples for accessing a variety of methods and properties. It is possible to define a script as a component. Doing so can be very useful when you wish to run one or more scripts within the context of a *GameObject*. Such a script is called a behavior.

To create a behavior for a *GameObject*, you need to have a class derived from the base class MonoBehaviour. Behaviors can be created through the Unity interface. Start by right-mouse clicking a part of the assets hierarchy and choosing *Create ➤ C# Script*. This will generate a behavior script for you and inserts some initial code.

Unity uses a messaging system that is purely based on C#. This system makes it possible to catch system-defined messages or to create your own custom messages. You can catch an enormous number of messages inside a behavior class. For that, you will need to implement the MonoBehaviour class. It is worthwhile to have a look at them. The flow messages that you will mostly use when writing script code are described in Table 4-2.

Table 4-2. *Flow Behavior Class Messages*

Message	Description	When
Awake()	This method is mostly used to initialize any variables or application state. The method is called after all objects in the scene are initialized. This allows you safely to access other referencing objects. It is recommended by Unity to use this method to setup references between scripts.	The method is only called once during the lifetime of the instantiated script. The Awake() is always called before the Start().
Start()	This method is mostly used to pass information back and forth. But it can also be used from initializing any variables or application state.	This method is called on the first frame when a script is enabled and just before any of the Update() methods are called. This method is only called once.
Update()	This method is the most commonly used function to implement scripts that alter the GameObject during runtime.	This method is called every frame after the Start() is called first. When a *GameObject* is inactive, this class is disabled and will not call the method.

There are some other messages that are interesting and most used next to the messages mentioned previously. These messages mainly focus on changes in the appearance and continuity of the *GameObject*. Table 4-3 describes these messages.

Table 4-3. *State Behavior Class Messages*

Message	Description	When
OnEnable()	Use this method to perform certain actions that are needed when the object is enabled or becomes enabled again.	This method is called when the object becomes enabled and active. It is called when the script is loaded and active.
OnDisable()	Use this method to perform certain actions that are needed when the object is disabled.	This method is called when the object becomes disabled and inactive. It is also called when the object is destroyed.
OnDestroy()	This method can be used to clean up and deinitialize variables.	This method is called when a scene is closed and/or the application ends.

As said, it is also possible to implement your own custom messages within your application. Implementing a custom message is relatively easy. You will need to define your own interface class derived from IEventSystemHandler with the message methods defined. For example:

```
using UnityEngine.EventSystems;

public interface IProcessEvents : IEventSystemHandler
{
    // functions that can be called via the messaging system
    void OnTrackUsersInProcess(Transform[] userPositions, int processId);
    void OnStartProcess(int processId);
    void OnEndProcess(int processId);
    void OnEndAllProcesses();
}
```

As you can see in the example, you can specify different message methods. These methods can contain simple and complex properties to pass information along with the message. This interface can then be implemented in your class as follows:

```
public class TaskVisualizer : MonoBehaviour, IProcessEvents
{
    public void OnEndAllProcesses()
    {
    }

    public void OnEndProcess(int processId)
    {
    }

    public void OnStartProcess(int processId)
    {
    }

    public void OnTrackUsersInProcess(Transform[] userPositions, int processId)
    {
    }
}
```

The final step will be issuing the message. For this we have a static helper class providing us with a method that allows us to send a message. The method is provided through the ExecuteEvents class. Its name is Execute, and it allows you to send a message to a specific *GameObject* gameObject. For example:

```
ExecuteEvents.Execute<IProcessEvents>(gameObject, null, (x, y) =>
x.OnStartProcess(1200));
```

There is a second method named ExecuteHierarchy that allows you to send a message up into the hierarchy of the specific *GameObject* gameObject. Here's an example of that method being invoked:

```
ExecuteEvents.ExecuteHierarchy<IProcessEvents>(gameObject, null, (x, y) =>
x.OnStartProcess(1200));
```

The *GameObject* class also provides several message methods. These methods correspond to the ones explained previously. They use a string to define the name of the message. The message method itself does not have to be defined in an interface and can be defined directly in the class, which is derived from MonoBehavior. The methods are listed in Table 4-4.

Table 4-4. *GameObject Message Methods*

Message method	Description
SendMessage	Calls the method name methodName on every MonoBehavior in the *GameObject*
SendMessageUpwards	Calls the method named methodName on every MonoBehaviour in the *GameObject* and on every one of its hierarchical parents
Broadcastmessage	Calls the method name methodName on every MonoBehavior in the *GameObject* or any of its children

Keep in mind that these methods in Table 4-4 are based on reflection and are much slower than the previous example for messaging.

Both system messages and custom messages are sent to all active objects in your scene, which implements them. The order in which they run is not possible to predict. You can't expect a certain message method to be called first in a specific object. You will need to implement your own state system to determine the order in which messages are handled over multiple objects.

Component Properties

Components allow you to specify properties in the Inspection window. A property in the Inspector window is drawn by using a property drawer. It is also possible to create your own custom property drawers. We will now focus on the properties that are built-in in Unity. An example of some properties of the component *Custom Controller* is shown in Figure 4-9.

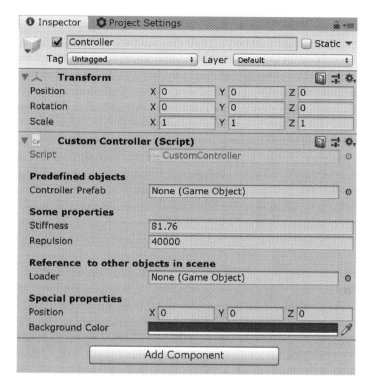

Figure 4-9. *An example of component properties in the inspector view*

To have a property appear in the Inspector window, you will need to make it public. Based on the type of property, a different UI is created. The following code example creates the properties as shown in Figure 4-9.

```
public class CustomController : MonoBehaviour
{
    [Header("Predefined objects")]
    public GameObject ControllerPrefab = null;

    [Header("Some properties")]
    public float Stiffness = 81.76f;
    public float Repulsion = 40000.0f;

    [Header("Reference  to other objects in scene")]
    public GameObject Loader = null;
```

```
    [Header("Special properties")]
    public Vector3 position;
    public Color backgroundColor = Color.blue;
}
```

In this case, we use the Header attribute to distinguish different sets of properties for this component. This example shows some different examples using properties. Properties like Stiffness and Repulsion can be used for configuration of the component through the Unity interface, while others like the position and the backgroundColor even allow you to select the value differently, based on the type it is. But it is also possible to use a *GameObject* reference. This can be handy to reference another existing *GameObject* in your scene. In this example, we reference a loader that will be shown when we are retrieving some values in the background. The Unity interface allows you to drag some *GameObject* from the scene into that field. This allows you to prevent using methods like GameObject.FindGameObjectsWithTag. Such a method allows you to find a *GameObject* based on a tag specified. But it is slow and expects you to fully manage the right tags. Such a *GameObject* can also be used for specifying a prefab. This allows you to instantiate from code a new *GameObject* based on that prefab. This can be useful if your component needs to create child *GameObjects* based on various predefined prefabs.

Camera

The camera used in your scene is the device through which the user views the world. In the case of a mixed reality application, the camera device is the Microsoft HoloLens.

After you start an application on the HoloLens device, the middle of the device is the (0, 0, 0) point in space of your scene from that point forward. This resets whenever you restart your application. This is the same for the direction of X, Y, and Z axes. The Z axis is the direction where you looked at when the application started up.

The camera is nothing more than an empty *GameObject* containing the *Camera* component. The *Camera* component needs some configuration before it can be used on a HoloLens device, as you can see in Figure 4-10.

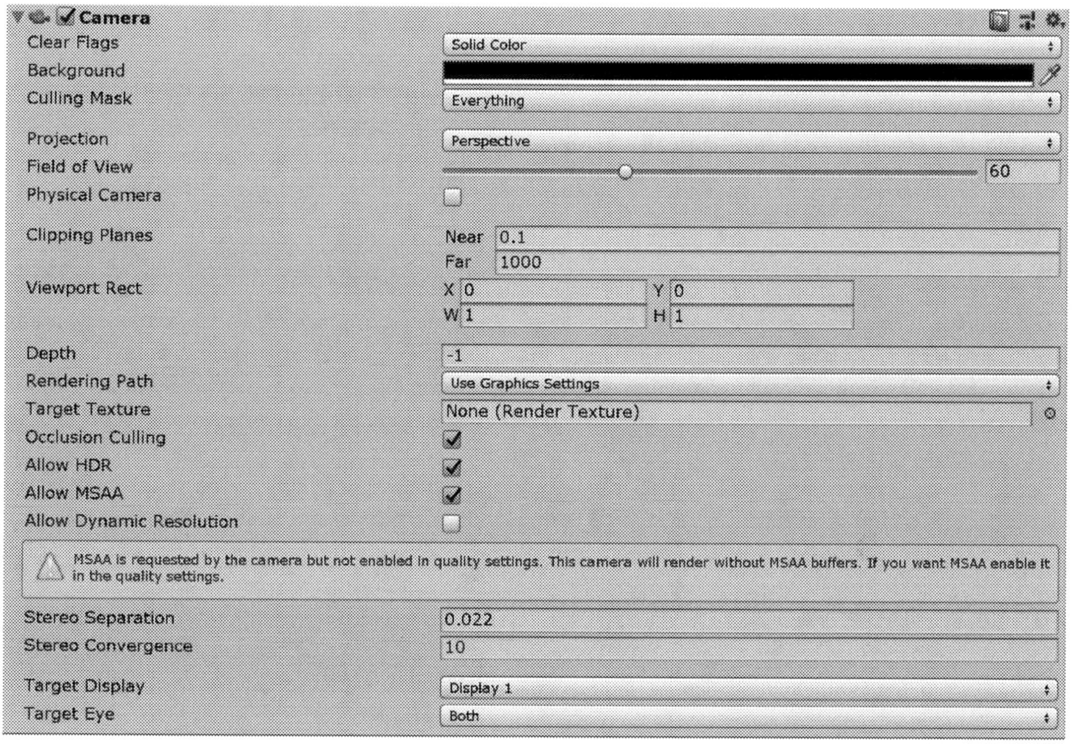

Figure 4-10. *The camera component*

A HoloLens device uses the color black as transparent. That means that we will need to set the *Clear Flags* on *Solid Color* and *Background* on the color *black*. Since HoloLens is mostly used within the range of 3-5 meters, you will need to make sure that near clipping is not set too high, because too high a setting will prevent the 3D world from being drawn for the user. You will need to set the *Clipping Planes Near* to, for example, 0,1. After using the configuration tool of the MRTK v2, a start structure containing the camera is created.

You can find the camera under *ImmersiveOffice365* ➤ *MixedRealityPlacespace* ➤ *Main Camera* under the hierarchy. You can access the camera from code as follows:

```
Vector3 headPosition = Camera.main.transform.position;
Vector3 gazeDirection = Camera.main.transform.forward;
```

The first line gets the current position of the device itself, while the second line retrieves the direction vector of where you look at. Both use a Vector3 class to express the value. But in the second case, it defines a direction and not a point in space.

Gaze Provider

This component is part of the MRTK v2 and is automatically added to the *GameObject* named *Main Camera*. This component takes care of visualizing the gaze cursor for the Microsoft HoloLens 2. It contains several settings, which can be seen in Figure 4-11.

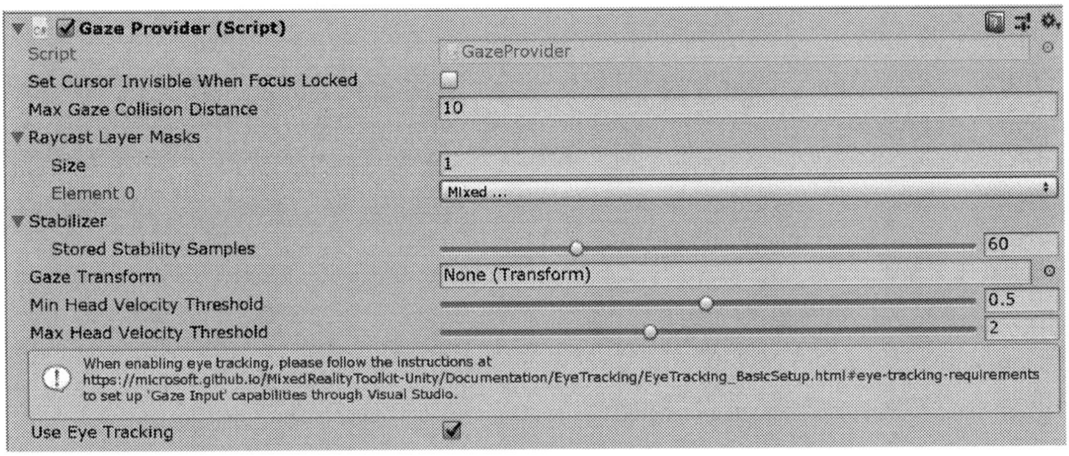

Figure 4-11. *The gaze provider component*

The gaze provider takes care of the gaze from the Microsoft HoloLens 2 itself as from the finger on the hand. It also supports the use of eye tracking. You can define which layers it should collide with objects by setting the Raycast Layer Masks. This component resolves a lot of headaches building a correct gaze cursor.

Spatial Understanding

An important part of Microsoft HoloLens is spatial understanding. The device can distinguish the environment by using multiple cameras and a depth camera. Unity provides two basic components for spatial mapping. The first component, called *Spatial Mapping Renderer*, is a script that allows you to define which material is used for occlusion and visualization of the environment. The second component, called *Spatial Mapping Collider*, is a script that allows you to collide with that spatial mapping.

In the next steps, you will add spatial understanding to the scene. To add these, create an empty *GameObject* in the root of your scene. Now select the *GameObject* and add both components through the *Add Component* button, as can be seen in Figure 4-12.

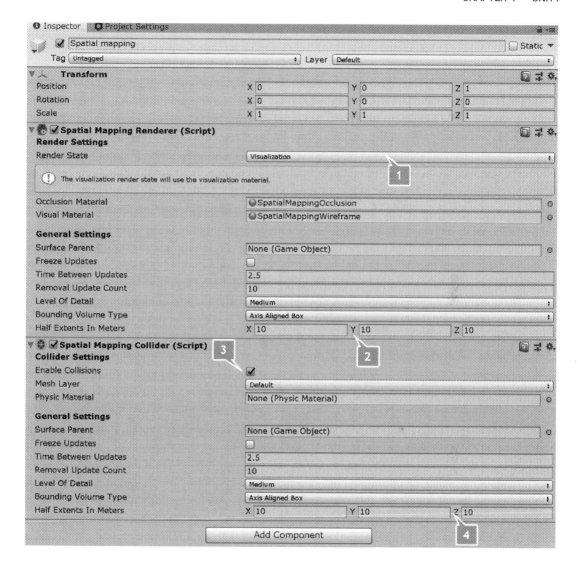

Figure 4-12. *The spatial mapping renderer and spatial mapping collider components*

Make sure that the *Render State* of the *Spatial Mapping Renderer* is set to Visualization. This will use the SpatialMappingWireframe material to draw your surroundings and make them visible to you in the application.

Make sure that Enable Collisions of *Spatial Mapping Collider* is checked. This allows you to hit the spatial mapping rendering with the gaze cursor.

Finally, for both components, set the `Half Extents in Meters` value to 10 in all directions. This size is the bounding volume used by the components to define the area in which spatial mapping reports physical surface changes.

Our First Hologram

Let's create our first hologram. We will start with something simple to display the rotating text message "Hello World!" approximately one meter in front of you.

Create an empty *GameObject* in the root of your scene. Rename the *GameObject* to HelloWorld! Select the *GameObject* and check the empty Inspector window. Press the *Add Component* button and search for the *Text Mesh* component. Make sure you configure the properties of that component as follows:

- **Text** = Hello World! Divide both words over two lines by pressing the Enter button in the text field.

- **Character Size** = 0.01

- **Anchor** = Middle center

- **Alignment** = Center

- **Font Size** = 500

Make sure that the properties of the Transform component of that GameObject are configured as follows:

- **Position** = 0, 0, 1

- **Rotation** = 0, 0, 0

- **Scale** = 0.2, 0.2, 0.2

The next step is creating a behavior script. We will first create a folder structure under Assets in the Project Window. That folder structure is named *App* ➤ *Scripts*. Add a new C# script called `Rotate`. Double clicking the C# script will open the Visual Studio 2019 editor. You will need to add the following code to that script:

```
using System.Collections;
using System.Collections.Generic;
using UnityEngine;
```

```
public class Rotate : MonoBehaviour
{
    public float Speed = 100f;

    void Update()
    {
        gameObject.transform.Rotate(Vector3.up * Speed * Time.deltaTime);
    }
}
```

This script calls the `Rotate` method on the *Transform* of the *GameObject* to rotate the object and thus the text. We use a calculation of direction `Vector3.up` multiplied by `Speed` and the time passed since the last `Update()` called `Time.deltaTime`.

Now go back to Unity. Open the HelloWorld! *GameObject* and press the *Add Component* button in the Inspector view. Select the *Rotate* script. The result of all these steps will be similar to what is shown in Figure 4-13.

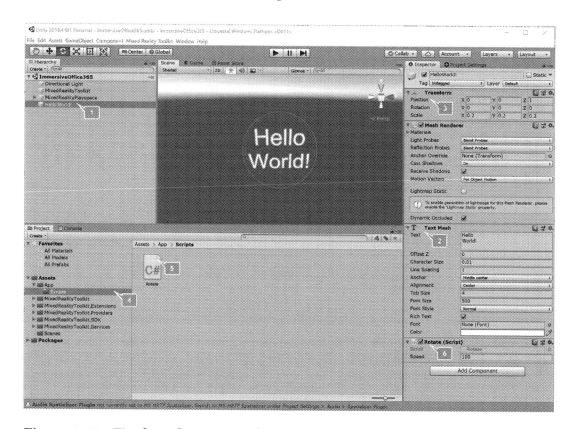

Figure 4-13. *Final result in Unity of our Hello World! application*

To test your application, you can press the Play button in the toolbar. The application will run within the Unity editor. Unity switches to the Game tab showing the text Hello World! rotating around, as can been seen in Figure 4-14.

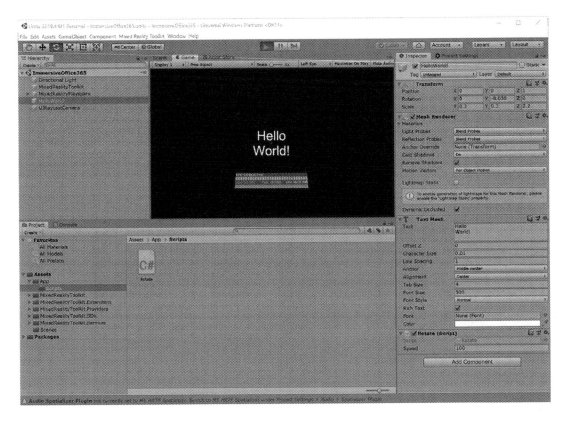

Figure 4-14.   *The result of the application running in game mode*

Press the Play button again to leave the Game mode and return to the Unity editor.

Build and Deploy

The next step is creating an application that can run on a Microsoft HoloLens emulator or a Microsoft HoloLens 2 device. This chapter goes into detail of building and deploying the application.

The application lifecycle of an application for Microsoft HoloLens is, in short, to do the following:

1. Create a scene in Unity

2. Build a Microsoft Visual Studio solution

3. Deploy that solution to a device

4. Run the solution on the device

Since we have our scene, the next step is building a Microsoft Visual Studio solution. We need to go to Build settings, as shown in Figure 4-15, via the main menu *File ➤ Build Settings.*

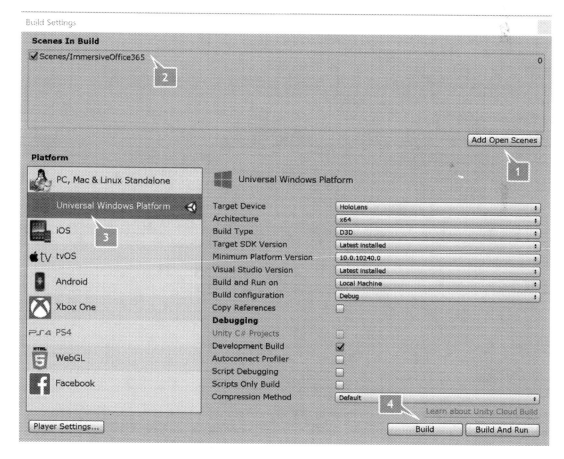

Figure 4-15. *Build settings dialog in Unity*

Due to the MRTK v2 configurator, most configurations are already set and ready to go. Check if the scene you are working on is visible and checked in the list. If not, then use the *Add Open Scenes* button to add the scene. If you have more than one scene, make sure that the scene that you want to start is listed at the top. We are building a UWP application. Make sure that *Universal Windows Platform* is selected as platform. Press the *Build* button at the bottom to create the Microsoft Visual Studio solution. You will need to specify a location for the build. It is preferable to create a folder called App in the project folder of the Unity project. As soon as the build is finished, a File Explorer with the location of the solution is opened.

Double-click the `ImmersiveOffice365.sln` file. This is the solution file for Microsoft Visual Studio. After the solution is opened, you will notice in the *Solution Explorer* window three projects, as you can see in Figure 4-16.

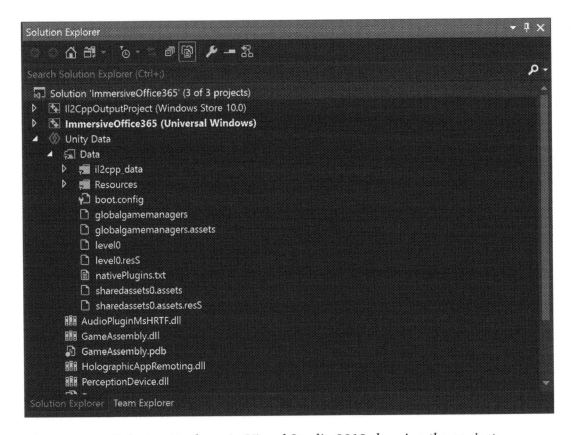

Figure 4-16. *Solution Explorer in Visual Studio 2019 showing the projects generated by Unity*

The projects are built based on IL2CPP. IL2CPP is an intermediate language to C++ and is developed by Unity as a scripting backend, which can be used as an alternative for Mono. When a project is built using IL2CPP, the intermediate language code is converted from scripts and assemblies to C++ before an actual native binary file is created. This makes it very suitable for building against several different platforms. Another advantage of building with IL2CPP is the increase of performance and security.

There is also a downside. Since the scripting is compiled to C++, your project does not contain any C# code anymore. While with earlier versions of Unity, only rebuilding the Microsoft Visual Studio solution was necessary when assets changed, currently changing script will require this too. This will lengthen the time during code debugging, which often requires making code changes. There are some solutions like remote debugging, but the fact is that we don't have control anymore over scripting in Microsoft Visual Studio.

Table 4-5 explains the purpose of each of the projects in the solution.

Table 4-5. *Projects in our Solution*

Project	Type	Contains
IL2CppOutputProject	Windows Store 10.0	This project contains the IL2CPP code based on the scripting and assemblies used in Unity.
ImmersiveOffice365	Universal Windows	This is the actual UWP project that runs the application on the device.
Unity Data	n/a	This project contains configurations and compiled scene assets.

Since we now have a solution containing projects based on IL2CPP, we need to build it natively as a UWP for a Microsoft HoloLens 2 device. That means we need to do some settings in the build dropdowns found in the toolbar, as shown in Figure 4-17.

Figure 4-17. *The toolbar in Visual Studio 2019 for building the solution*

The first selection is the type of solution. There are several options that are explained Table 4-6.

Table 4-6. *Possible Solution Types*

Build Type	Description
Debug	This option creates a version that you can debug. It contains the debug information and profiler support.
Release	The Release build optimizes the code for better performance. For Microsoft HoloLens projects it can make a huge difference when building for Release instead of for Debug. This can in some cases improve the quality of run from 40 FPS to 60 FPS.
Master	This type of build is used for generating a solution that is Microsoft Store ready and allows you to submit your application. The profiler support is completely stripped out.
MasterWithLTCG	LTCG stands for Link-Time Code Generation. LTCG is used to perform whole-program optimization. This build setting tells the linker to apply program optimization and LTCG for only the affected files by an edit, instead of the whole project. This will build quicker than Master itself.

The second and third dropdowns specify for which processor and to which target we are building. The options are given in Table 4-7.

Table 4-7. *Processor Options*

Build target	Processor	Description
Device	ARM	This will build and/or run a version to a device connected via USB.
Remote Machine	ARM	This will build and/or run a version to a device available in the network, based on an IP address.
HoloLens 2 Emulator 10.0.18362.1019	x86 or x64	This will build and run to the HoloLens 2 emulator. You will need to specify x86 or x64.

When the build is generated for a Microsoft HoloLens 2 device, you will need to specify the processor to ARM. The HoloLens 2 is an ARM device.

Hello World!

The final step is to build and deploy the Hello World! application to the Microsoft HoloLens 2 device. Make sure you have selected the following: Debug, ARM, and Device. Make sure that the Microsoft HoloLens 2 is connected via USB and recognized by your build machine. Right-click the solution in the Solution Explorer and select the option Deploy Solution. If the solution is not yet built, it will be built for you.

Put on the Microsoft HoloLens 2 and look for the just-installed application in the menu. Run the application. After the Unity logo, a Hello World! text is seen rotating around the Y-axis, as shown in Figure 4-18.

Figure 4-18. Hello world! on a Microsoft HoloLens 2 device

Keep in mind that we have not yet implemented any interactions. The text will always appear one meter in front of our first look direction when the application is started.

CHAPTER 5

Unity Advanced

Now that we have learned to master Unity to develop an application for HoloLens, we get to the more advanced scenarios. In this part, we go into threading and the use of plugins.

Threading

I was very surprised when I started developing for mixed reality devices like the HoloLens using Unity. Unity is a single-threaded computing application. For me, working mostly with multithreaded application development, it was like going back in time. Why on earth is this application single-threaded? Are there even benefits to using such a system? Yes, there are! There is a very good reason for it.

Multithreaded applications take advantage of the capabilities of the CPU of your computer system and use parallelism. It allows you to process many different threads to execute all kind of different tasks. Because these threads run in parallel, programming applications using that are somewhat different than normal. Running multiple threads allows you to divide different tasks in your application at the same time. The main thread from which those threads are started gets the results returned. Because you never know which thread is finished first, you must consider that when handling the results of those threads, especially when tasks or results are depending on each other. There are several advantages of having different threads running parallel. Your main thread, which mostly runs your user interface, will perform when, for example, a thread is executing a lot of calculations or retrieving some information and is depending on the speed of the current connection. Another advantage is the improvement in performance by simultaneously executing the computation and I/O operations. Also, when correctly used in code, it minimizes the number of system resources used. Finally, it allows simplifying of programming structure. Since threads run a specific task, the code is written in the context of the task and its used objects. This creates better and more readable code.

© Alexander Meijers 2020
A. Meijers, *Immersive Office 365*, https://doi.org/10.1007/978-1-4842-5845-3_5

Using multithreading works well if the number of tasks is low and manageable overseen. Code written for game development mostly contains a great number of small tasks to be executed at once. Using multithreading, a thread per task, would cause many threads with a short lifetime running simultaneously. That can push your processor capacity to its limits and will result in performance loss. This is caused by something called context switching. Context switching is the process of saving the state of an executing thread, switching forward to another thread to give it computing power, and switching back again to the saved thread. In other words, multiple threads are sharing the same computing space.

For that reason, Unity as a game development platform is based on a single-threaded principle compared to concurrency. Single-threaded means that the execution of all your running tasks is shared by the same thread. For each running task, an instruction goes in and a result comes out at a time. The more running tasks, the more work needs to be performed by the CPU. That means you need to look very closely at which tasks are needed at the current context and which tasks are not. Because tasks are built within scripts used on *GameObjects*, the execution of the void Update() method is called for each active *GameObject*. Having long-term operations running within this method can cause the application to run slow and even freeze for some time. There are two options for you as a developer:

- *Coroutines*: These methods can be executed in pieces by borrowing time from the main thread.

- *Plugins*: Plugins allow you to create additional UWP libraries, which can be included in your project and can execute multithreaded tasks.

Based on the preceding theory of single-threaded versus multithreaded, you can divide the following type of tasks into one of these two options.

Type of task	Option
Complex calculations and algorithms	Plugin
Machine learning & AI services	Plugin
Game related code	Coroutines
Small tasks within the user interface like animations, changing values over time and other	Coroutines
File operation access	Plugin
Accessing web services depending on network communication and service provider	Plugin

Coroutines

As explained earlier, the void Update() method of each active *GameObject* is called for each frame displayed by Unity. With normal behavior, this method is called approximately 30 times per second. A coroutine can pause and continue its execution over each of those frames displayed by Unity. This allows a coroutine to spread the complete run of a method across multiple frames, which are also used by Unity in its messaging system to call each void Update() method of each active *GameObject*. This allows coroutines to run their execution concurrent to the system. But keep in mind that this is still running in a single main thread and is not comparable to multithreading.

Coroutines are particularly useful when doing, for example, animations in the user interface. Let's say we have a method that changes the position of a *GameObject* one meter in distance forward. The method will look like the following:

```
protected void MoveForward()
{
    Vector3 initialPos = gameObject.transform.position;

    for(float posZ = 0; posZ <= 1f; posZ += 0.01f)
    {
        gameObject.transform.position = initialPos + new Vector3(0, 0, posZ);
    }
}
```

If we run the method at once from the void Update() method, it would be completely executed within a single frame update. That means that we wouldn't see the actual animation and we are holding up other *GameObjects* that need to be updated too in that same frame update. Hence there is the possibility of freezing objects.

To implement the same method that can be used as part of a coroutine, we need to change the declaration of the method. The return values become an IEnumerator object. Then we specify within the for loop a yield return null. At that point, the method will pause. At the next frame update, it continues from that same location.

```
protected IEnumerator MoveForward()
{
    Vector3 initialPos = gameObject.transform.position;

    for (float posZ = 0; posZ <= 1f; posZ += 0.01f)
```

```
    {
        gameObject.transform.position = initialPos + new Vector3(0, 0, posZ);

        yield return null;
    }
}
```

All the values of properties are kept in the same state during the pause of the method. This allows you to spread the execution of the code in the for loop of that same method across multiple frame updates.

The following is a code example that shows you how to start this method via a coroutine by hitting a key on the keyboard during runtime.

```
void Update()
{
    if (Input.GetKeyDown("m"))
    {
        StartCoroutine("MoveForward");
    }
}
```

But it is also possible to run the animation as soon as the GameObject is created by calling StartCoroutine("MoveForward") in the void Start() method. A coroutine can be stopped in different ways. These are as follows:

- When the method that is called from the Coroutine is finished without a yield

- Calling the method Monobehaviour.StopCoroutine with the name of the specific coroutine

- Calling the method Monobehaviour.StopAllCoroutines will stop all running coroutines for that *GameObject*

- When the MonoBehaviour object is destroyed

- When the attached *GameObject* is disabled

Normally, a coroutine will pick up the method in the next frame update. But it is also possible to postpone the continuation of the method by using WaitForSecondsRealtime(.1f) in the yield call. This will postpone the time set in that method.

```
protected IEnumerator MoveForward()
{
    Vector3 initialPos = gameObject.transform.position;

    for (float posZ = 0; posZ <= 1f; posZ += 0.01f)
    {
        gameObject.transform.position = initialPos + new Vector3(0, 0, posZ);

        yield return new WaitForSecondsRealtime(.1f);
    }
}
```

In the preceding example, we wait a tenth of a second before we continue the method. Keep in mind that this is in the next frame update after that specified time.

Plugins

Normally you would use scripting in Unity to create all different types of functionalities. But Unity also allows you to include external written code using plugins. A plugin is also called a dynamic-link library or DLL. Unity has two distinct types of plugins that can be used in your application:

- *Managed plugins*: These plugins are managed .NET assemblies. They only support features that are supported by the .NET framework against which they are compiled. There are different forms of these plugins depending on for what platform you are building an application.

- *Native plugins*: These plugins are platform-specific libraries using native code. This allows you to call operating system- or platform-specific functionalities. Native plugins will perform better than managed plugins, since they are optimized for the specific platform you are developing for.

This book focuses primarily on managed plugins for our application.

Since Unity version 2019.2.x and higher, only IL2CPP scripting backend is supported for building projects. Unity has stated that it is almost impossible to maintain two different platforms, and therefore decided that scripting used in Unity is always compiled to IL2CPP. That means that building and deploying the solution from Visual Studio to a HoloLens device will optimize the application, since it is using C++. But it also means that debugging is not easy anymore as when you normally would debug .NET code in Visual Studio. Making any changes to the code requires you to fully generate the Visual Studio solution before you can run it on the HoloLens device.

It is common to use managed plugins when building applications for the Universal Windows Platform. In the past, we had plugins on .NET scripting backend. Nowadays we are encouraged to use plugins on IL2CPP scripting backend. But the latter requires extensive knowledge of C++ and is much more difficult to implement. While the first, plugins on .NET scripting, is part of the legacy documentation, it does not necessarily mean that you are not allowed to use them. For Unity, it shouldn't matter which platform and computer language are used for building your plugin. And indeed, it is still possible to use these .NET scripting backend plugins. The classes and methods from these plugins can still be used from scripting in Unity.

In our application, we will be using a plugin based on a .NET DLL. This plugin will contain code that will not run within the Unity Editor. Therefore, we need an additional placeholder plugin. This placeholder requires the following:

- The placeholder plugin is also based on a .NET DLL.

- The placeholder plugin should have the same name as the first plugin.

- The same namespace needs to be used.

- The same classes and methods need to be used, but they can contain dummy code.

Both plugins need to be placed at specific locations within the assets folder of your Unity project. The plugin needs to be placed in the following folder:

Assets/Plugins/WSA

The placeholder plugin needs to be placed in the following folder:

Assets/Plugins

Some additional settings need to be set per file, which is explained later in this chapter. In the following steps, I will explain what is needed for both plugins for your project. Let's start with the plugin:

1. Start Visual Studio 2019. The dialog as shown in Figure 5-1 will appear. If Visual Studio does not show the dialog, open it via the main menu *File* ➤ *New* ➤ *Project*.

2. Type Class Library in the search field to find the project template for .NET standard related projects.

3. Select the project template called *Class library (.NET standard)*.

4. Press the *Next* button to continue to the next step.

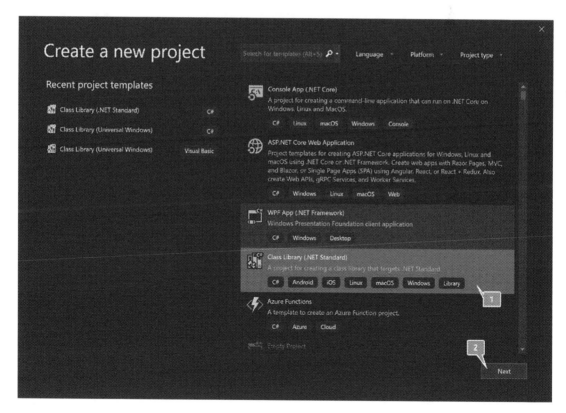

Figure 5-1. *Create a new class library (.NET Framework) project.*

In the next step, as seen in Figure 5-2, we need to configure the project settings.

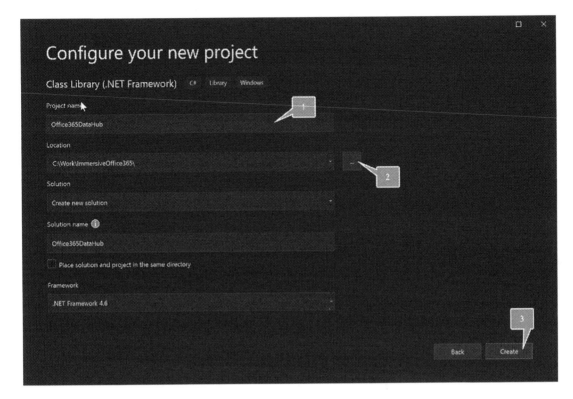

Figure 5-2. *Configure your new project*

1. Fill in a *Project Name*. Enter Office365DataHub as the project name.

2. Select a location for your project. Since we will have multiple projects, it would be wise to put them all under the same folder. In my case this is the ImmersiveOffice365 folder. The solution name will be filled in automatically.

3. Press the *Create* button to create the project.

Now let's start writing some code. We are going to create a manager class. But we need to have only one instance of that class present in our project. Therefore we start creating a templated singleton class. The singleton pattern restricts the instantiation of a class to one true single instance. This allows us to always get the same instance of that manager.

You will notice that the project contains a generated `Class1.cs` file. We remove this file from the project before we start adding our own classes.

Create a new code *Class* file via the solution explorer using right-click the project and select *Add* ➤ *New* Item. Call the new class `Singleton.cs`.

The following code describes a singleton. It contains a `static` method that returns the single instance of `class` T. An instance of `class` T is created if there are not yet any present. The constructor of the `class` is set to protected to prevent instantiating the `class` T from outside the `Instance` method.

```
namespace Office365DataHub
{
    public class Singleton<T> where T : new()
    {
        private static T instance;

        protected Singleton()
        {

        }

        public static T Instance
        {
            get
            {
                if (instance == null)
                {
                    instance = new T();
                }

                return instance;
            }
        }
    }
}
```

Create another new code *Class* file via the solution explorer using right-click the project and select *Add* ➤ *New* Item. Call your new class `Manager.cs`. This class will contain the actual code accessing the Office 365 data. But for now, to explain the part about using plugins in Unity, we will keep it to access a certain web page through an HttpClient using asynchronous code. Copy the following code to your newly created class file. It contains the right namespaces needed and the basic frame of the class using the earlier created Singleton template class.

```
using System.Net.Http;
using System.Threading.Tasks;
using Windows.Foundation;

namespace Office365DataHub
{
    public class Manager : Singleton<Manager>
    {
    }
}
```

Accessing a web service can take some time. It depends on the web service itself if any security handshake needs to be done and the amount of data to be transferred. Therefore, calling a web service is best done by using asynchronous calls. That means that we are going to call our method from a new thread. Since our method needs to pass some results back, we are going to use a callback method. Using a callback method allows us to pass a method as a property to another method. The definition of such a method is done by using the keyword delegate in the method definition.

Add the following code to define a callback by using a delegate definition. The callback will return the result as a string.

```
public delegate void OnGetSomeInformationCompleted(string result);
```

Now we need to define the actual method retrieving our information from a web call using HttpClient. The method is defined as an asynchronous method returning nothing. The property url contains the URL we will request through the HttpClient class. The property onGetSomeInformationCompleted is called with the result coming from the request. Add the following method to the Manager class:

```
protected async Task GetSomeInformationAsync(string url,
OnGetSomeInformationCompleted onGetSomeInformationCompleted)
{
    string result = "";
```

```
    using (var client = new HttpClient())
    {
        HttpResponseMessage response = await client.GetAsync(url);

        if (response.IsSuccessStatusCode)
        {
            result = await response.Content.ReadAsStringAsync();
        }
    }

    onGetSomeInformationCompleted(result);
}
```

We need to implement one more method called GetSomeInformation. This is the method that will call the GetSomeInformationAsync method from a new thread. This is also the method that will be publicly accessible and called from the scripting in Unity.

The method has the same properties that are passed along to the second method. We use the Windows.System.Threading.ThreadPool.RunAsync to create a work item on a new thread. This work item calls the GetSomeInformationAsync method. Copy the following method to the Manager class:

```
public void GetSomeInformation(string url, OnGetSomeInformationCompleted
onGetSomeInformationCompleted)
{
    IAsyncAction asyncAction = Windows.System.Threading.ThreadPool.
    RunAsync(
        async (workItem) => { await GetSomeInformationAsync(url,
        onGetSomeInformationCompleted); });
}
```

The result is shown in Figure 5-3. We now have two classes, Singleton and Manager, defined in our project. The next step is compiling the project and producing a DLL, which can be imported into Unity. Make sure you have *Debug* and *Any CPU* selected from the top dropdowns. Then build the project to generate the DLL.

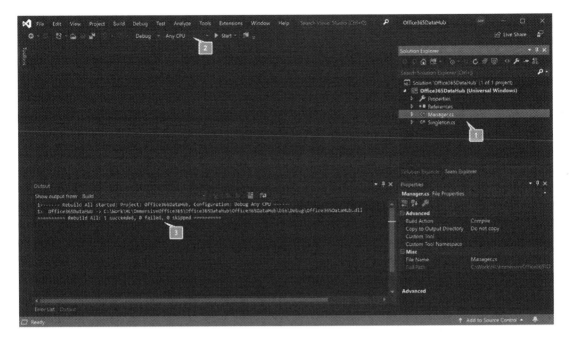

Figure 5-3. *Build a debug version of the plugin*

In this next step, we are going to create the placeholder plugin. This plugin is based on a .NET standard DLL:

1. Start Visual Studio 2019. The dialog will appear, as shown in Figure 5-4. If Visual Studio does not show the dialog, open it via the main menu *File ➤ New ➤ Project.*

2. Type Class Library in the search field to find the project template for .NET standard related projects.

3. Select the project template called *Class library (.NET standard).*

4. Press the *Next* button to continue to the next step.

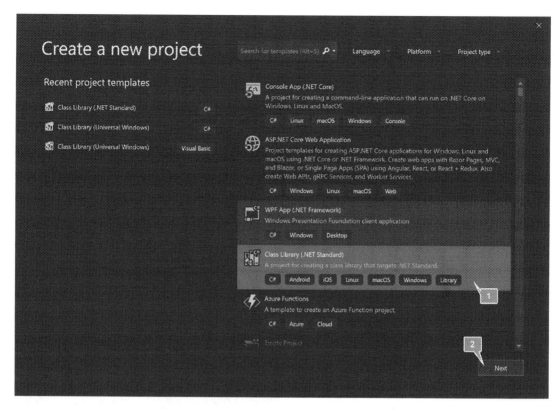

Figure 5-4. *Create a .NET standard library*

In the next step, as seen in Figure 5-5, we need to configure the project settings.

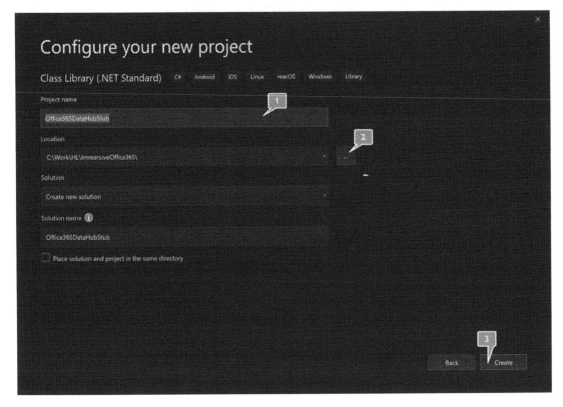

Figure 5-5. *Configure the .NET standard library project*

1. Fill in a *Project Name*. Enter Office365DataHubStub as the project name.

2. Select a location for your project. Since we will have multiple projects, it would be wise to put them all under the same folder. In my case this is the ImmersiveOffice365 folder. The solution name will be filled in automatically.

3. Press the *Create* button to create the project.

You will notice that the project contains a generated Class1.cs file. We remove this file from the project before we start adding our own classes.

The placeholder plugin needs to have the same name as the UWP plugin. It also needs to have the same methods and classes defined in the same namespace. This means that we need to configure the project settings, as can be seen in Figure 5-6.

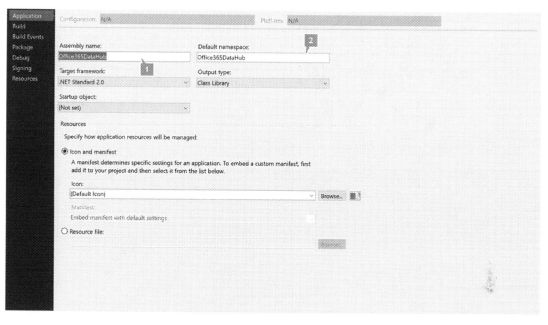

Figure 5-6. *Configure project settings of the .NET standard library project.*

1) Right-click the project and select properties.

2) Change both the *Assembly Name* and *Default namespace* to
   Office365DataHub.

Just like the previous project, we need to add the same classes to this placeholder plugin. Create a new code *Class* file via the solution explorer using right-click then project and select *Add ➤ New* Item. Call your new class Singleton.cs Copy the following code to that file. The code for the Singleton template class will stay the same.

```
namespace Office365DataHub
{
    public class Singleton<T> where T : new()
    {
        private static T instance;

        protected Singleton()
        {

        }
```

```
        public static T Instance
        {
            get
            {
                if (instance == null)
                {
                    instance = new T();
                }

                return instance;
            }
        }
    }
}
```

Create another new code *Class* file via the solution explorer; right-click the project and select *Add* ➤ *New* Item. Call your new class Manager.cs. This class would normally contain the code for accessing the web service. But since this will be a placeholder, also called a stub, the code will be somewhat different. Copy the following code to create the framework of the class:

```
namespace Office365DataHub
{
    public class Manager : Singleton<Manager>
    {

    }
}
```

We need to add the same definition of the callback as we have in the other plugin. Copy the following code into the class Manager:

```
public delegate void OnGetSomeInformationCompleted(string result);
```

The second method that is called from the scripting in Unity is GetSomeInformation. In this example, we return the given parameter url to the callback method. Add the following method to the class Manager:

```
public void GetSomeInformation(string url, OnGetSomeInformationCompleted
onGetSomeInformationCompleted)
{
    onGetSomeInformationCompleted(url);
}
```

The result is shown in Figure 5-7. We now have two classes, Singleton and Manager, defined in our project. The next step is compiling the project and producing a DLL, which can be imported into Unity. Make sure you have *Debug* and *Any CPU* selected from the top dropdowns. Then build the project to generate the DLL.

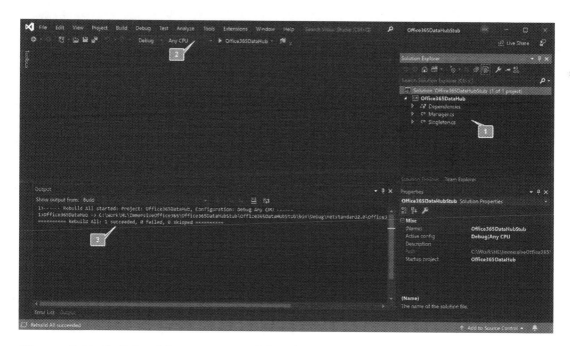

***Figure 5-7.** Build a debug version of the plugin*

Open the Unity project that was created in the previous chapter. Create two new folders under Assets. The first folder is called Plugins. Create the second folder WSA as a subfolder under Plugins. WSA stands for Windows Store Apps. Drag the UWP DLL named Office365DataHub into the folder Assets/Plugins/WSA. Drag the placeholder DLL named `Office365DataHubStub` into the folder `Assets/Plugins`. The result is shown in Figure 5-8.

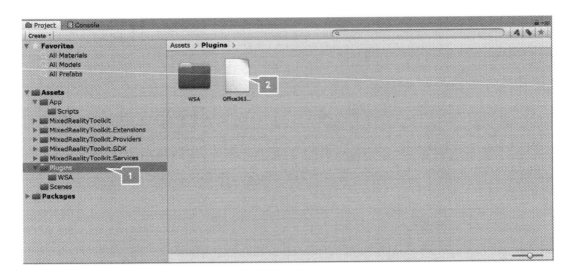

Figure 5-8. *Add the plugins in the assets folder to your Unity project*

Select the placeholder DLL, the one in the `Assets/Plugin` folder, in the *Project* tab. The properties of that file will appear in the *Inspector* window, as seen in Figure 5-9. Make sure that the following settings are met for the plugin:

- **Include platforms** – This defines which platforms the DLL is available too. Since it is a placeholder DLL, only the option *Editor* should be checked.

- **CPU** – Any CPU

- **OS** – Any OS

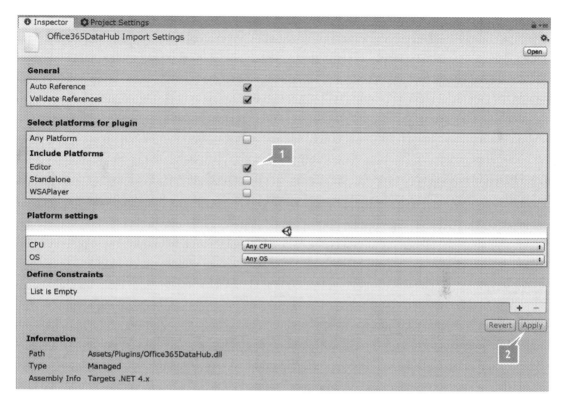

Figure 5-9. *Configure the settings of the placeholder plugin*

When the changes are made, press the *Apply* button to acknowledge the settings for the plugin.

Select the UWP DLL, the one in the `Assets/Plugins/WSA` folder, in the *Project* tab. The properties of that file will appear in the *Inspector* window, as seen in Figure 5-10. Make sure that the following settings are met for the plugin:

- **Include platforms** – Only the option *WSAPlayer* Is checked.

- **SDK** – Any SDK

- **ScriptingBackend** – Any scripting backend

- **Don't Process** – This option needs to be unchecked. Otherwise you will receive compiler errors when you build the solution from Unity.

- **Placeholder** – Select the previously configured placeholder. It will be found, since it uses the same name as this .NET standard DLL.

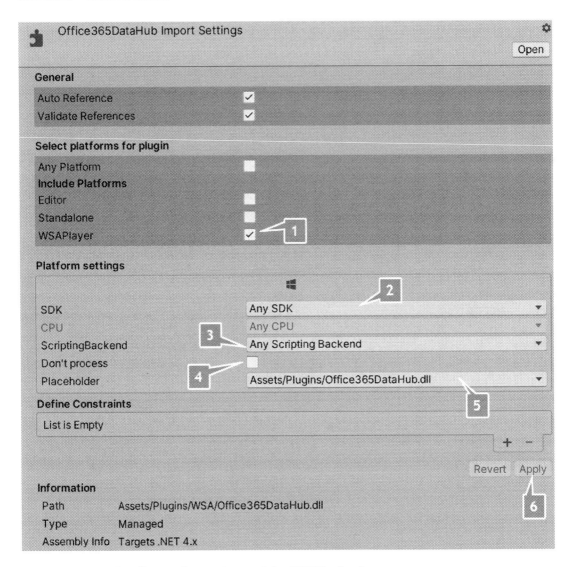

Figure 5-10. *Configure the settings of the UWP plugin*

When the changes are made, press the *Apply* button to acknowledge the settings for the plugin. Now both plugins are configured and ready for use.

Let's use the Manager class from a scripting file in Unity. Create a new C# scripting file in Unity called SomeInformation, which we will add to the HelloWorld! *GameObject.* The scripting file will call GetSomeInformation method on the Manager class and outputs the result onto the TextMesh in the HelloWorld! *GameObject.*

```
using UnityEngine;

public class SomeInformation : MonoBehaviour
{
    string text = "";

    private TextMesh mesh = null;

    // Start is called before the first frame update
    void Start()
    {
        mesh = gameObject.GetComponent<TextMesh>();
    }

    // Update is called once per frame
    void Update()
    {
        if (mesh != null)
        {
            mesh.text = text;
        }
    }
}
```

The TextMesh from the HelloWorld! *GameObject* is retrieved in the Start() method and the text property of the TextMesh is updated in the Update() method.

The main thread used by Unity is not thread-safe. This means that all calls to the Unity API need to be done from the main Unity thread. Synchronizing data back from a separate thread requires another form of implementation.

For that reason, we define a separate property called text in the class. The result returned from the callback method is stored in that property. The application would fail if we tried to set the text property of the TextMesh directly from the callback. Copy the following method in the SomeInformation class:

```
private void OnGetSomeInformationCompleted(string result)
{
    if (result.Length > 100)
    {
```

```
        text = result.Substring(0, 100);
    }
    else
    {
        text = result;
    }
}
```

Add the following code in the Start() method just below the row that retrieves the mesh from the *GameObject*:

```
Office365DataHub.Manager.Instance.GetSomeInformation("https://www.
microsoft.com", OnGetSomeInformationCompleted);
}
```

This row will instantiate the Manager from the Office365DataHub namespace and calls the GetSomeInformation method. The result is returned in the OnGetSomeInformationCompleted.

Now drag the scripting file onto the HelloWorld! *GameObject* or use the *Add Component* button in the *Inspector* window. The result would be the same as seen in Figure 5-11.

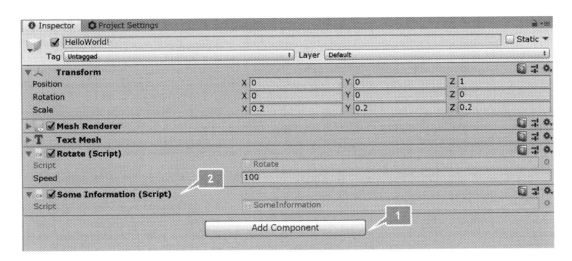

Figure 5-11. *Add the script to the HelloWorld GameObject*

When you start the scene in Unity, the placeholder plugin is used. You will see that, since the Hello World! text is replaced by the URL specified in the call to the `Office365DataHub.Manager.Instance.GetSomeInformation` method. If you build the solution to a Visual Studio solution, deploy it to a HoloLens device, the UWP plugin is used. This will show the first 100 characters of the page requested by the URL.

Using a plugin can be very useful, since you have a lot of functionality present that is normally not present in Unity. The downside is that you are not able to test such functionality from the play mode of Unity. On the other hand, you can test the UWP plugin extensively using a UWP test application outside Unity and the HoloLens device. It also allows you to still use C# code in the backend because Unity does not compile the UWP DLL.

CHAPTER 6

HoloLens

This chapter goes into more detail of Microsoft HoloLens specific elements during development using Unity and Visual Studio. This incorporates tools and available packages. The second part of this chapter goes into more detail on how to create interaction with your objects and environment by using spatial understanding, gestures, gaze, and eye tracking.

Tools and Packages

To make your life a little bit easier when developing applications for HoloLens, there are several different toolkits, tools, and packages that you can use. The chapter also explains how the Windows Device Portal can help you when developing applications.

Unity Store

Let's start with the Unity Store. The Unity Store is a great place to find all kinds of different packages. These packages are called Assets. Depending on the functionality of the item, the Asset contains different elements. These include *GameObjects*, shaders, script, DLLs, and many others. You will need a Unity account to access the Unity Store. This doesn't have to be a paid account. Keep in mind that not all Assets in the Unity Store are free. But some of the Assets are worth the money they ask. You always have the chance to check out the contents of the Asset. In some cases, the company or person who has put the Asset in the Unity Store has a link to a website with more information about the Asset. In Figure 6-1 you can see the Asset Store tab next to the Scene and Game tab.

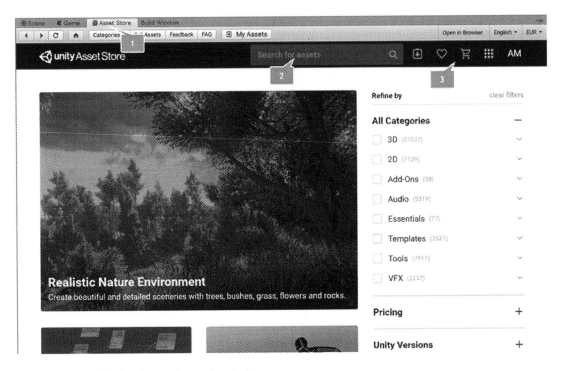

Figure 6-1. *Unity Asset Store in Unity*

As soon as you click the tab, it logs in automatically and shows the latest packages available for you. The tab contains several functionalities. It is possible to search for a specific package or packages that apply to the used keywords.

	Item	Description
📟	My Assets	This will show all the Assets that you have bought from the Unity Store. The list allows you to download the Assets or import them into your currently open project.
♡	My favorites	Assets that you found in the Asset Store and are interesting can be flagged as favorites. They will appear in the list when this icon is clicked.
🛒	Cart	The shopping cart contains all Assets you want to buy. Even an Asset that is free needs to be bought through the shopping cart.

Importing Assets

Assets are stored as packages. These packages use the extension `unitypackage`. There are different ways of getting a package inserted into your project:

- *Import from Asset Store*: When you have bought an Asset, you can import it into your currently open project by clicking the Import button.

- *Project window*: Import via right-click menu Import package ➤ Custom package.

- *Main menu*: Import via Assets ➤ Import package ➤ Custom package.

- *Import by dragging*: A downloaded package can be dragged into Unity. Unity will automatically import the package.

Unity does not have something like a versioning system that makes it easy to update a package. You will need to check for a package that the owner expects from you when you install it. Some packages require you to remove all the folders created in your project to prevent issues when recompiling the project. The Mixed Reality Toolkit is an example of that.

Mixed Reality Toolkit

The Mixed Reality Toolkit, nowadays called MRTK, is an open source toolkit that is available for all mixed reality devices like the Microsoft HoloLens and the Windows Mixed Reality immersive headsets. It is a toolkit that allows you to more easily implement applications for devices. Support for gestures, gaze, voice, and spatial understanding are some examples of it. Specifically for Microsoft HoloLens 2, the MRTK has been released as a completely new toolkit under the name MRTK v2. It contains the latest functionality to support all the new features of Microsoft HoloLens 2 like gestures and eye tracking. Nowadays this toolkit is under the flag of Microsoft instead of some good folks from the community. It is still possible to contribute to the MRTK v2 platform. But since Microsoft is the best party to implement their own device functionality, for me this decision is the best so far.

It also has some faulty code removed like the singleton implementation for a script. But it also has functionality removed like Newtonsoft, which allowed easy access and handling JSON files.

Microsoft has made a special page on docs for getting your app ready for HoloLens 2. This page describes the different steps required for migrating your current application to HoloLens 2 using the MRTK v2. Read more about it here: `https://docs.microsoft.com/en-us/windows/mixed-reality/mrtk-porting-guide`.

There is another toolkit offered. It is called the XRTK and is a direct fork of the MRTK v2. This toolkit is maintained by some great MVPs and people from the mixed reality community. Their goal is to create a true mixed reality approach that coverts AR, XR, and VR completely. It supports OpenVR on all platforms that support the standard as for native SDK implementations. Therefore this toolkit supports multiple types of devices with a single codebase. They work closely with the MRTK v2 to follow their roadmap to ensure the best result. The migration path from MRTK v2 to XRTK is not that difficult. The differences are mainly the namespace and some missing scripts in prefabs. It is an interesting toolkit to keep a close watch on and see how this develops in the next few years. And who knows, maybe even interesting to migrate to.

The MRTK v2 can be downloaded from GitHub. At the time of writing, the toolkit is at release version 2.1.0. Always keep in mind that when building with the MRTKv2, use an LTS version of Unity and a release build form the MRTK v2. The documentation specifies which Unity version is required for the selected MRTK v2 version. That combination will give you the best result, performance, and support.

The MRTK v2 consists of three important packages containing the functionality of the toolkit:

```
Microsoft.MixedReality.Toolkit.Unity.Foundation.{version}.unitypackage
Microsoft.MixedReality.Toolkit.Unity.Tools.{version}.unitypackage
Microsoft.MixedReality.Toolkit.Unity.Extensions.{version}.unitypackage
```

The Tools and Extensions are optional and only need to be installed if you require functionality from those packages. There is also a package available with examples. Needless to say, this package is also optional.

```
Microsoft.MixedReality.Toolkit.Unity.Examples.{version}.unitypackage
```

In Figure 6-2 you will see the result when the packages, except for the example package, are installed in your project.

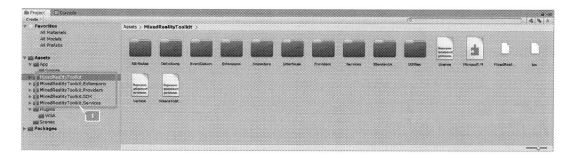

Figure 6-2. *The project windows containing some of the MRTK v2 packages installed in the project*

Updating to a new version of the MRTK v2 requires you to remove all the previously generated files. So be careful when doing changes to one of those files, since they will be overwritten or deleted.

Interaction

Interacting with the real world using a HoloLens device creates a true immersive experience for an end user. HoloLens offers spatial understanding, implementation of different gestures, gaze, eye tracking, and the use of voice. It really depends on what you want to achieve with your application. In some cases, like in industry, it is not useful to use voice since you have too much sound from your surroundings. Another thing to remember is how people can interact with your application. Do they need to have their hands continuously free or are they able to use gestures all the time? This will determine which of the interactions will be used in your application. The following interactions are available:

- Gaze

- Pointers

- Hand gestures

- Near interactions

- Speech

- Eye tracking

149

And don't forget spatial understanding. That part especially will allow you to interact with your application in a more commonly expected way for your users. Think of placing objects on the wall or a table, which allows end users to interact with your application as they would normally do if they were using, for example, paper.

Objects and Object Container

Now Office 365 data is in 2D and on a computer screen. We would like to bring that data into 3D space and interact with it. That means we need to define a certain model for our data to be present in that 3D space. That model will be built from objects and object containers. Each object represents some Office 365 data. Think about a document, a person, an email, or something else. The object container represents a collection of those objects. In some cases an object container contains only the same type of objects. But it is not uncommon that object containers contain different types of objects. In that case, we have a certain relationship between those objects in our application.

If we translate this back into Unity using the MRTK, we can use *GameObjects* and object collections. MRTK contains different script classes for object collections. Each of those scripts has one or more different surface types that allow you to represent the objects in that collection in some specific way. Depending on how you want the user to experience the data, different surface types will suit the solution.

Create an empty *GameObject* called Visual in the root. This will become our root *GameObject* for our object collections. Let's start with creating our object collections. We want to represent a collection of people from the company and a collection of people who will be forming a team. We have created two prefabs for both types of collections.

Download the `prefabs.unitypackage` from the following GitHub location:

```
https://github.com/ameijers/ImmersiveOffice365/tree/master/Unity/
Chapter%206/UnityPackages
```

Import the unitypackage via the main menu option Assets ➤ Import package ➤ Custom package...

The prefabs can be found in the Project Window under Assets ➤ App ➤ Prefabs. Drag the *PeopleContainer* under the GameObject *Visual*. Rename it to *People*. Drag the *TeamContainer* under the GameObject *Visual*. Rename it to *Team*.

You will find a prefab called *Person* under the folder Assets ➤ App ➤ Prefabs. Now drag the prefab multiple times under the GameObject *Person* to create different persons.

Rename each of the instances to a person's name. In Figure 6-3 you will see the steps to be taken and the result of adding the object collections and objects.

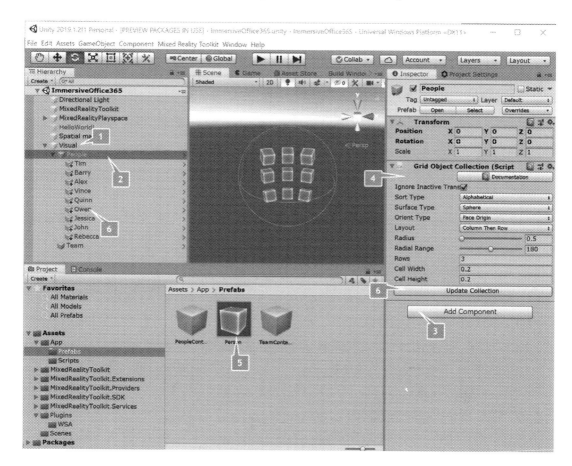

Figure 6-3. *The final result of creating two object collections and several persons*

The next part of this chapter starts implementing the interaction between those objects and object containers. That includes interactions like taking out a certain object from one object container to another object container.

It also goes more in depth with regard to gaze, hand gestures, and eye tracking.

Input System

The MRTK uses an input system. This input system is an architectural model for interaction with *GameObjects*. The input system looks rather complex, since the MRTK is written for different input sources of different devices. In our case, we only want to implement for HoloLens 2. But using the input system will create elements that can be used to get it to work on immersive headsets or other devices.

The input system of the MRTK is extensively described at GitHub. For more information about the different elements we discuss, you can check that documentation.

There are several important elements within the input system. Each of them is described in the following table.

Element	Description
Device manager	The device manager contains providers to all kind of different input sources: input sources like HoloLens, mixed reality immersive headsets, joysticks, or other. Providers are registered through the *Registered Service Providers Profile*. This can be found when you open the Mixed Reality Toolkit component in the MixedRealityToolkit *GameObject*. These providers will automatically activate when detected by the device manager and will generate input events.
Input events	The input system contains several input event interfaces. These event interfaces can be used by creating your own classes derived from MonoBehaviour, which implements one or more interfaces. An example is the SourceDetected and SourceLost events implemented by implementing the IMixedRealitySourceStateHandler. There are more input events available. Examples are Source Pose Changed, Input Down, Input Up, Speech Keyword Recognized, Gesture Updated, Hand Joints Updated, and others.
Input actions	It is possible to use a more global system for reacting to inputs from device sources. Input actions make it possible to call some application logic from a specific device source that is producing an input. This allows you to bind business logic to some specific action like *Select*, *Menu*, *Grip Pose* and others instead of using the Input events. Input events are more complex, since you have to rely on several *GameObjects* in your scene to react and resolve the event.
Controller	Controllers are a gateway for accessing different input events. Controllers are created for each device that is registered and available as input. As soon as the device is not available anymore, the controller is destroyed too. It is possible to have Pointers attached to controllers. If that is the case, they will be used to determine the focused object and have Pointer events raised on it.

(continued)

Element	Description
Pointer	A Pointer allows you to point out a *GameObject* by using your hand. Pointers are attached to a Controller. They are automatically instantiated based on the configuration of the *MixedRealityPointerProfile*. There are different types of pointers, like a Far Pointer and a Near Pointer.
Cursor	The cursor is the visual indication where the pointer is hitting the *GameObject*. It also shows you in what state your hand is. The cursor can be changed in the Mixed Reality profile.
Focus	Focus means that an event created by a pointer is redirected to the *GameObject* that currently has the focus.
Interactable	This is a component that can be added to a *GameObject*, allowing you to alter its visual state based on events. It listens to certain events like focus, enter, exit, input down, input up, and others.

Our application will be using Input events over Input actions, since we want to work from the context of the data. That means that events are handled at a *GameObject* level instead of globally. How some of these elements relate to each other is shown in Figure 6-4.

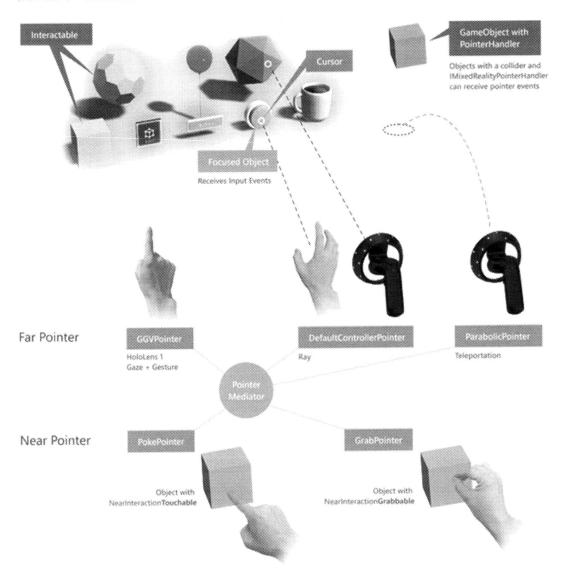

Figure 6-4. *An overview of how the input system of MRTK works*

We will now go deeper into describing each of the important elements used by our application to interact with Office 365 data.

Input Event Life Cycle

There is a clear event life cycle of input events created by the input system. This is most important at script level because interfaces are implemented at classes derived from the MonoBehaviour class. In the diagram shown in Figure 6-5, you can see the different steps of the life cycle.

Figure 6-5. *The event life cycle of an event in the MRTK input system*

Every event fired by the MRTK input system is following the event life cycle:

- *Input event occurred*: The MRTK input system recognizes an input event coming from one of the registered and activated devices.

- *Global input handlers*: It is possible to register a certain object to receive global input events. That means that it will always receive these events without being focused on and having an input event handler interface implemented. These objects get the events fired first.

- *Registered active pointers*: The following steps are executed for each registered and active pointer:

    - The input system will fire the events on the *GameObject* that is active and has the focus.

    - The process ends when the input event is marked as used. At that point, no other *GameObjects* will receive callbacks.

- *Registered fallback input handlers*: The input system will call each fallback registered input handler when all the preceding are not found.

The Unity event system is used by the input events from the input system. Therefore the system will search upward through the parents of the *GameObject* looking for an input event interface if none is found at the *GameObject*. Also, keep in mind that Pointer input events are not handled the same, since they are only fired when the *GameObject* is in focus by that pointer.

Gaze

The gaze is the first form of input when using a HoloLens device. It can be compared with using your mouse to point to something at your screen. The gaze allows us to point to an object in 3D space. This allows us to determine which object interactions need to take place.

There are forms of gaze when using the MRTK:

- *Head gaze*: This gaze is based on the direction where the head or camera is looking—meaning the direction in which the device is pointed by the wearer. This form of gaze is active on devices that do not support eye tracking, like Microsoft HoloLens 1 or where the ability of eye tracking is not yet enabled for the user.

- *Eye gaze*: This gaze is based on the direction where the user is looking with his/her eyes.

Both forms of gaze are provided by the class `GazeProvider`.

The provider needs to be configured. Open the inspector view of the MixedRealityToolkit *GameObject*. You will find the specific configurations of your application using the MRTK as a component under this *GameObject*. The default settings are mostly enough for your application. These settings are read only and grayed out. To change the configuration settings, you will need to clone them first, as shown in Figure 6-6.

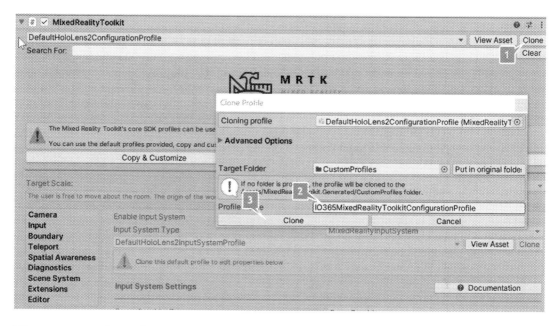

Figure 6-6. *Clone the MixedRealityToolkit profile*

Click the *Clone* button next to the current selected profile. Fill in the name *IO365MixedRealityConfigurationProfile* as new name. Press the *Clone* button to clone the profile. We now do the same for the input system profile, as shown in Figure 6-7.

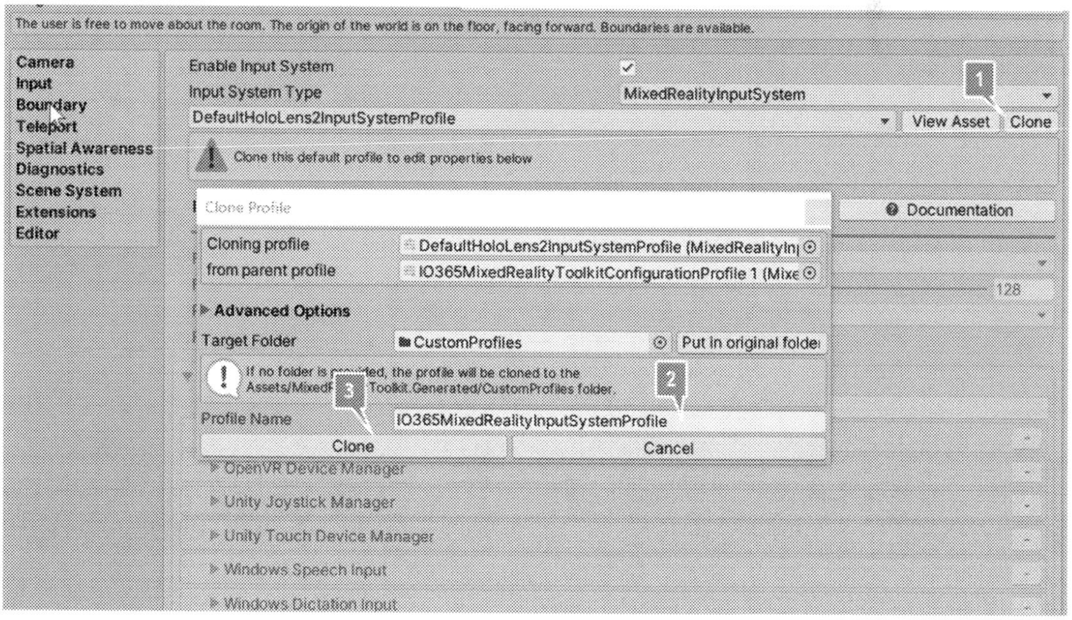

Figure 6-7. *Clone the input system profile*

Click the *Clone* button next to the current selected profile. Fill in the name *IO365MixedRealityInputSystemProfile* as the new name. Press the *Clone* button to clone the profile.

Keep on repeating this process till you have cloned the configuration settings you want to change.

Open the tab Pointer and clone the pointer using the *Clone* button. Use the name *IO365PointerProfile*. Now you will be able to change the settings of the pointer.

All these configurations are stored by default under Assets ➤ MixedRealityToolkit. Generated ➤ CustomProfiles.

To make any changes in the MRTK configuration of your application, you will need to clone each configuration part separately. While you can only copy and customize once from a default configuration profile, each configuration part in the profile can be cloned more than once. This allows you to create different configurations of specific functionality within a single profile.

We will not be making any changes yet, since we want to use the default settings. But this technique allows you to change the cursor used or even write your own GazeProvider class based on the IMixedRealityGazeProvider interface.

The following code shows how to check if the gaze is hitting an object:

```
using Microsoft.MixedReality.Toolkit;
using UnityEngine;

public class ObjectTracker : MonoBehaviour
{

    void Update()
    {
        Vector3 gazeDirection = Vector3.zero;
        GameObject target = null;
        Vector3 origin = Vector3.zero;
        Vector3 pointer = Vector3.zero;

        if (CoreServices.InputSystem.GazeProvider.GazeTarget != null)
        {
```

```
            gazeDirection = CoreServices.InputSystem.GazeProvider.
            GazeDirection;
            target = CoreServices.InputSystem.GazeProvider.GazeTarget;
            origin = CoreServices.InputSystem.GazeProvider.GazeOrigin;
            pointer = CoreServices.InputSystem.GazeProvider.GazePointer.
            Position;
        }
    }
}
```

There are a few important methods and properties on the GazeProvider class that are used in the preceding code. The GazeTarget returns the *GameObject* that is hit by the gaze. It is important to understand that you are not hitting the *GameObject* itself, but the collider of the *GameObject*. If the *GameObject* does not have a collider, the *GameObject* is handled as if it was not there. That means that the gaze goes through the object until it hits another *GameObject* with a collider.

The GazeOrigin is the position of gaze coming out of the HoloLens device. The GazePoint.Position gives us the position where the gaze hits the collider of the *GameObject*. The GazeDirection is the direction from the GazeOrigin to the GazePoint. Position returned as a vector.

Pointers and Focus

Pointers are used to interact with *GameObjects*. Think of grabbing, touching, or pointing to an object. Pointers are registered via the Mixed Reality Toolkit Profile. Each registration is based on the prefab for the pointer, the controller type, and the handedness. The prefab determines the visualization and behavior of the pointer. The controller type determines for which type of controllers the pointer is supposed to be used. The handedness determines if it is registered for the left, right, or both hands.

Therefore each controller, which is created by the registration of the device, can contain one or more pointers. The input system uses something called pointer mediation to determine which pointer needs to be active. This depends completely on the behavior of the user. An example is that the system mediates between whether the user wants to press a button or grab an object, and determines which pointer is becoming active and which pointer will be inactive.

There are two types of pointers of interest for building applications for HoloLens:

- *Near pointer*: This is the most commonly used type, since it describes the interaction with objects that are close enough to the user to grab or to touch them.

- *Far pointer*: This type of pointer is used to interact with objects that are out of reach for the user. This allows a user to interact with objects without the need to approach them. Far pointers can become interesting when combined with grabbing. Think of looking at an object that is far away and then executing the grab interaction in the air to grab the object.

The input system has a separate class called `FocusProvider`. This class is not derived from `MonoBehaviour` and used as such. But it is called from within an `Update()` call. In each frame the class iterates over all available and active pointers. For each of those pointers, it maintains the focused object. In some cases, two objects can have the focus when a pointer is used by both hands.

This class uses ray casting to determine for each pointer which object it is currently hitting. If an object is hit, it will also fire events for getting focus and focus lost.

Hand Gestures

The MRTK supports all types of hand gestures. It supports hand gestures for Microsoft HoloLens 1 and Microsoft HoloLens 2. The following table gives an overview of the hand gestures and for which device they can be used.

Type	Description	HoloLens 1	HoloLens 2
Gestures	These are input events based on the hands of the user. These are the basic gestures like the tap gesture and tap and hold gesture, which have been present from the beginning of HoloLens. This allows you to implement behaviors like hold, navigation, and manipulation.	Yes	Yes
Hand tracking	Hand tracking allows you to track both hands based on the joints, palm, and index finger.	No	Yes
Near interaction	Near interaction is based on the hand tracking type and gives you some default interactions with objects like grab and touch.	No	Yes

We will be focusing on near interaction with hand tracking for our application. Just like the gaze, hand tracking uses a profile called Hand Tracking Profile. This profile can be found under the Input System Profile ➤ Hand Tracking and describes the different forms of visualization. You can visualize the joints of the hand by enabling the option *Enable Hand Joint Visualization* and defining the prefabs for a joint, palm, and fingertip. You can visualize the complete hand by enabling the option *Enable Hand Mesh Visualization* and specifying the prefab for the hand mesh. You can see an example of the latter in Figure 6-8.

Figure 6-8. *An example of hand mesh tracking enabled*

These options can be useful when testing your scene and interactions inside the Unity Editor. But keep in mind that if you do not have any need for visualizing joints and hands in the final application, keep the options unselected. Using the visualization will influence the performance of your application.

You will need to be careful if you want to define your own prefabs for joint, palm, fingertip, and hand mesh. Since these prefabs are redrawn every frame, having complex code running in your *GameObjects* can have a major impact on performance.

The hand tracking classes can be used when you want to have full control over the hands' position and rotation. To get these values, you can request a `MixedRealityPose` struct for each individual hand joint. This struct contains a series of properties describing the hand joint. The following table shows the available values.

Property	Description
Position	The position of the pose of the hand joint
Right, Up and Forward	Respectively, the X, Y, and Z axis of the pose in world space coordinates
Rotation	The rotation of the pose
ZeroIndentity	This is a predefined value that can be used for calculating a Six Dof transform. In principle, it's only used for mixed reality headsets.

It is possible to retrieve these values through a hand controller or using the available utility classes. It depends on if you have a hand controller available. An example of having a hand controller available is when you are in a class that has one or more input event interfaces implemented. The following example shows how to get the joint pose information:

```
using Microsoft.MixedReality.Toolkit.Input;
using Microsoft.MixedReality.Toolkit.Utilities;
using UnityEngine;

public class HandTracking : MonoBehaviour, IMixedRealitySourceStateHandler
{
    public void OnSourceDetected(SourceStateEventData eventData)
    {
        IMixedRealityHand hand = eventData.Controller as IMixedRealityHand;

        if (hand != null)
        {
```

```
        if (hand.TryGetJoint(TrackedHandJoint.Wrist, out
        MixedRealityPose pose))
        {
            Vector3 positionOfWrist = pose.Position;
        }
    }
}

public void OnSourceLost(SourceStateEventData eventData)
{
}
}
```

Placing this object on a *GameObject* in the scene will result in receiving the SourceDetect and SourceLost events of one or both hands.

If no controller is available, you can use the utility classes to retrieve the hand joint pose data. The following code shows how you can do that:

```
using Microsoft.MixedReality.Toolkit.Input;
using Microsoft.MixedReality.Toolkit.Utilities;
using UnityEngine;

public class HandTracking : MonoBehaviour
{
    public void Update()
    {
        if (HandJointUtils.TryGetJointPose(TrackedHandJoint.Wrist,
        Handedness.Any, out MixedRealityPose pose))
        {
            Vector3 positionOfWrist = pose.Position;
            IMixedRealityHand whichHand = HandJointUtils.
            FindHand(Handedness.Any);
        }
    }
}
```

In this code example, the static member `HandJointUtils.TryGetJointPose` is used to retrieve the position and the static member `HandJointUtils.FindHand` to determine which of both hands is returned.

Near Interaction

Near interactions can be described as complex hand gestures packed into a script component to allow you to quickly and easily implement them on your *GameObjects*. The MRTK already has two near interactions called touches and grabs. Both are raised by the `PokePointer` or the `GrabPointer`, respectively. The following need to be ensured to have near interactions implemented correctly:

- The pointer that needs to raise the event needs to be registered in the Mixed Reality Toolkit Profile.

- The *GameObject* that implements the near interaction is required to have a collider component.

- The near interaction script component is added to the *GameObject*.

- Add an additional script component that listens to the events generated by the near interaction to add your own business logic.

Our model contains objects and a collection of objects where the objects are different types of data from Office 365. In the example we are building, we have created several persons. In the next step, we will implement the grab near interaction on those objects, allowing us to pick out a person and move it from the people collection to the team collection.

We need to make sure that the GrabPointer is registered in the Mixed Reality Toolkit Profile. This should be registered as the default. Check the profile and make sure it looks the same as in Figure 6-9. Navigate to Input ➤ Pointers ➤ Pointer options.

Pointer Prefab	PokePointer	⊙	-
Controller Type	Articulated Hand		
Handedness	Any		

Pointer Prefab	GrabPointer	⊙	-
Controller Type	Articulated Hand		
Handedness	Any		

Figure 6-9. *Registration of the GrabPointer in the Mixed Reality Toolkit Profile*

Make sure it is defined with *Articulated Hand* as Controller Type.

Since we have created prefabs for our objects and object collections, we need to add components at the prefab level, as shown in Figure 6-10. Go to Assets ➤ App ➤ Prefabs. Click the *Person* prefab. Now press the Open Prefab button in the Inspector view to open the prefab for editing. Use the Add Component to add the *Near Interaction Grabbable* script component to the prefab. This will automatically add it to all instances of the prefab in the scene.

Figure 6-10. *Adding the Near Interaction Grabbable script to the Person prefab*

165

Finally, we need to add an additional script that handles the events coming from the GrabPointer. This requires the implementation of the IMixedRealityPointerHandler interface, as you can see in the code below. This interface handles both grab as touch near interaction events. Create a new class under Assets/Apps/Scripts called ObjectDataBehavior. Add the following code to that class:

```
using Microsoft.MixedReality.Toolkit.Input;
using Microsoft.MixedReality.Toolkit.Utilities;
using UnityEngine;

public class ObjectDataBehavior : MonoBehaviour,
IMixedRealityPointerHandler
{
    public void OnPointerClicked(MixedRealityPointerEventData eventData)
    {
    }

    public void OnPointerDown(MixedRealityPointerEventData eventData)
    {
    }

    public void OnPointerDragged(MixedRealityPointerEventData eventData)
    {
    }

    public void OnPointerUp(MixedRealityPointerEventData eventData)
    {
    }
}
```

We need to add the class as a component to the Person prefab. Go to Assets ➤ App ➤ Prefabs. Click the *Person* prefab. Now press the Open Prefab button in the Inspector view to open the prefab for editing. Use the Add Component to add the *ObjectDataBehavior* script component to the prefab.

Let's write some business logic to accommodate grabbing a person from one collection and placing it into another collection. We want to allow the user to grab a person and drag it over to another collection. When the dragging fails due to dragging to a location without a collection, we need to attach the person back to its initial collection. Therefore we need a reference to that initial location. Add the following code to the ObjectDataBehavior class:

```
private Transform initialCollection = null;
```

As soon as the person is grabbed by the user, the OnPointerDown event is fired. In this event, we store the initial collection and make sure that the Person *GameObject* is detached from its parent to move it around freely. Replace the OnPointerDown code in the ObjectDataBehavior class with the following code:

```
public void OnPointerDown(MixedRealityPointerEventData eventData)
{
    // store the collection
    initialCollection = gameObject.transform.parent;

    // detach from the collection
    gameObject.transform.parent = null;
}
```

The event OnPointerDragged is fired as long as the user is holding onto the Person *GameObject*. We set the position and rotation of the grabbing to the Person *GameObject*, which gives the feeling you are holding it in your hand. Replace the OnPointerDragged code in the ObjectDataBehavior class with the following code:

```
public void OnPointerDragged(MixedRealityPointerEventData eventData)
{
    // follow the position and rotation of the pointer during dragging
    gameObject.transform.position = eventData.Pointer.Position;
    gameObject.transform.rotation = eventData.Pointer.Rotation;
}
```

The event OnPointUp is fired when the user lets go of the Person *GameObject*. At that moment, we need to do several steps. Since we know that the collections have a GridObjectCollection component, we look for all the collections in the scene under

the *GameObject* Visual. Replace the `OnPointerUp` code in the `ObjectDataBehavior` class
with the following code:

```
public void OnPointerUp(MixedRealityPointerEventData eventData)
{
    // determine if there is a nearby collection
    GridObjectCollection[] objects = initialCollection.parent.GetComponents
    InChildren<GridObjectCollection>();

    float distance = 1f;
    GameObject closedObject = null;

    foreach(GridObjectCollection obj in objects)
    {
        GameObject go = obj.gameObject;

        float dist = Vector3.Distance(go.transform.position, gameObject.
        transform.position);
        if (dist < distance)
        {
            distance = dist;
            closedObject = go;
        }
    }

    // update the parent to the closest collection
    if (closedObject != null)
    {
        gameObject.transform.parent = closedObject.transform;
    }
    else
    {
        gameObject.transform.parent = initialCollection;
    }

    // update the collection it is attached to
    GridObjectCollection goc = gameObject.transform.parent.GetComponent<Gri
    dObjectCollection>();
```

```
    if (goc != null)
    {
        goc.UpdateCollection();
    }
}
```

Then we determine per found collection which one has the shortest distance to the Person *GameObject*. That will become the new collection. If none is found, the initial collection is used again. We need to update the view of the `GridObjectCollection` to present the change.

Interactable

Do you want to create more interactive menus, buttons, and other objects? Normally you would build the logic yourself to get it to work. But with the MRTK you have the `Interactable` component. This component allows you to respond to all kind of different interactions like touch, focus, speech, eye ray, and more by making changes in how the object is visualized. This technique uses something called Visual Themes. Visual Themes allow you to have more control over UX Assets in response to different state transitions. Think of changing the color and depth of a button when hovering over it.

To make use of the `Interactable` component, the configuration is divided into the following sections:

- *General*: This contains some general settings. It allows you to enable the component, on which input action it needs to respond, and the type of selection mode.

- *Profiles*: This part allows you to define multiple combinations between a target *GameObject* and one or more *Visual Themes* in combination with *States*. This allows you to define different visualizations between certain states. An example is a button that visually changes depending on which state is active. States would be none, focus, pressed, and disabled.

- *Events*: Events allow you to define different rules based on events fired on certain objects. These rules allow you to call method and properties within the context of that object. An example could be calling a custom function defined in one of the components on the object when the `OnClick()` event occurs. It can be used for nonvisual-related changes and gives you more grained control over the process of events and business logic.

Eye Tracking

With HoloLens 2, we finally have eye tracking as a form of input. It allows us to engage with objects by looking at them. Using eye tracking can make your application smarter, since you know what the user is looking at. This could be interesting to use when walking around a 3D model of Office 365 data, to determine which part of the data is the most important. This can be achieved by measuring how often the user is looking at some of the data.

To get eye tracking to work in your scene and application, some requirements need to be met:

- It requires an *Eye Gaze Data Provider* for the input system.

- The option Use Eye Tracking in the `GazeProvider` needs to be set to true.

- You will need to enable the capability GazeInput in your application. This is a capability that you need to set in Visual Studio or through the MRTK build tool. The capability is not yet present under the capabilities of the build window in Unity.

- The eyes of the current user need to be calibrated. Normally when using HoloLens 2 with a new user, the process of calibration is automatically started. But it is also possible to detect if the current user has calibrated their eyes. If not, you could provide a message explaining that your application requires eye calibration before using it.

- Eye tracking permissions must be met. When your application is started up for the first time, the HoloLens 2 will ask the user to give permissions to use eye tracking. This is requested only once, and is valid for each user using that application on that specific device. You can always change a denied eye tracking request by resetting it in the settings menu on the HoloLens under Settings ➤ Privacy ➤ Apps.

The following steps explain where you can check if the *Eye Gaze Data Provider* is added and correctly set. You will need to go into the Mixed Reality Toolkit Profile. Select Input ➤ Input System settings ➤ Input Data Providers. An example is shown in Figure 6-11.

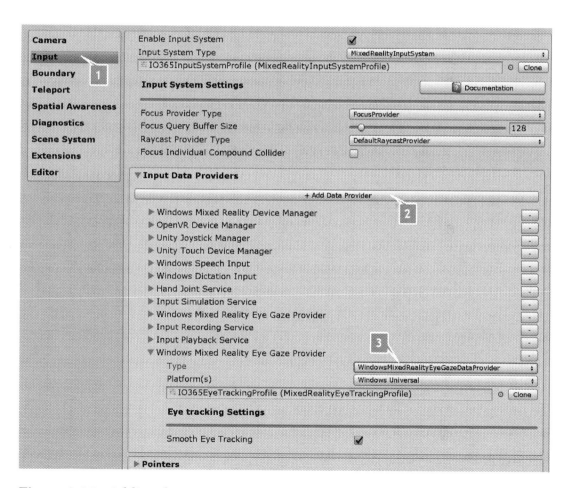

Figure 6-11. *Adding the Eye Gaze Data Provider to the configuration*

In this example it is present. But if it were not, you need to execute the following steps.

Press the Add Data Provider button to add a new data provider. Open the new data provider and select the type `Microsoft.MixedReality.Toolkit.WindowsMixedReality. Input ➤ WindowsMixedRealityEyeGazeDataProvider`. Make sure that you have selected Windows Universal as one of the platforms.

The `GazeProvider` script component can be found under the *GameObject* MixedRealityPlayspace ➤ Main Camera. Make sure that the option Use Eye Tracking is enabled.

Using eye tracking does not require any more scripting to be included in your project. But it is possible to access the eye gaze data. You can simply use the `MixedRealityToolkit.InputSystem.EyeGazeProvider` class. Several properties are exposed, giving you interesting information about eye tracking like `GazeOrigin`, `GazeDirection`, and `Hitinfo`. The property `IsEyeGazeValid` can be checked to determine if the data returned is valid.

It is also possible to validate if eye tracking is currently on by `UseEyeTracking`, and if there is a valid calibration of the user's eyes with `IsEyeCalibrationValid`.

Run Your Application

The final step is to build and deploy your application to the Microsoft HoloLens 2 device. Use the Build Settings window as you have used before to build your Visual Studio solution. Open the Visual Studio solution and make sure you have selected the following: Debug, ARM, and Device. Make sure that the Microsoft HoloLens 2 is connected via USB and recognized by your build machine. Right-click the solution in the Solution Explorer and select the option Deploy Solution. If the solution is not yet built, it will be built for you. Put on the Microsoft HoloLens 2 and look for the just-installed application in the menu. Run the application and try to move a person block from one visual collection to the other visual collection by grabbing it with your hand.

CHAPTER 7

HoloLens Development

This chapter goes into more detail of HoloLens development using Unity and Visual Studio. This incorporates the architecture of your application and what you will need to debug your application.

Application Architecture

To understand how your applications run and behave you will need to understand the architecture and lifecycle of your application. There are several parts you need to understand, to get a grip on how your application acts in certain conditions. A mixed reality application is built using Unity and Visual Studio. The application runs mainly on the Unity engine using scripts on *GameObjects* and possibly on code that is written outside the Unity space to perform, for example, other functionality that is not available via Unity. In our case, that is using DLLs to run asynchronous calls to web services due to the single thread mechanism of Unity.

Scripting Lifetime

Unity works with an event system using event functions. Event functions are called at a certain time once or more, depending on the function, to execute scripting in a MonoBehaviour-derived class in the current running scene. This order is called the order of execution. The order in which those event functions are called influences how your application responds. That means you need to understand the order and when each function is called, as you are building a mixed reality application using Unity. Which events are called differs from running the application outside or inside the Unity Editor.

© Alexander Meijers 2020
A. Meijers, *Immersive Office 365*, https://doi.org/10.1007/978-1-4842-5845-3_7

There is no particular order in which objects inside a scene receive the events. You can't assume that object X is called before object Y. To resolve such issues, you can make use of the Singleton pattern. Do not use the Singleton pattern on a class derived from MonoBehaviour, since that will result in unexpected behavior due to timing issues.

In Figure 7-1 you see a diagram of the different phases of the scripting lifecycle in Unity. The same diagram shows some of the most important user callbacks and the order in which they are called during the phase.

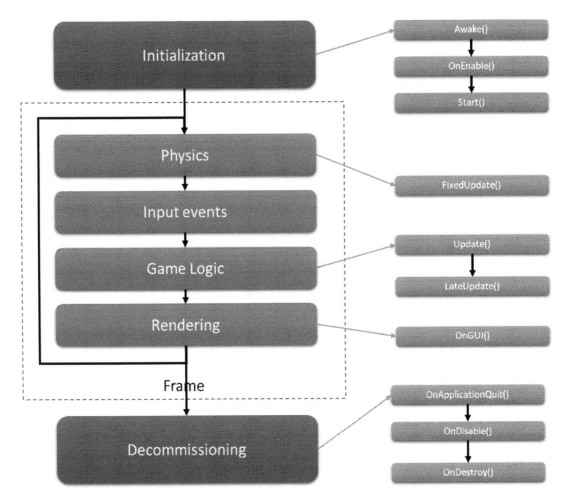

Figure 7-1. *Scripting lifecycle in Unity for applications*

The several phases shown in the diagram are described as follows:

- *Initialization*: The Initialization phase is called for each object in the scene when the scene is loaded the first time. Objects added later to that scene are handled in the same way. These events are all called once before the object proceeds to the next phase. Several different phases are passed through during each frame cycle.

- *Physics*: The Physics phase handles all events related to the physics of objects in the scene. Think of processing animations, triggers, and collisions, but also the call to `yield WaitForFixedUpdate`.

- *Input events*: This phase handles the implemented `OnMouse` events.

- *Game Logic*: The Game Logic phase is supposed to be used for handling all game logic in your application. Think of updating the location of an object or data presented from a source or specific functions. This phase is also used to process moves for animations. Yields methods and coroutine methods like `yield null`, `yield WaitForSeconds`, and `yield StartCoroutine()` are also handled in this phase. Most of your code will happen in the `Update()` method. But keep in mind that since these methods are called for each frame cycle, heavy code can cause disruption and performance issues in your application.

- *Rendering*: The Rendering phase is used for rendering the scene, the graphical user interface, and *Gizmos*. *Gizmos* can be used as a visual aid for debugging your scene. It allows you to draw all kind of different graphical objects like lines, cubes, text, and others. *Gizmos* can only be used when running in the Unity Editor. It is not available in your application outside the Unity Editor. In that case, you will need to write your own code to draw lines, cubes, and other graphical output.

- *Decommissioning*: This phase takes care of cleaning everything up. The events called are mostly for quitting the application, and disabling and destroying objects.

Custom Events

It is also possible to create your own events in Unity by using *UnityEvents* or C# events. Both can be used for different types of functionality like content driven callbacks, predefined calling events, and decoupling of systems. Decoupling of systems is a very important one. Unity scripting code can easily and quickly become entangled, hard to read and convert to complex systems where objects are relying on each other by deep links. Using an event system can prevent this.

Both event systems use the same principle. You define and create an event. Then you add listeners to your event. Listeners are callbacks that you register for a certain event. As soon as the event is invoked, all registered listeners are called.

Let's first start explaining UnityEvents. There are two types of supported function calls with *UnityEvents*:

- *Static*: These function calls are set through the UI of Unity. They use preconfigured values defined in that UI. When the event is invoked, the preconfigured value in the UI is used.

- *Dynamic*: These function calls use the arguments that are sent from the scripting code. This is bound to the type of UnityEvent. The filters used in the UI filter the available callbacks and show only valid calls for the event.

UnityEvents are added to a class derived from MonoBehaviour. Their behavior is the same as standard .NET delegates.

It requires you to create, for example, a new script called EventManager. The script needs to have the UnityEngine.Events implemented and a UnityEvent property defined as follows:

```
using UnityEngine;
using UnityEngine.Events;

public class EventManager : MonoBehaviour
{
    public UnityEvent actionEvent;

    public EventManager()
    {
    }
```

```
public void DoAction()
{
}

public void DoAction(int id)
{

}
}
```

Add the script to an empty GameObject in your scene and open the Inspector window. Add a new listener through the UI by clicking the + symbol, as shown in Figure 7-2.

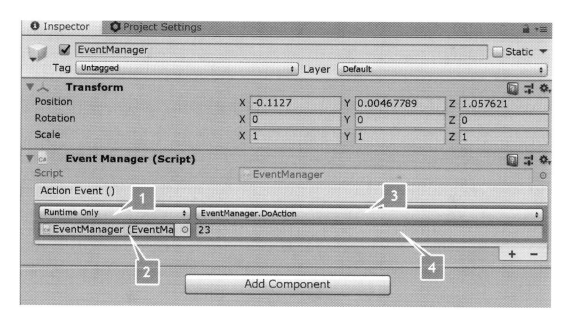

Figure 7-2. *A static function event added through the UI of Unity*

Select the type *Runtime Only* or *Editor and Runtime*, which determines if the listener only works in runtime or both editor and runtime. In this example, I have dragged the EventManager *GameObject* into the Object field. That allowed me to select the DoAction(int id) method defined in that class. Since this is a static function call, I must define its value in the UI.

By default, an event is registered without arguments and binds to a void function. It is also possible to use arguments for your event. *UnityEvents* can be specified with up to four arguments. For that, you will need to define a custom UnityEvent<> class that supports the multiple arguments. Open the EventManager script file and add the following code above the definition of the EventManager class:

```
Using UnityEngine;
using UnityEngine.Events;

[Serializable]
public class IDEvent : UnityEvent<int>
{
}
```

Add an instance of this custom UnityEvent class to the EventManager class.

```
public class EventManager : MonoBehaviour
{
    public IDEvent idEvent;
}
```

Select the *EventManager* GameObject in the hierarchy and check the Inspector window. The event will now appear in the Event Manager script component, as shown in Figure 7-3. Press the + sign to add a new event. Leave *Runtime only* as type. Drag the EventManager GameObject into the Object field.

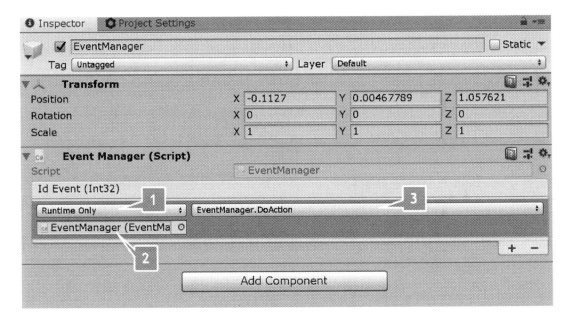

Figure 7-3. *A dynamic event is added through the UI of Unity*

In this case, you will notice that when you select the function it shows all dynamic functions at the top in the dropdown. That is done through the filtering mechanism, based on your custom-defined event. You also do not need to specify a value. The value is set through the Invoke() method on the event by calling idEvent.Invoke(23);.

Make sure that the custom UnityEvent class is defined with [Serializable]. Otherwise, it will not appear in the Inspector window of the UI of Unity.

Using UnityEvents is easy and allows you to create an event system for your application by only using the UI interface of Unity. UnityEvents are easy for people who use drag and drop or when they are creating Unity Editor plugins.

But UnityEvents are not built as native code and therefore are less well performing and use more memory then C# events. If you do not need to use UnityEvents, use C# events instead. The following code shows an example how to use C# events:

```
public class NativeEventManager
{
    public static NativeEventManager instance;

    public event Action myEvent;
    public event Action<int> myIdEvent;

    public static NativeEventManager Instance
    {
        get
        {
            return instance != null ? instance : instance = new
            NativeEventManager();
        }
    }
    protected NativeEventManager()
    {
        myEvent += DoAction;
        myIdEvent += DoAction;
```

```
        myEvent.Invoke();
        myIdEvent.Invoke(23);
    }

    public void DoAction()
    {

    }

    public void DoAction(int id)
    {

    }
}
```

As you can see, it is almost the same principle as working with UnityEvents. But it allows me to use the singleton pattern, since the class does not have to be derived from MonoBehaviour. And that allows me to invoke the event from any location in my application.

```
NativeEventManager.Instance.myEvent.Invoke();
NativeEventManager.Instance.myIdEvent.Invoke(23);
```

Time and Framerate

Most of the work takes place in the Update() event of MonoBehaviour-derived classes. The event allows you to handle data and use scripts to execute certain tasks. In some cases these tasks require timing. Think of moving a certain hologram over time or other time-based actions. While the normal framerate for Microsoft HoloLens is around 60 frames per second, its stability and number are influenced by several factors:

- The current actions of the CPU

- Using video streaming or Miracast will downgrade the framerate by half.

- Complex and long execution of code written in the Update() event running inside a single framerate

Even if the system is stable enough, it does not guarantee that the length of time between two `Update()` event calls is always the same. Moving an object using the `Update()` event will cause an irregular speed, since the time between two `Update()` calls are not the same.

This can be resolved to scale the size of the movements by the frame time. The frame time is available through the property `Time.deltaTime`. The following is an example of code using this property to compensate for the irregularity of framerates:

```
using UnityEngine;

public class MoveObject : MonoBehaviour
{
    public float distancePerSecond = 0.1f;
    void Update()
    {
        gameObject.transform.Translate(0, 0, distancePerSecond * Time.
        deltaTime);
    }
}
```

The property `distancePerSecond` specifies the distance that the object is moving per second. Multiplying this by the delta time of the framerate will assure that the object is moving the same speed over time. In this case, it is 10 centimeters per second.

Physics in the application makes use of a fixed timestep to maintain accuracy and consistency during the run of the scenario. The system uses a kind of alarm, which will define when physics is doing the calculations. Physics are updated when the alarm goes off. It is possible to change the time of the fixed timestep by using the `Time.fixedDeltaTime` property. A lower value will result in more frequent updates of the physics but will result in more load on the CPU.

The system takes care of an accurate simulation of physics due to the fixed timestep. But if framerates drop due to various reasons, it can cause issues for the regular updates to be executed, which will result in frozen objects or graphics that get out of sync. As soon as the framerate time takes longer than the maximum allowed timestep, the physics engine stops and gives room for the other steps taken place in the `update()` event.

It is also possible to slow down the time, to allow animations and script to respond at a slower rate. For this, Unity has a Time Scale property. The Time Scale property controls how fast time is executed relative to real time. A value above 1 will speed up the execution time, while a value below 1 will slow down the execution time. Time Scale is not really slowing down the execution time, but changes the values of both properties `Time.deltaTime` and `Time.fixedDeltaTime` to achieve the same result. Time Scale is set through the `Time.timeScale` property.

With Microsoft HoloLens it sometimes happens that you want to record or stream the video output. Both situations will drop the current framerate by half. That means that your application runs at only 30 frames per second. This is caused by the capturing mechanism of the camera. The performance will also drop, and other visual effects like drifting can take place. There seems to be a solution for this with Unity. Unity provides a `Time.captureFramerate` property. When the property is set higher than zero, the execution time will be slowed down and frame updates will be executed at a precise regular interval. This can result in better recording or streaming. Nowadays it is possible to stream the output of the Microsoft HoloLens 2 using Miracast to other devices like a laptop without having a framerate drop.

Unity DOTS

DOTS stands for Data-Oriented Technology Stack, and at the time of writing still is in preview. With DOTS it is possible to fully utilize the latest multicore processors without the need for knowledge of complex programming. In Figure 7-4 shows an architectural overview of Unity DOTS.

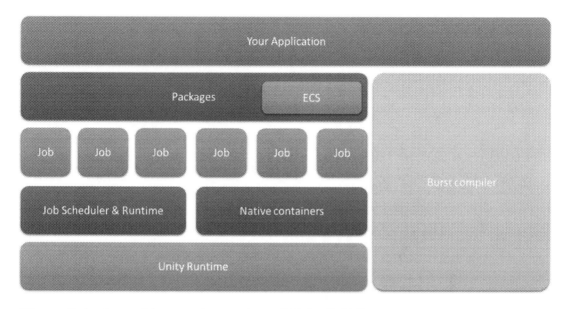

Figure 7-4. *An architectural overview of Unity DOTS*

DOTS include several features:

- *C# Job System*: This system is used for running multithreaded code efficiently using C# scripting. It allows users to write safe and fast code by exposing the native C++ Job System through C# scripting.

- *Entity Component System*: This system allows programmers to write high-performance code. It takes care of everything for you and allows you to focus mainly on writing your code for data and behavior in your application.

- *Burst compiler*: This compiler can produce highly optimized native code across multiple platforms by using a new LLVM-based backend compiler.

Due to these features, programmers can write multithreaded code with massive performance gains running inside a sandbox. There are several advantages to using this system. It is easier to build scenes with complex simulations that run on a large set of different hardware. Code can be more easily reused due to moving from object-oriented to data-oriented design.

Debugging

Creating applications for HoloLens will not always go as smoothly as you want. This chapter explains how you can debug your application, even when it is running on a HoloLens device or running in the HoloLens emulator.

Lifecycle of Application

Deploying a Unity project results in a Visual Studio project using IL2CPP. IL2CPP stands for Intermediate Language to C++. The problem with that is that each part of the script files is converted to native code running in your project. When you look at your project, you will notice that it does not generate the same classes, functions, and properties. This makes it very hard to debug your code. You instead want to debug the script files which are written in C#. Debugging your scripts can be done at two levels:

- Debugging your script files in the Unity Editor

- Debugging you script files when your app runs at a device or emulator

Debugging with Unity

Debugging with Unity is one of the easiest forms of debugging your C# scripts with a managed debugger. But it requires you to run your solution in the Unity Editor. While that is OK when testing basic stuff like scene setup, camera, and other Unity specific functions, as soon as you are accessing external code or want to test gestures outside the Unity Editor, you will need to start debugging script on your device or emulator.

This method of debugging does not require any additional configurations except for having the Unity Editor and Visual Studio. Open your project in Unity and double-click a C# script that you would like to debug, as shown in Figure 7-5.

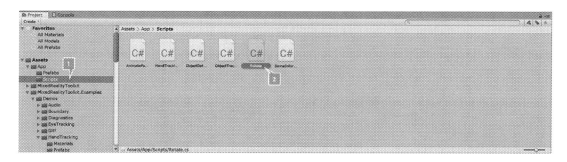

Figure 7-5. *Double-click the script you wish to debug*

That will start a Visual Studio, which allows you to start a managed debugger. When Visual Studio has loaded all the scripts from the project, the double-clicked script is selected.

Press the play button in the Unity Editor to start your project in Unity, as shown in Figure 7-6.

Figure 7-6. *Start the project in the Unity Editor by pressing the play button*

Now switch back to Visual Studio and place your breakpoint at the code. Select debug in the dropdown box of the debug bar. Finally, click Attach to Unity in the dropdown box of the debug bar, as shown in Figure 7-7.

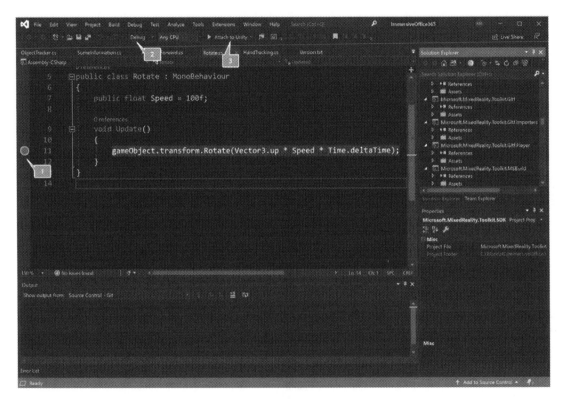

Figure 7-7. *Set the breakpoint and attach the managed debugger to Unity*

The managed debugger will start, and your breakpoint is hit as soon as the code is executed, as shown in Figure 7-8.

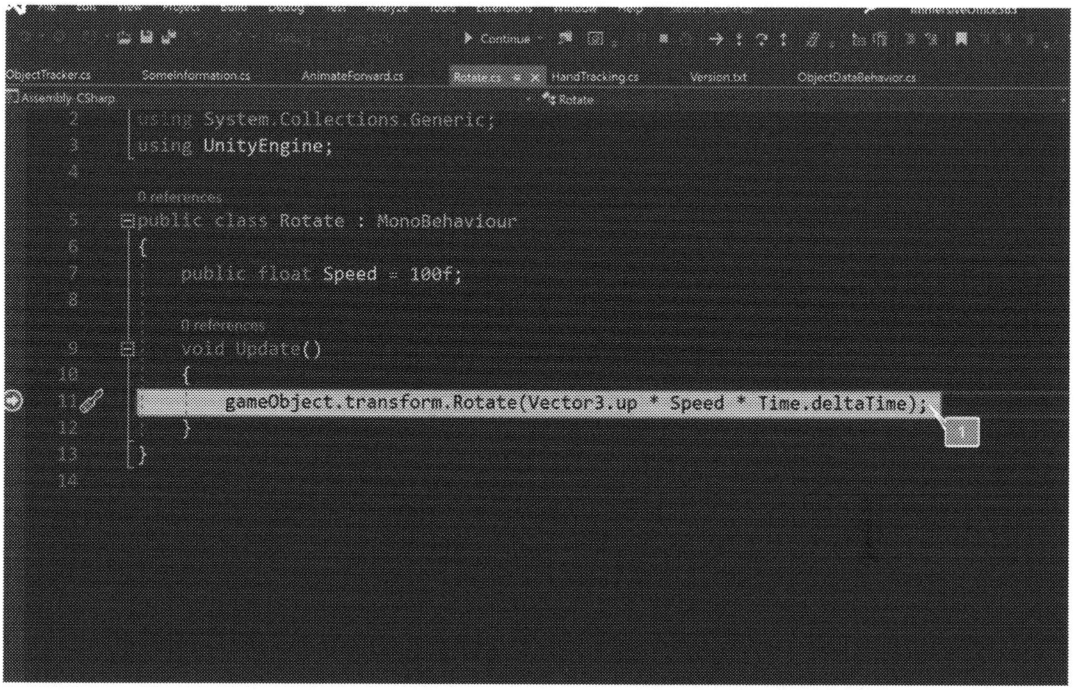

Figure 7-8. *The managed debugger hits the breakpoint, allowing you to debug the C# script*

Debugging at Your Device or Emulator

The following will describe how we can debug our scripts when running the application on a Microsoft HoloLens 2 device or in the Microsoft HoloLens 2 emulator. Before we can start debugging, some settings and prerequisites must be met to get it to work.

We need to configure the player settings in the project settings of our Unity project, as shown in Figure 7-9.

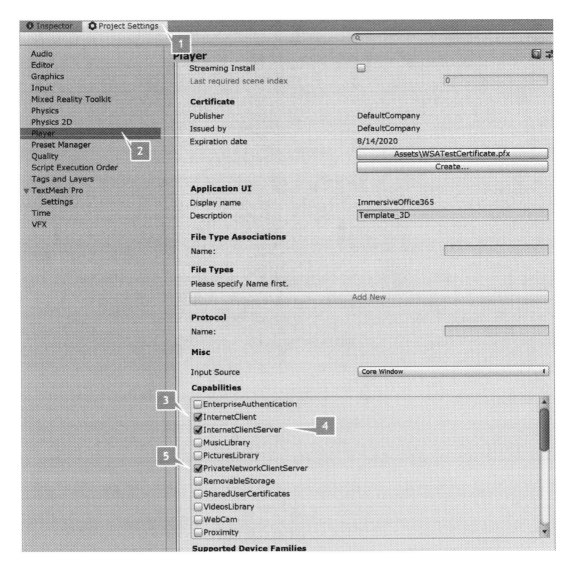

Figure 7-9. *Configuring the Player settings of the Unity project*

Select the menu option Edit ➤ Project settings. The Project Settings tab is opened next to the Inspector window. Select at the left the option Player. In the player settings, go to the tab publishing settings and view the capabilities. Make sure that the following capabilities are enabled:

- InternetClient

- InternetClientServer

- PrivateNetworkClientServer

These capabilities will allow the debugger to connect through the network capabilities of the device or the emulator.

The second thing we need to do is configure several settings in the build window before we start generating the Visual Studio solution. Select the menu option File ➤ Build Settings to open the build settings dialog, as shown in Figure 7-10.

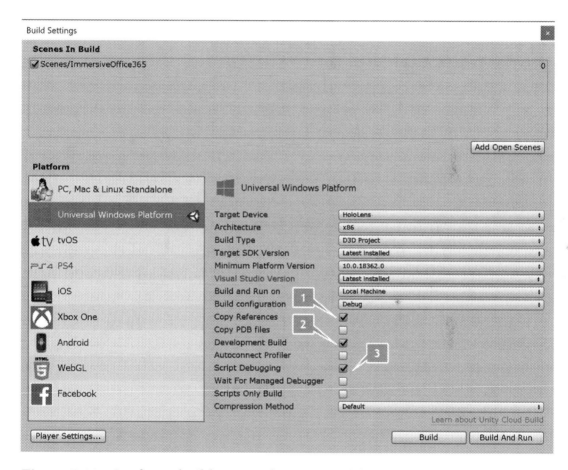

Figure 7-10. *Configure build settings for managed debugging*

Make sure that the options Copy References, Development Build, and Script Debugging are selected.

There is also an option called Wait for Managed Debugger. This option will pop up a dialog in your device or emulator and will wait till you have connected a managed debugger. Till then, your application will not continue unless you press the close button in the dialog. An example is shown in Figure 7-11. In some situations this can be handy, but for now we'll leave the option disabled.

Figure 7-11. *This dialog will be shown when the option Wait For Managed Debugger is selected*

The last thing you need to take care of is making sure that Visual Studio is not blocked by the firewall on your machine. Make sure that Visual Studio is allowed to put anything through via TCP and UDP.

Build the Visual Studio solution and open it in Visual Studio. Depending on the target device, you will need to configure the dropdown boxes for building the solution in Visual Studio. This can be seen in Figure 7-12.

Figure 7-12. *Configure the build settings for building and deploying to the device or emulator*

In this example, we will be debugging the app using a Microsoft HoloLens 2 Emulator. Select Debug and x86 from the dropdown boxes at the top. Select the HoloLens 2 Emulator as the target.

Build the application using the configured build settings in Visual Studio. Deploy and run the application on the device or in the emulator. Although you can run the debugger, you don't need it. Our debug session will be running from a second instance of Visual Studio. Deploy and run the application to the emulator. When the application is started, you will see the emulator as shown in Figure 7-13.

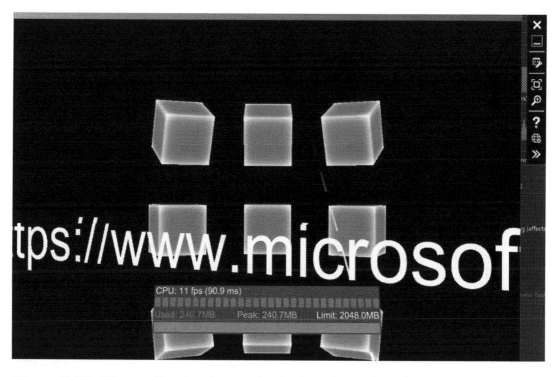

Figure 7-13. *The application is running in the Microsoft HoloLens 2 emulator*

As soon as your application is running, go back to your Unity project. Select one of the scripts by double-clicking, as shown in Figure 7-14.

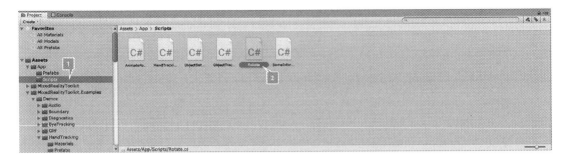

Figure 7-14. *Double-click the script you want to debug to open Visual Studio*

This will open another Visual Studio, as shown in Figure 7-15.

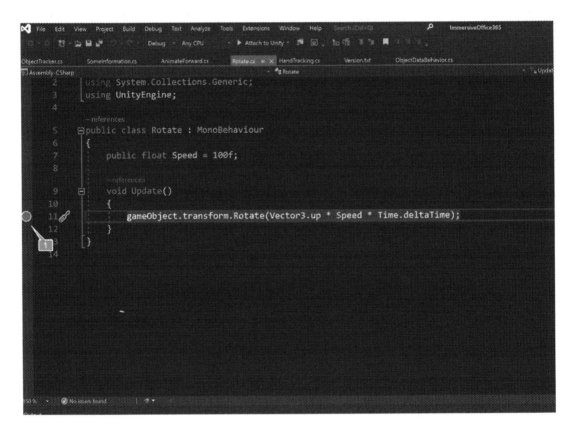

Figure 7-15. *Visual Studio as the managed debugger with a breakpoint set in C#*

This time, we have the C# scripts in front of us. Place your breakpoint at the row that you want to debug into.

We need to attach the debugger to the running instance of the application on the device or the emulator. Select from the menu Debug ➤ Attach Unity Debugger. This will pop up a dialog showing all running instances of Unity and applications, as shown in Figure 7-16.

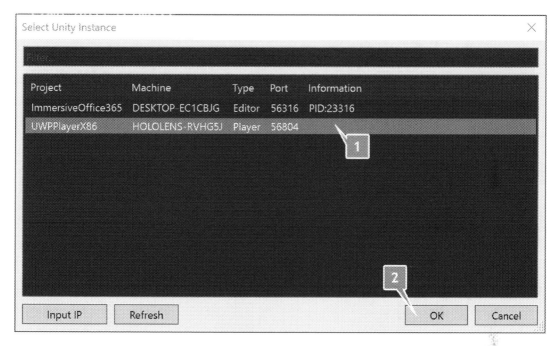

Figure 7-16. *Select the instance running on the device or emulator*

If you instead click Attach to Unity at the top of Visual Studio, that would connect to the Unity instance by default, rather than showing all available instances.

There are some issues with different versions of the Microsoft HoloLens 2 emulator that cause the device not to appear when you want to connect your managed debugger. At the time of writing this book we used the Visual Studio 2019 version 16.4.2 and the Microsoft HoloLens 2 emulator version 10.0.18362.1042 together with Windows 10 version 1909 build 18363.535. Make sure you are using at least the same or higher versions.

Select the instance running on your device or emulator. The managed debugger will start and your breakpoint is hit as soon as the code is executed, as shown in Figure 7-17.

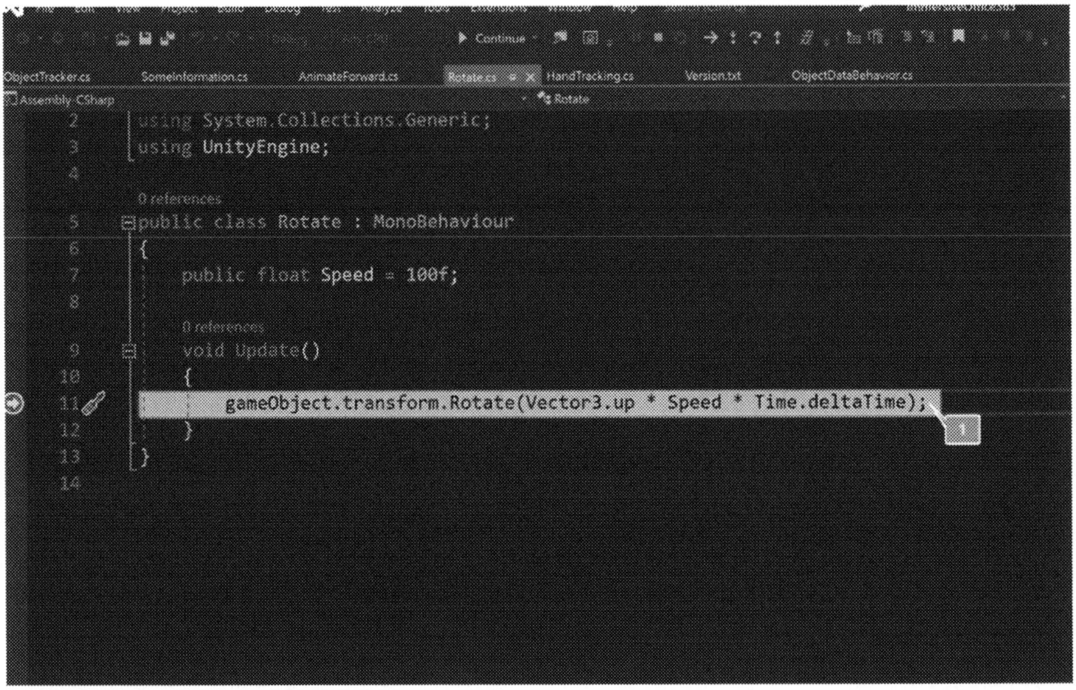

Figure 7-17. *The managed debugger hits the breakpoint, allowing you to debug the C# script*

This technique allows you to debug your C# scripts using a managed debugger. Keep in mind that changing the C# scripts will require a solution build from Unity and a build and deploy from Visual Studio.

Performance monitoring

Building applications for devices like the Microsoft HoloLens requires a certain skill to think further than only programming and creating scenes in Unity. Everything you do has an impact on how the CPU, GPU, and the HPU are utilized. Using, for example, more CPU can impact the performance of your application. But it can also impact the battery life of the device. It is possible to build applications that literally drain your batteries in less than 1 hour.

Heavy scenes will affect the framerate of your applications. Normal applications should run around 60 frames per second (fps). The lower the fps, the more unstable your application becomes. Instability could develop into drifting of holograms, color changes, and even hanging holograms.

There are several techniques that can help to create better performing applications for Microsoft HoloLens 2. This book we will not go into detail. Check the appendices for references to improvements to your application.

Microsoft HoloLens offers different performance tools through the Windows Device Portal:

- *Performance tracing*: Performance tracing captures Windows Performance Recorder (WPR) traces from your device. There are several profiles available to choose from. To perform a trace, you can select the profile and start tracing. As soon as you want to stop tracing, click the stop link and wait till the complete trace file has been downloaded.

- *Viewing processes*: You can view all the running processes through the processes page. Each process has memory in use, CPU utilization, and the account that is used to run the process specified. This list contains both application processes as system processes.

- *System performance*: This allows you to view current system metrics as graphs of different systems in your device in real time. Metrics like system-on-chip power and system power utilization, GPU utilization, percentages of CPU used, how many I/O read and writes are happening, network connectivity, memory, and the number of frame rates per second. The information shown can differ if you are running on an emulator or HoloLens device.

An example of the graphical interface for system performance is shown in Figure 7-18.

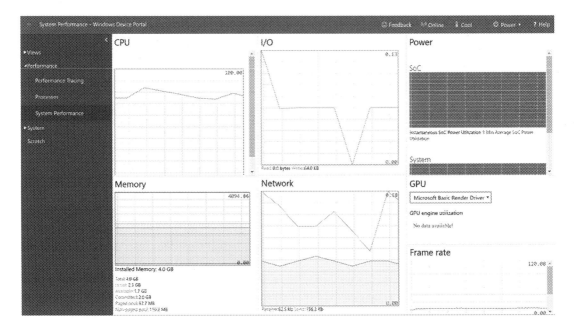

Figure 7-18. *An example of the system performance graphs on an emulator*

CHAPTER 8

Visualization

The power of mixed reality allows us to create 3D immersive experiences. This is something that requires a different way of visualization of data, content, and relationships. And it doesn't stop there. We also need to think about how we interact with that environment. How are we going to add actions like adding a user to a specific site? This chapter goes into details of data representation, how social networks can be shown, and what kinds of models are available.

Data Visualization

The first step is understanding how you get to data visualization by using a visualization model. The image in Figure 8-1 is an overview that explains different steps needed to get data into the 3D space. This diagram shows a high-level overview of a model explaining what you need to consider when you are working with data visualization.

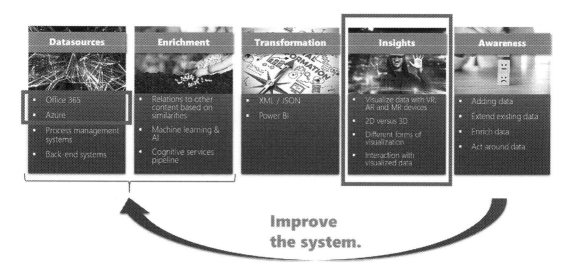

Figure 8-1. *Overview of the visualization model showing how to get data into the 3D space*

© Alexander Meijers 2020
A. Meijers, *Immersive Office 365*, https://doi.org/10.1007/978-1-4842-5845-3_8

You need to start identifying the different data sources you want to use in your application. Data sources can be anything from back-end systems, to process management systems, to cloud services like Azure and Office 365. This book is focusing on data coming from Office 365 as a data source.

The second phase is called Enrichment. Enrichment is used to make sense out of your data. But it is also used to bring data together based on similarities. Think of creating relationships between content based on the same type or based on different types. Another way of enriching data is by using machine learning and artificial intelligence. An example would be creating new data based on your existing data from one or more data sources, using predictive machine learning models.

Transformation is the next phase. In this phase you will need to transform the result of the enrichment phase into a uniform model that can be understood by your application. Transformation is a necessary step to get all your data in an understandable format that can be used. Since your application will retrieve data through a separate thread, you need to transfer the data from one thread to another thread.

The most important part of this model is the Insights phase. This phase is all about displaying the data in some sort of way from 2D space to 3D space using, a mixed reality device like Microsoft HoloLens 2. Based on the type of data, the role of the user, and the purpose of the information, you will need to decide what kind of visualization you want to use. This phase also comprehends how the user will interact with the data. Microsoft HoloLens 2 now supporting natural gestures will open doors for you as implementer to create a diverse set of near actions to interact with the data in 3D space.

The final phase is called the Awareness phase. This phase is all about the actions flowing out of interactions on the data in 3D space. In some cases this can result in changes of the original data source. Think of dragging a user onto a Teams site in 3D space; this has two actions. The first one is changing the view in 3D space for the user, to show that the user is added and belongs to that Teams site. The second action would be adding the user as an actual Team member to the Teams site in the data source.

As mentioned, the Insights phase is the most important and interesting phase of the visualization model. It is all about getting your data in 3D space and understanding how to interact with it. That phase has been divided into six parts you need to understand, and which can influence how you build your application. An overview of the Insights phase is shown in Figure 8-2.

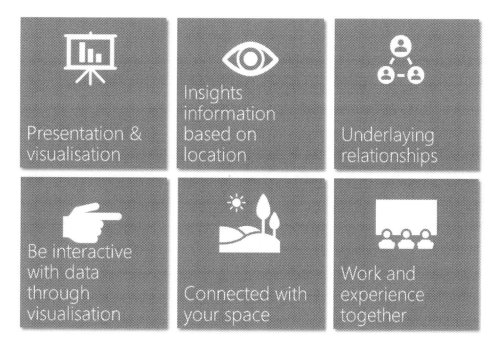

Figure 8-2. *The Insights phase overview*

Each of the parts will help you to shape your application, and is explained in the following.

Presentation and visualization

You will need to think about how you want to represent the data in 3D space. This depends on several important factors, which are influenced by the content, the purpose of the application, and the person or persons using the application. These factors are as follows:

- *Type of content*: The type of content will influence how you want to present it to the user and how the user is going to interact with it. Content can be visualized in different ways, like spread out over a table or cluttered against several walls in a room.

- *Dynamic or static*: In some situations content is dynamic, which means it can change a lot or it is building up due to different requests for the content, which expands the visualization.

- *Different views*: Sometimes different visualizations of the content are required to achieve your goal with the application. You need to think about which visualizations you require and how or when transitions between these different visualizations take place.

- *Purpose*: What do you want to achieve with the application? What is the user going to do? Which actions does the user need to perform on the content? These are all questions that will influence how the data is presented.

- *Role of user*: This is an important one. A person with a financial role is more interested in data presented as a 3D diagram, while a person with the manager role is more likely interested in seeing the data spread out over visualized departments to give better insights.

- *Context*: it is important to understand that you only visualize content that is part of the context in which the user is operating. Too much content cluttered together in a 3D space will cause loss of interest or will cause the user to deviate from doing the tasks you had in mind.

Information Based on Location

Making the information in your application location based allows you to create a more immersive experience. Microsoft HoloLens 2 allows you to use different types of information from the device to implement in your experience. Think of using the location of the user by tracking the location of the device and the direction in which the user is looking in the real world against real-life objects. But also tracking the position of one or both hands and type of near actions you are performing can be used.

An example would be defining the importance of content based on where the user is in comparison with the content. You could also use the eye tracking to determine which content is more interesting than others by creating a kind of content head map. Based on that information, you could provide additional content or allow drilling down to underlying content, knowing what the user is looking for.

Some content is displayed in the form of panels that are floating around the user or within the context of an object. Make sure that when you use panels, the user has the choice of locking the panel in a certain location in their environment or keeping it floating around.

Underlying Relationships

You would be surprised how many interesting underlying relationships can be found in your content. And these relationships will help in different ways. They could help you in transitions between different visualizations, drill down into content, open new related content, refer to existing content in the 3D space, and more.

Be Interactive with Data Through Visualization

Microsoft HoloLens 2 offers so many new ways of interaction with content and your 3D space. There are several different ways to interact with content, which can be combined in any way:

- *Natural gestures*: Natural gestures allow you to use predefined near and far interactions. But it is also possible to create your own near interactions. An example would be using your flat hand moving up under a cube to open it and show the information spread out around you. The possibilities are endless.

- *Eye tracking*: Eye tracking could be a way of interacting with your data. By looking at certain content for some time you could open a menu or drill down to underlying data or move to the next view.

- *Speech*: The device will understand any command from single words to complete sentences to control your actions. Due to the onboard AI chip, you don't have to be connected anymore with the cloud to have the speech translated to understandable commands.

- *Head movement*: Head movement is not a real interaction. But since you can track the location of the device and the direction in which the device is pointing, you could use this as interaction inside your application.

In some cases it would be wise to use different forms of interaction. But be aware of not overdoing it. Too much could result in unclarity for the user, which results in your application not being used in the correct way.

Another way of interaction with content is done through menus. Menus allow you to control, for example, the scene or a specific piece of content in the scene. Following is a helpful diagram explaining when and where to use menus.

Location	How	Target
Hand menu	The menu pops up around the hand when you turn the inside of a flat hand toward you.	Scene
Floating menu	This menu is always present and is floating at a certain distance away from the user.	Scene or Object context
Arm menu	Think of having one or more buttons if you look at the inside of your arm. It can be compared with the start menu button on your wrist.	Scene
Popup menu	The menu pops up somewhere around the object due to some interaction with the object.	Object context
Object menu	The object has a small holographic element indicating the presence of a menu. A menu will open by interacting with that holographic element.	Object context

There are several things you need to be aware of when creating and using menus. Keep menus simple. Avoid using submenus, even in the first level. Think about the user who needs to operate the menus. Make sure that the menus are easy to access and not too small. Make sure it is obvious that it is a menu. It wouldn't be the first time that a user gets stuck due to unclarity of available controls and options. Make sure what the purpose is of a menu item when using only graphical representation. If the menus could be difficult to reach with natural gestures, allow them to be controlled by speech as an additional interaction. And keep the way to implement menus consistent through the whole application. Nothing is so confusing as when menu options are different in naming or location inside your application.

The MRTK has several great buttons that allow your user to interact with the application. They are easy to implement and have a consistent look and feel for the user. They also integrate all-natural gestures and can be controlled by speech.

Connected with Your Space

A mixed reality device is aware of its surroundings. Microsoft HoloLens 2 uses several cameras to create a spatial map and understand your environment. It can indicate where walls, ceiling, floor, and raised platforms like chairs and tables are. Using your real-life environment will make your application even more immersive than ever. Connecting the information to a table, door, walls, and even as an overlay on a real-life object will make it a truly immersive experience for the user. But make sure it fits your application. True immersive experiences are only created when the real world and virtual objects are blended correctly.

Work and Experience Together

While most applications are built for the use of a single user, multiuser environments are getting more and more interesting. These environments allow you to work and experience the same content together. And this doesn't have to be in the same location. A shared experience can be from seeing each other interacting with the content or operating around the same content from different perspectives. An example could be searching together to find something through different parts of the content in different directions.

Social Networks

When we talk about immersive experiences with the modern digital workplace, it all comes to the point of correct visualization of data, content, and relationships. One of them is how social networks are presented and used. An Office 365 environment comes very close to a social network. This chapter goes somewhat deeper into how this could work.

Let's start with the theoretical concept for analyzing social networks. For that, we have social network analysis. Social network analysis is a process of defining and exploring social networks by using network theory and graph theory. Network theory is all about relationships between objects in structured and unstructured ways represented by a graph, whereas graph theory is finding and defining the mathematical structures in relationships between those objects. A graph is in its turn built from nodes and edges, where nodes are the objects and edges are the defined relationships between the objects.

That sounds familiar because we are using Microsoft Graph for accessing data from Office 365. Microsoft Graph is based on this concept of network theory and graph theory.

Within Office 365 nodes represent the actors, people, messages, documents, and other content that are part of the network. Edges are all about the relationships, collaborations, and interactions between those nodes.

Figure 8-3 shows an example of visualizing a social network. This example is just one of many possibilities when it comes to visualizing a content network based on nodes and edges.

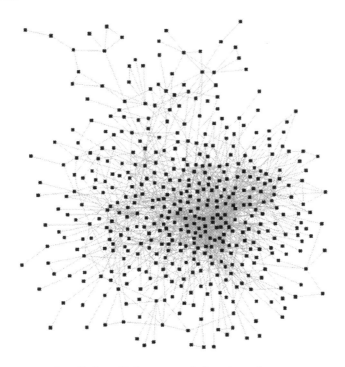

Figure 8-3. *An example of visualizing a social network*

Modeling and visualizing the network allows us to get a better understanding of the network and its complex relationships. By doing that, it helps us to better control the content, focusing on content that is important and leaving out content that is not relevant at that time.

Be aware that even if in some cases the content is not relevant, it depends on the role, purpose, situation, and task you are performing. The same content can be relevant in other situations. So never rule out content based on assumptions.

There are several important steps that can help to visualize your network. One of them is classification or categorization and the other is the weight.

Classification or categorization is a way of putting objects into categories. Categories are mostly defined based on classes, types, similarities, or common criteria. Categorization allows you to create order in the chaos of objects. It is up to you to look for those similarities and common criteria in your content network. Categorization can help with learning, making decisions, and making predictions. These are important when you build an application around content.

Weight focuses more on the relationship and interactions between objects. It gives certain importance to the relationship. Importance of the relationship is based on the context in which the relationship is defined. Think about relationships between people based on how they collaborate over documents, mail, and messaging services. In this case the weight could be measured based on the number of interactions. But it depends on the purpose of the application and the content that is visualized.

Models

There are many more possibilities to the visualization of content networks like in Figure 8-3. Strangely enough, the world around us can help us to define a visualization model. An example is how cities are structured and built up. See if it is possible to transform your content into city suburbs where blocks of houses represent classified content and the streets are the relationships between other classified content. You will need to decide how your content is visualized. And that decision is based on the type of content, classifications, weight, and many more factors. It is impossible to talk about every available model and the combinations between different models in this book. It is up to your imagination to come up with something that works for you.

This chapter discusses a more intelligent model based on a force-directed graph, to comprehensively create a more complex and dynamic content network.

Force-Directed Graph Model

We want to show relationships between people based on how they work together in our application. For that we need to identify how people are related to each other. We can get such relationships based on interactions between people on different content using Microsoft Graph. Microsoft Graph uses machine learning to identify similarities based on interactions between people on content like documents, presentations, emails, and many other content forms. Think of people who have been working together on a document, sending emails to each other, or have been chatting by messaging. In some cases, it could be that they have a relationship because one person created a document and the other has read it.

In this situation, we have a many-to-many relationship between people. To bring such a many-to-many relationship into the 3D space, we can use a force-directed graph model. A force-directed graph model is several algorithms that allow you to draw data and their underlying relationships in a two- or three-dimensional space. An example of a social network two-dimensional visualization using a force-directed graph drawing algorithm is shown in Figure 8-4.

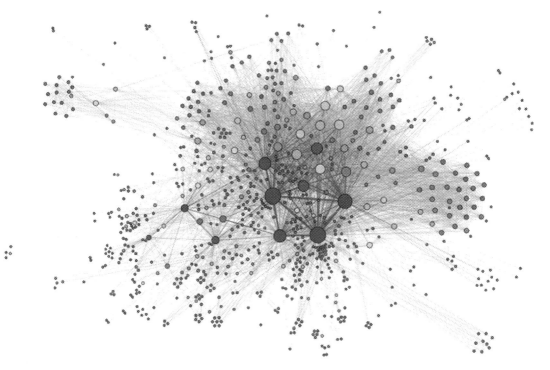

Figure 8-4. *An example of social network two-dimensional visualization using a force-directed graph. Sourced from Wikipedia*

These drawing algorithms assign forces to the edges drawn between the nodes. We could define the following when we apply this to known users in Office 365.

Each node in the model represents a person. Each edge in the model represents a relationship between two persons based on interactions. Each node added to the model is positioned in 3D space with a `Vector3` coordinate. As soon as we add additional nodes with a relationship to an already added node, each node position defined by a `Vector3` in the model is recalculated by the algorithm.

Since the algorithm is based on assigning forces between nodes and edges, it will try to keep edges mostly the same length with the least number of crossings.

In this example, we will be using a force-directed graph algorithm built using .NET code. The force-redirected graph project was started by *Woong Gyu La* and inspired on the Springy project of Dennis Hotson. It is completely written in C# and rather easy to implement within a Unity project. You can find a unitypackage to implement the force-directed graph based on the project of Woong Gyu La under

```
https://github.com/ameijers/ImmersiveOffice365/tree/master/Unity/
Chapter%208/UnityPackages.
```

Download the unitypackage and import it into the project. That will create a subfolder `ForceDirectedGraph` in the assets folder. The project also contains some demo code to use in your application. But since we are going to use it inside Unity, this will be mostly different from the example provided. The result of adding the force-directed graph code is shown in Figure 8-5.

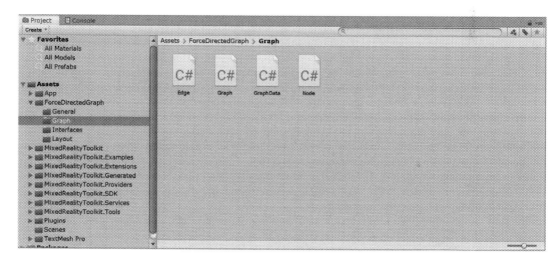

Figure 8-5. *Force-directed graph algorithm .NET code added to Unity project*

We will be introducing a new class called `GraphController`. This class will be our main entry point of the application, containing the flow of our application. We will first start adding code needed to create a force-directed graph represented by *GameObject* objects.

Create the subfolder `Assets/App/Scripts/Graph`. Create a script called `GraphController`.

We will need to make use of the force-directed graph code by adding a using to the specific namespace called `EpForceDirectedGraph.cs`. We didn't change the namespace in these project files, allowing us to support future updates of the *EpForceDirectedGraph. cs* project. Add the following code to the GraphController file:

```
using EpForceDirectedGraph.cs;
using System;
using System.Collections;
using System.Collections.Generic;
using UnityEngine;
using UnityEngine.XR.WSA.Input;

public class GraphController : MonoBehaviour
{
    public float Stiffness = 81.76f;
    public float Repulsion = 40000.0f;
    public float Damping = 0.5f;
    public float Threshold = 0.1f;
}
```

We also need to define several properties that allow us to tune the visualization and appearance of the force-directed graph. We have the following properties.

Property	Description	Value
Stiffness	This value is used for the stiffness of the spring of an edge.	90.55f
Repulsion	Node repulsion rate	50000.0f
Damping	Damping rate	0.7f
Threshold	This value is used to stop the physics iteration at a certain point. Without this, the algorithm will indefinitely continue to move.	0.1f

The next step requires us to define a renderer class that will draw the nodes and edges. Normally we would create the graphical nodes and edges using this renderer class. Except with Unity, this will work differently. Each node and edge is represented by a GameObject in our scene. Since edges are always between nodes, drawing the line between both nodes only requires the Vector3 positions of those nodes. Therefore we only need to be aware of the nodes in our scene and update those accordingly in our renderer class. The edges will automatically follow the new Vector3 positions of the nodes.

We need to add two additional properties to our GraphController class. The first is a dictionary of GameObject objects representing the nodes uniquely defined by their names. The second property is called NodeUpdate and defines the timing in which nodes need to be updated graphically. The third property called ScaleFactor helps us to scale the visualized model in 3D space.

```
public class GraphController : MonoBehaviour
{
    public Dictionary<string, GameObject> gameNodes = new
    Dictionary<string, GameObject>();
    public float NodeUpdate = 0.05f; // in seconds
    public float ScaleFactor = 0.003f;
}
```

We need to create a renderer class named GraphRenderer. This class is derived from the abstract class AbstractRenderer, which implements the IRenderer interface. That abstract class has several virtual methods defined, which can be overloaded to perform the render updates by the force-directed graph algorithm.

Create a new script file called GraphRenderer.cs in the Assets folder App/Scripts/Graph. Add the following code to that file:

```
using EpForceDirectedGraph.cs;
using System.Collections;
using System.Collections.Generic;
using UnityEngine;

public class GraphRenderer : AbstractRenderer
{
    private GraphController controller = null;

    public GraphRenderer(GraphController controller,  IForceDirected
    forceDirected) :  base(forceDirected)
    {
        this.controller = controller;
    }

    public override void Clear()
    {
    }
```

209

```
protected override void drawEdge(Edge iEdge, AbstractVector iPosition1,
AbstractVector iPosition2)
{
    if (controller.gameNodes.ContainsKey(iEdge.ID))
    {
        GameObject gameEdge = controller.gameNodes[iEdge.ID];

        GameObject source = controller.gameNodes[iEdge.Source.ID];
        GameObject target = controller.gameNodes[iEdge.Target.ID];

        LineRenderer line = gameEdge.GetComponent<LineRenderer>();

        if (source != null && target != null & line != null)
        {
            line.SetPositions(new Vector3[] { source.transform.
            position, target.transform.position });
        }
    }
}

protected override void drawNode(Node iNode, AbstractVector iPosition)
{
    if (controller.gameNodes.ContainsKey(iNode.ID))
    {
        GameObject gameNode = controller.gameNodes[iNode.ID];

        // use localPosition, since you can determine the precise
        location by the transform of the gameobject which these
        // nodes are child of
        gameNode.transform.localPosition = new Vector3(iPosition.x *
        controller.ScaleFactor, iPosition.y * controller.ScaleFactor,
        iPosition.z * controller.ScaleFactor);
    }
}
}
```

We need to access the list of GameObject nodes created when the nodes were created. This requires us to reference the GraphController class from the constructor of the renderer class.

Only the methods drawNode(Node iNode, AbstractVector iPosition) and drawEdge(Edge iEdge, AbstractVector iPosition1, AbstractVector iPosition2) need to be overridden. The first method is called for each node changing. The exact GameObject belonging to the node is looked up and its position is set based on a ScaleFactor property. The second method is setting the positions of the line based on the connected nodes of the edge.

In the following step, we will add the necessary properties for the force-directed graph:

```
public class GraphController : MonoBehaviour
{
    private ForceDirected3D fdg = null;
    private Graph graph = null;
    private GraphRenderer graphRenderer = null;
}
```

Create a new method called Initialize. This method will initialize the classes Graph and ForceDirected3D. We also create an instance of the GraphRenderer class with a reference to the GraphController and the ForceDirected3D instance.

```
public class GraphController : MonoBehaviour
{
    private void Initialize()
    {
        graph = new Graph();
        fdg = new ForceDirected3D(graph, Stiffness, Repulsion, Damping);
        fdg.Threshold = Threshold;
        graphRenderer = new GraphRenderer(this, fdg);
    }
}
```

Add the Update method to the GraphController. The Draw method on the GraphRenderer is called with a timestep update called NodeUpdate. The Update method will do a recalculation based on the algorithm and will redraw each node and edge by calling the methods in your GraphRenderer class.

```
public class GraphController : MonoBehaviour
{
    // Update is called once per frame
    void Update()
    {
        graphRenderer.Draw(NodeUpdate);
    }
}
```

We are almost there. We need two methods for adding new nodes and edges to our visualization model. The methods are respectively called CreateNode and CreateEdge. Both node and edge are represented by GameObject objects. We need to have two public properties in our GraphController class that are the prefabs of both objects.

```
public class GraphController : MonoBehaviour
{
    public GameObject NodePrefab = null;
     public GameObject EdgePrefab = null;
}
```

Let's start with creating a node. Creating a node only requires a unique identifier. This will help us to identify the correct node when drawing the nodes in the model. We start with creating the actual NodeData and Node objects that are used by the force-directed graph algorithm. The NodeData object contains information regarding the mass and label. The Node object is the actual node in the algorithm. It requires the NodeData and a unique identifier. Once created, the node is added to the graph object.

The second step is creating the actual GameObject representing the node. That GameObject is created based on a prefab object defined by the property NodePrefab. The node is stored in the dictionary of gameNodes, which is used by the GraphRenderer class. Add the method CreateNode to the GraphController class as follows:

```
public class GraphController : MonoBehaviour
{
    public GameObject CreateNode(string id = "")
    {
        // Create node in graph
        NodeData data = new NodeData();
```

```
        data.mass = 10.0f;
        data.label = "node";
        string newId = id != "" ? id : Guid.NewGuid().ToString();
        Node newNode = new Node(newId, data);
        Node createdNode = graph.AddNode(newNode);

        // create unity node object
        GameObject go = GameObject.Instantiate(NodePrefab);
        go.transform.parent = gameObject.transform;
        gameNodes[createdNode.ID] = go;

        return go;
    }
}
```

We require some means to add data to the GameObject representing the node. That data can be used to display, for example, a name of the node. For this, we need to create a component called NodeInformation that can be added to the node GameObject. The class is a container for the actual Node object. Create a new script file NodeInformation. cs in the Assets subfolder App/Scripts/Graph. Add the following code:

```
using EpForceDirectedGraph.cs;
using System;
using System.Collections;
using System.Collections.Generic;
using UnityEngine;

public class NodeInformation : MonoBehaviour
{
    public Node node;
}
```

We require that the GameObject has a component added that is based on the NodeInformation class. When the node GameObject is instantiated, the component is retrieved and assigned with the Node class from the algorithm. This requires adding the following code to the CreateNode method:

```
public class GraphController : MonoBehaviour
{
    public GameObject CreateNode(string id = "")
    {
        // Create node in graph
        ...

        NodeInformation nodeInfo = go.GetComponent<NodeInformation>();
        nodeInfo.node = createdNode;

        return go;
    }
}
```

This allows us to create, for example, a TextMesh in the prefab used for the node GameObject, which is filled by the value of the node property. Additional properties can be added later.

The second method is for creating an edge. Creating an edge requires having the references to both source and target Node objects. We start with creating the actual EdgeData and Edge objects, which are used by the force-directed graph algorithm. The EdgeData object contains information regarding the length and label. The Edge object is the actual edge in the algorithm. It requires the EdgeData, source, target, and a unique identifier. Once created, the node is added to the graph object.

The second step is creating the actual GameObject representing the edge. That GameObject is created based on a prefab object defined by the property EdgePrefab. The edge is stored in the dictionary of gameNodes, which is used by the GraphRenderer class. Add the method CreateEdge to the GraphController class, as follows:

```
public class GraphController : MonoBehaviour
{
    public GameObject CreateEdge(Node source, Node target)
    {
        // create edge in graph
        EdgeData data = new EdgeData();
        data.label = "edge";
```

```
        data.length = 60.0f;
        Edge newEdge = new Edge(Guid.NewGuid().ToString(), source, target,
        data);
        Edge createdEdge = graph.AddEdge(newEdge);

        // create unity edge object
        GameObject go = GameObject.Instantiate(EdgePrefab);
        go.transform.parent = gameObject.transform;
        gameNodes[createdEdge.ID] = go;

        return go;
    }
}
```

We need to have some means to add data to the GameObject representing the edge. That data can be used to display, for example, the weight or other information of the edge. For this, we need to create a component called EdgeInformation, which can be added to the edge GameObject. The class is a container for the actual Edge object. Create a new script file EdgeInformation.cs in the Assets subfolder App/Scripts/Graph. Add the following code:

```
using EpForceDirectedGraph.cs;
using System.Collections;
using System.Collections.Generic;
using UnityEngine;

public class EdgeInformation : MonoBehaviour
{
    public Edge edge = null;
}
```

We require that the GameObject has a component added that is based on the EdgeInformation class. When the edge GameObject is instantiated, the component is retrieved and assigned with the Edge class from the algorithm. This requires adding the following code to the CreateEdge method:

```
public class GraphController : MonoBehaviour
{
    public GameObject CreateEdge(Node source, Node target)
```

```
    {
        // create edge in graph
            ...

        EdgeInformation edgeInfo = go.GetComponent<EdgeInformation>();
        edgeInfo.edge = createdEdge;

        return go;
    }
}
```

Before we start connecting this to an actual data source containing data from Office 365, we start with some sample data. The following method CreateSampleData creates several nodes. Then it creates several edges where it randomizes the source and target nodes. Add the CreateSampleData method to the GraphController class as follows:

```
public class GraphController : MonoBehaviour
{
    private void CreateSampleData()
    {
        List<Node> nodes = new List<Node>();

        for(int i= 0; i < 50; i++)
        {
            GameObject go = CreateNode();
            NodeInformation nodeInfo = go.GetComponent<NodeInformation>();
            nodes.Add(nodeInfo.node);
        }

        System.Random rand = new System.Random((int)Time.time);

        for (int j = 0; j < 50; j++)
        {
            int sourceIndex = rand.Next(50);
            int targetIndex = rand.Next(50);

            if (targetIndex != sourceIndex)
            {
```

```
            CreateEdge(nodes[sourceIndex], nodes[targetIndex]);
        }
    }
}
}
```

Add the Start method to the GraphController class. In that method we will call the Initialize and CreateSampleData method. This will be called as soon as the GraphController GameObject is instantiated.

```
public class GraphController : MonoBehaviour
{
    void Start()
    {
        Initialize();
        CreateSampleData();
    }
}
```

We have finalized all the scripting we need to create an example of a force-directed graph visualization. The next steps are creating the necessary prefabs and the implementation of an example with the GraphController class using the algorithm. Let's start with creating the prefab for a node, as shown in Figure 8-6.

Figure 8-6. *Creating a node prefab for the force-directed graph visualization*

Right-click in the hierarchy and select 3D object ➤ Cube. This will create a cube
GameObject in the scene. Select the GameObject and view the components in the
Inspector view. Make sure that the scale is set in all directions to 0.1, which is one
centimetre in size, as shown in Figure 8-6. Add the Node Information component via the
Add Component button. Drag the newly created GameObject into the Assets folder App/
Prefabs. That will automatically create a prefab from your GameObject.

We need an additional prefab called Edge, which is shown in Figure 8-7.

Figure 8-7. *Create an edge prefab for the force-directed graph visualization*

Create an empty `GameObject` in your scene. Add the Edge Information component via the *Add Component* button. We need to add the Line Renderer component, since this object represents a line. Make sure that you have created a material for the color of the line. Drag the material on the material field in the Line Renderer component. Also change the width of the line to `0.05` or lower, depending on how thin you would like to have the line. Drag the newly created `GameObject` into the Assets folder `App/Prefabs`. That will automatically create a prefab from your `GameObject`.

The final step is creating an example that uses these prefabs to present the force-directed graph visualization. We still have some other GameObjects active, which will cause some interruptions. Let's deactivate those first. You will need to deactivate the *HelloWorld!* and the *Visual* GameObjects by changing the active flag checkbox left from the name of the object in the Inspector window.

Add a new empty `GameObject` to the scene and call it `Graph`. Add the `GraphController` component via the *Add Component* button. Now drag the `Edge` prefab on the Edge Prefab property of the GraphController script in the Inspector window. Do the same for the Node prefab on the Node Prefab property. You can see the result in Figure 8-8.

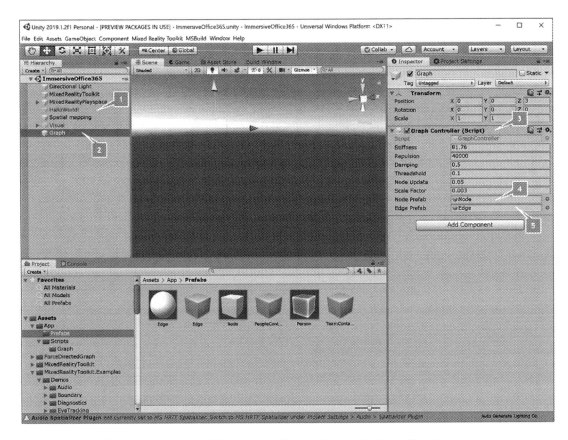

Figure 8-8.   *Create a demo of the force-directed graph visualization*

We are all set to give it a try in the Unity Editor. Make sure everything is saved and run the application by clicking the Play button. The result of our code is demonstrated in Figure 8-9.

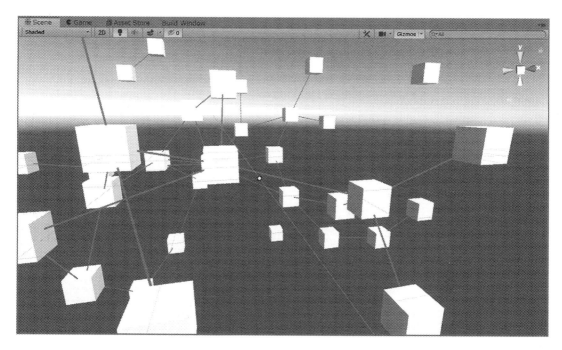

Figure 8-9. *An example of a force-directed graph using random nodes and edges*

The way we have set up this type of visualisation in classes can be repeated for all different types of visualizations. By creating a new `GraphController` type class for each new visualization, we have a selection of which we could instantiate during specific interactions in our application.

You have now implemented a rather complex system to visualize data as a force-directed graph. At the moment we are only using demo data. In the next chapter we will focus on creating a social app that uses Office 365 data in conjunction with this type of visualization.

CHAPTER 9

Building a Social App

This chapter goes into more detail on getting content from Office 365 to start building a social app. This social app will incorporate several functionalities as described in the different scenarios at the beginning of the book.

App Architecture

It is important to understand the app architecture (Figure 9-1) before we start creating code to access Office 365. Our application is a Microsoft HoloLens 2 app, which is a Universal Windows app, built with Unity. Unity itself is a single-threaded environment. As explained before, we want to do true asynchronous calls. These calls are moved to a separate DLL called Office365Hub.

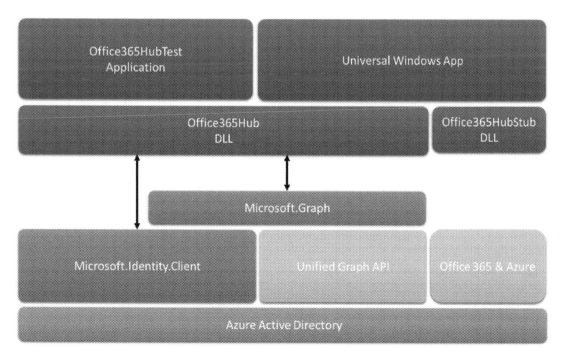

Figure 9-1. *Application architecture overview*

© Alexander Meijers 2020

A. Meijers, *Immersive Office 365*, https://doi.org/10.1007/978-1-4842-5845-3_9

The Office365Hub DLL uses several .NET framework functionalities that are not allowed with Unity. Therefore, we have an additional Office365HubStub DLL containing only the class definitions.

The Office365Hub DLL uses a `Microsoft.Identity.Client` library to implement authentication with Azure Active Directory. It also provides the user token, which can be used to access different endpoints in the unified graph API. The `Microsoft.Graph` library is used to access data from Office 365. Based on the user token, delegated permissions and permissions of the user, data is returned to the Office365Hub DLL.

The GitHub project also contains an Office365HubTestApp project, which is an ordinary Universal Windows app, to test the code written in the Office365Hub DLL on a desktop computer. This test application allows us to quickly test the authentication and results of the methods without the need to go through the whole process of creating, deploying, and running the Microsoft HoloLens 2 application. This book will not go further into detail of that test application, since it speaks for itself on how to use it.

Accessing Unified Graph API

Previous chapters explained using separate dynamic link libraries to perform the queries to our data source like Microsoft Graph. They also discussed how to execute a true asynchronous call using separate threads inside these DLLs. This chapter goes into detail about how to retrieve different types of objects from the Microsoft Graph via the unified graph API.

Authentication

The first step in using the unified graph API requires us to log on through the Azure Active Directory. Using an application that uses the unified graph API requires you to have an App registration. The App registration is nothing more than a registration describing the application and its permissions. As soon as the application tries to authenticate based on the user logging in, the App registration is checked and determines how the application can be used.

Open the Azure portal in a browser, using the URL `https://portal.azure.com`, and log in with the same credentials as your own Office 365 tenant. You will need to have administrator rights in the Azure portal. Open the Azure Active Directory service in the portal, as shown in Figure 9-2.

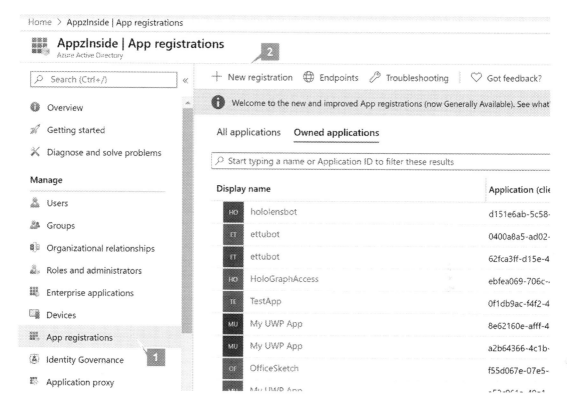

Figure 9-2. *Create a new app registration in the Azure portal*

Select App registrations and click the New registration button at the top of the right window. This will open a new screen, as shown in Figure 9-3, which allows you to create a new App registration.

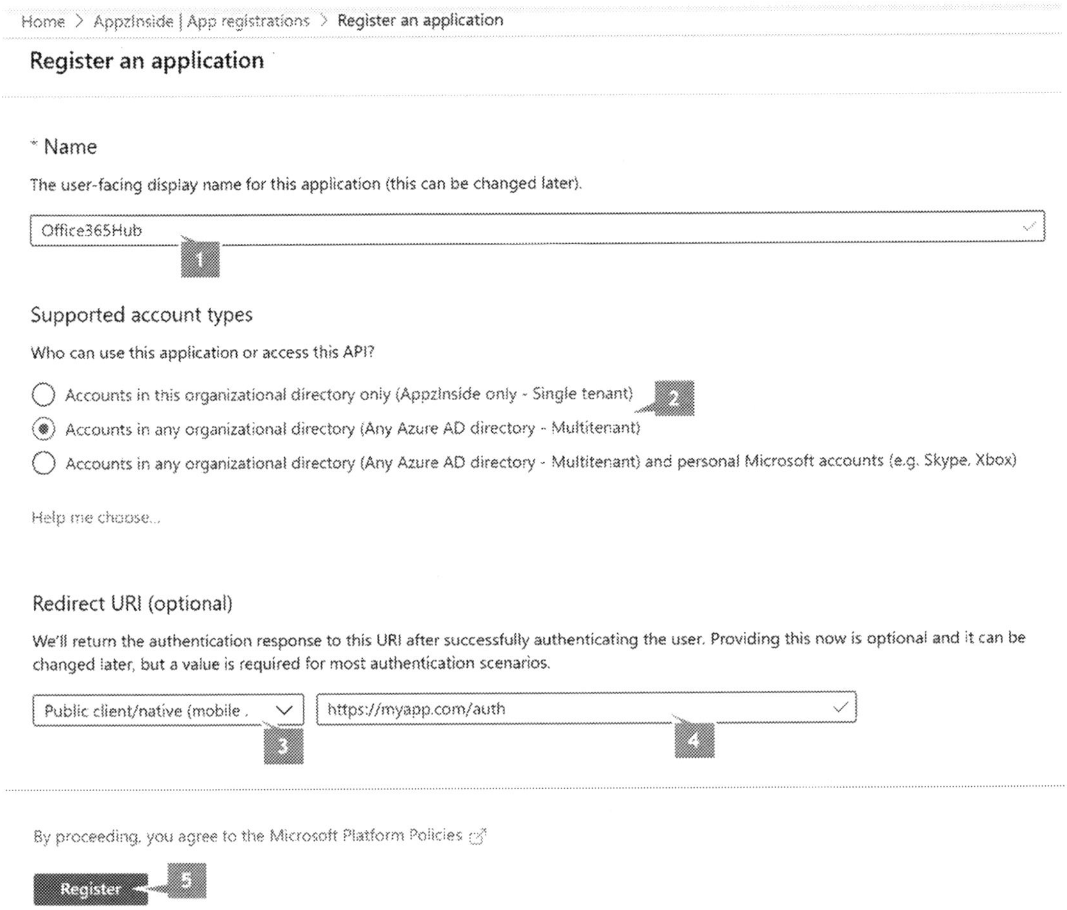

Home > AppzInside | App registrations > Register an application

Register an application

---

* Name

The user-facing display name for this application (this can be changed later).

| Office365Hub | ✓ |

1

Supported account types

Who can use this application or access this API?

◯ Accounts in this organizational directory only (AppzInside only - Single tenant)   **2**

◉ Accounts in any organizational directory (Any Azure AD directory - Multitenant)

◯ Accounts in any organizational directory (Any Azure AD directory - Multitenant) and personal Microsoft accounts (e.g. Skype, Xbox)

Help me choose...

Redirect URI (optional)

We'll return the authentication response to this URI after successfully authenticating the user. Providing this now is optional and it can be changed later, but a value is required for most authentication scenarios.

| Public client/native (mobile . ∨ | https://myapp.com/auth   ✓ |

3   **4**

By proceeding, you agree to the Microsoft Platform Policies ⎘

[Register] ◀ **5**

Figure 9-3. *Register an application via the Azure portal*

Enter the name Office365Hub as the name for the App registration. In the next step, you need to select one of the supported account types, depending on the target group of the application. The first option allows your app only to be used by people inside your tenant. The second option allows your app to be used across multiple tenants. The third option is the same as the second, but allows personal accounts next to the work accounts.

It does not mean that users can access data across tenants while creating a multitenant app. It only means that the app can be used in different tenants. Users in tenants require consent for all rights before using the app. And then users still require having the rights themselves. Users with access in more than one tenant need to give consent for each tenant separately.

While the option for *Redirect URI* is optional, we require you to have one. Our application will be matching based on a URI to determine if the app can access the Microsoft Graph on behalf of the user. Make sure you have selected *Public client/native (mobile & desktop)*. Any valid URI is allowed. We choose `https://myapp.com/auth`.

Press the Register button to register the app. The registration will appear in the list. Select the `Office365Hub` App registration to view its information, as shown in Figure 9-4.

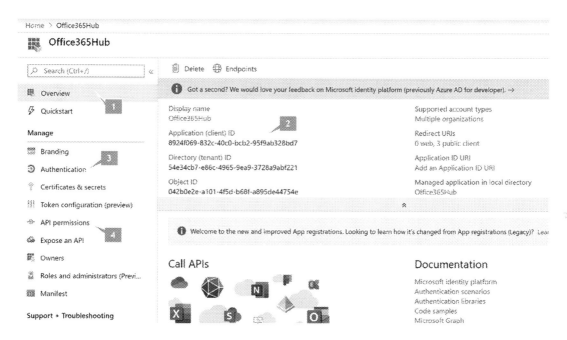

Figure 9-4. *Overview of the registered app*

Under the tab *Overview* you will find common information regarding the registration. An important part is the *Application ID*, also called *Client ID*. We will need that when authenticating against the Microsoft Graph. The *Authentication* tab shows which platform configurations are selected and the supported account type. The API permissions allow you to define which permissions, delegated or application, are set for the App registration.

Delegated permissions are used when a user is authenticating against your app. The user requires, per tenant, to consent with each of them before they can use the app.

Application permissions are used when you authenticate based on the app. This is mostly used for apps that do not require information from the logged-on user or when the app needs to visualize data that most users do not have access to.

It is also possible to grant admin consent for the tenant. This can only be done by an administrator. Users do not have to consent anymore when an admin consent is given.

Nowadays we do not have to specify delegated permissions in the Azure portal. It is also possible to specify them in your application.

NuGet Packages

The Office365Hub DLL needs to have several NuGet packages installed before we can start writing code. An overview of all the required packages is shown in Figure 9-5.

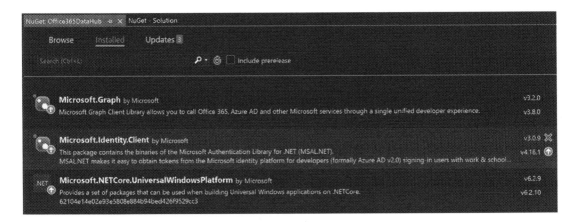

Figure 9-5. *Overview of the required NuGet packages*

Right-click the project in Visual Studio and choose *Manage NuGet packages*. Add the following required packages:

- **Microsoft.Identity.Client** – This contains the authentication library for .NET, also called MSAL.NET, and is required to log on to Azure Active Directory. At the time of writing this book, we are on version 3.0.9.

- **Microsoft.Graph** – This library allows you to access Office 365, Azure AD, and other Microsoft service through a unified API. At the time of writing this book, we are on version 3.2.0.

In the past it was a complete nightmare combining the right versions of each package in combination with the `Microsoft.NetCore.UniversalWindowsPlatform` package. This was caused by several changes made to the process of authentication using MSAL and the development of the Microsoft Graph API. This resulted often in having a low version with less functionality to access certain content in Office 365. Today we can finally use the latest versions of all the packages, which gives us a ton of information.

Authentication

We start by creating an AuthenticationHelper class, which contains all properties and methods to authenticate against Azure AD with MSAL.NET. The class is based on the singleton pattern. It contains several properties that determine how the authentication is executed. The UserLogon property specifies if we want a user to log on or that the application logs on using a client secret and the tenant ID. The UseBetaAPI allows us to control which API is used. Keep in mind that the API can change when you are using the beta version.

```
namespace Office365DataHub
{
    public class AuthenticationHelper
    {
        private static AuthenticationHelper instance = null;

        private string token = "";

        public string TokenForUser = null;
        public DateTimeOffset Expiration;
        public bool UseBetaAPI { get; set; }
        public bool UserLogon { get; set; }

        public string Token
        {
            get { return token; }
        }

        private AuthenticationHelper()
        {
            Authentication = new Authentication();
            UseBetaAPI = false;
        }
```

```
        public static AuthenticationHelper Instance
        {
            get
            {
                if (instance == null)
                {
                    instance = new AuthenticationHelper();
                }

                return instance;
            }
        }
    }
}
```

We have specified a class **Authentication**, which contains several variables that are used for authenticatiProperty	Description	Required by
ClientId	The client ID specified on the *Overview* tab page of the App registration	User
ClientSecret	Client secrets are not created by default. Go to the *Certificates & secrets* tab to create a new client secret. Copy the client secret before you leave the page. You will not be able to view it again.	Application
TenantId	The directory or tenant ID specified on the *Overview* tab page of the App registration	Application
RedirectUri	All specified redirect URIs can be found under the *Authentication* tab.	Both
Scopes	All required scopes need to be defined here in a `string[]` collection. You can use the same names as you will find under the tab *API permissions*. Keep in mind that changing the scopes will require the users to give their consent again.	User
ser		

The following code needs to be added:

```
namespace Office365DataHub
{
    public class Authentication
    {
        public string ClientId;
        public string ClientSecret;
        public string TenantId;
        public string RedirectUri;

        public string[] Scopes;
    }

    public class AuthenticationHelper
    {
        public Authentication Authentication { get; set; }

            ...

    }
}
```

A valid `GraphServiceClient` object is required, to execute a query to the Microsoft Graph via the unified graph API. This requires a user token. The token is returned when the user logs on successfully. The following code uses the `PublicClientApplicatioBuilder` class to create a new authentication object based on the `ClientId` and `RedirectUri`. The object is used to retrieve all the accounts. The token is retrieved by using the first account in the list of returned accounts and the scopes.

This will generate a login screen for the user, where username and password need to be filled in. Several scenarios can happen:

- *No consent given*: The user has no consent given, and no admin consent was given by an administrator. The user is presented with the permissions and requested for consent.

- *Consent given*: The user has given consent in the past or admin consent was given by an administrator.

- *Permissions changed*: The user is required to give consent again, or
  the administrator needs to give admin consent again. The user is
  presented with the permissions and requested for consent.

In all cases where the user must give consent, the user is required to have those same
permissions in the tenant. If not, the user is not able to give consent and use the app. So
be aware of requesting too many or too high-level permissions for your app.

```
namespace Office365DataHub
{
    public class AuthenticationHelper
    {
        /// <summary>
        /// Get Token for User.
        /// </summary>
        /// <returns>Token for user.</returns>
        public async Task<string> GetTokenForUserAsync()
        {
            var app = PublicClientApplicationBuilder.Create(Authentication.
            ClientId).WithRedirectUri(Authentication.RedirectUri).Build();

            var accounts = await app.GetAccountsAsync();
            AuthenticationResult result;
            try
            {
                result = await app.AcquireTokenSilent(Authentication.
                Scopes, accounts.FirstOrDefault()).ExecuteAsync();
                TokenForUser = result.AccessToken;
            }
            catch (MsalUiRequiredException)
            {
                result = await app.AcquireTokenInteractive(Authentication.
                Scopes).ExecuteAsync();
                TokenForUser = result.AccessToken;
            }
```

```
            return TokenForUser;
        }
    }
}
```

The final step is creating the Microsoft Graph client GraphServiceClient object. Based on the property UseBetaAPI, one of the URLs is used. For the beta API, we use the https://graph.microsoft.com/beta. For the release API, we use the https://graph.microsoft.com/v1.0.

```
namespace Office365DataHub
{
    public class AuthenticationHelper
    {
        private GraphServiceClient graphClient = null;

        public GraphServiceClient GetAuthenticatedClient()
        {
            if (graphClient == null)
            {
                // Create Microsoft Graph client.
                try
                {
                    graphClient = new GraphServiceClient(
                        UseBetaAPI ? "https://graph.microsoft.com/beta" :
                        "https://graph.microsoft.com/v1.0",
                        new DelegateAuthenticationProvider(
                            async (requestMessage) =>
                            {
                                token = await GetTokenForUserAsync();

                                requestMessage.Headers.Authorization = new
                                AuthenticationHeaderValue("bearer", token);

                            }));
                    return graphClient;
                }
```

```
        catch (Exception ex)
        {
            Debug.WriteLine("Could not create a graph client: " +
            ex.Message);
        }
    }

    return graphClient;
    }

    }
}
```

A DelegateAuthenticationProvider is used to create the client based on
the user token. The user token is retrieved by the previously explained method
GetTokenForUserAsync and added as bearer in the authentication header of the call.

Get Users

Let us start by getting people from an Office 365 environment. We want to have a clean
and uniform data model that can be used in Unity. We do not want to depend on a data
model that is part of a library. For that, we create our own data objects. Create a folder
Entities in the project. Create a new file called BaseEntity.cs in the folder Entities.
Copy the following code into the BaseEntity file:

```
namespace Office365DataHub.Entities
{
    public class BaseEntity
    {
        public string Id = "";
    }
}
```

Each data entity in our model is derived from the BaseEntity class. Create a new file called PersonEntity.cs in the Entities folder and copy the following code:

```
namespace Office365DataHub.Entities
{
    public class PersonEntity : BaseEntity
    {
        public string FullName = "";
        public string Surname = "";
        public string GivenName = "";
        public string JobTitle = "";
        public string Department = "";
        public string OfficeLocation = "";
        public string PhoneNumber = "";
        public string EmailAddress = "";
    }

    public class PersonEntityCollection : List<PersonEntity>
    {
    }
}
```

All methods that apply to people will be part of a class PeopleService. Create a folder called Services. Create a file called PeopleService.cs in the folder Services and copy the following code:

```
using Microsoft.Graph;
using Office365DataHub.Entities;
using System;
using System.Collections.Generic;
using System.IO;
using System.Linq;
using System.Threading.Tasks;

namespace Office365DataHub.Services
{
    public class PeopleService : Singleton<PeopleService>
    {
```

```csharp
public delegate void OnGetPersonCompleted(PersonEntity person);

public void GetCurrentUser(OnGetPersonCompleted onGetPersonCompleted)
{
    System.Threading.Tasks.Task.Run(
        () => GetPersonAsync(new Entities.PersonRequest(),
        onGetPersonCompleted));
}

public void GetPerson(Entities.PersonRequest request,
OnGetPersonCompleted onGetPersonCompleted)
{
    System.Threading.Tasks.Task.Run(
        () => GetPersonAsync(request, onGetPersonCompleted));
}

public async Task GetPersonAsync(string id, OnGetPersonCompleted
onGetPersonCompleted)
{
    PersonEntity person = null;

    var graphClient = AuthenticationHelper.Instance.
    GetAuthenticatedClient();

    if (graphClient != null)
    {
        User user = id == "" ? await graphClient.Me.Request().
        GetAsync() : await graphClient.Users[id].Request().
        GetAsync();

        person = new PersonEntity()
        {
            FullName = user.DisplayName,
            Surname = user.Surname,
            GivenName = user.GivenName,
            JobTitle = user.JobTitle,
            Department = user.Department,
            OfficeLocation = user.OfficeLocation,
            PhoneNumber = user.MobilePhone,
```

```
                EmailAddress = user.Mail,
                Id = user.Id
            };
        }

        onGetPersonCompleted(person);
    }
}
}
```

Each call always consists of at least two methods. One part contains the actual call encapsulated into an asynchronous method. In this case it is `public async Task GetPersonAsync(string id, OnGetPersonCompleted onGetPersonCompleted);`. The method uses the `GraphServiceClient` to retrieve the user based on the ID. The call `graphClient.Users[id].Request().GetAsync();` returns a `Person` object, which is then copied into our data entity `PersonEntity`.

The other method is not asynchronously defined and uses `System.Threading. Tasks.Task.Run` to perform the actual call. One or more callback methods is used to return the result when the asynchronous call is finished. This technique is necessary, since Unity does not understand asynchronous methods.

A part of a person is their profile picture. This requires a separate data entity object as shown in the following code, which can be copied into a new file `PhotoDetail.cs` in the folder `Entities`.

```
namespace Office365DataHub.Entities
{
    public struct PhotoDetail
    {
        public int? Width;
        public int? Height;
        public byte[] Photo;

    }
}
```

Getting the profile picture requires two separate calls to the Microsoft Graph. The first call gives us information back about the profile photo, like `Width` and `Height`. The second call gives us a stream back with the actual photo. To get the photo as an array requires us to copy the Stream to a MemoryStream. The MemoryStream can easily be converted to an array using the MemoryStream .ToArray() method. Add the methods GetPhoto and GetPhotoAsync in the PeopleService class as follows:

```
namespace Office365DataHub.Services
{
    public class PeopleService : Singleton<PeopleService>
    {
        public delegate void OnGetPhotoCompleted(PhotoDetail photo);

        public void GetPhoto(string userId, OnGetPhotoCompleted
        onGetPhotoCompleted)
        {
            System.Threading.Tasks.Task.Run(
                () => GetPhotoAsync(userId, onGetPhotoCompleted));
        }

        public async Task GetPhotoAsync(string userId, OnGetPhotoCompleted
        onGetPhotoCompleted)
        {
            onGetPhotoCompleted(await GetPhotoAsync(userId));
        }

        public async Task<PhotoDetail> GetPhotoAsync(string userId)
        {
            PhotoDetail detail;

            var graphClient = AuthenticationHelper.Instance.
            GetAuthenticatedClient();

            try
            {
                ProfilePhoto photo = await graphClient.Users[userId].Photo.
                Request().GetAsync();

                Stream photoStream = await graphClient.Users[userId].Photo.
                Content.Request().GetAsync();
```

```
        using (MemoryStream ms = new MemoryStream())
        {
            photoStream.CopyTo(ms);
            detail.Photo = ms.ToArray();
        }

        detail.Width = photo.Width;
        detail.Height = photo.Height;
    }
    catch (Exception)
    {
        detail.Width = 0;
        detail.Height = 0;
        detail.Photo = null;
    }

    return detail;
    }

  }
}
```

We have now implemented all the parts to retrieve the profile picture of a single person. We need to make several changes to get this implemented in the PeopleService.GetPersonAsync method. We need to add a property to the PersonEntity class, as shown in the following code:

```
public class PersonEntity : BaseEntity
{
    public PhotoDetail PhotoDetail;
}
```

Also add the row ,PhotoDetail = await GetPhotoAsync(id) into the GetPersonAsync method, as shown in the following. Don't forget to copy the comma before the row.

```
namespace Office365DataHub.Services
{
    public class PeopleService : Singleton<PeopleService>
```

```
{
    public async Task GetPersonAsync(string id, OnGetPersonCompleted
    onGetPersonCompleted)
    {
        ...

        if (graphClient != null)
        {
            ...
            person = new PersonEntity()
            {
                ...

                , PhotoDetail = await GetPhotoAsync(id)
            };
        }
    }
}
```

Getting the profile photo at the same time shouldn't be a problem. But you can imagine that requesting and converting the stream will take some time. Therefore, it can be interesting not to get the photo at the time you retrieve the person but to get the photo in a separate thread and update it in the interface accordingly.

Related People

In this second example, we want to retrieve related people. As explained in previous chapters, related people are people who have a connection with a user in some way. Their relationship can be based on any form like how they have worked together on a document, their mail traffic, and many other relationships originated by collaboration in Office 365.

Each relationship is based on one person related to another person. A person can have relationships with more than one person. Since we need to keep track of the person from whom we initially want to have the related people, we use a class called RelatedPeopleRequest, which is given to the method and is also returned in the callback methods. This allows us to have the person available inside the callback next to the related people. Create a folder called Data. Copy the following code into the file RelatedPeopleRequest.cs in the folder Data:

```
using Office365DataHub.Entities;

namespace Office365DataHub.Data
{
    public class RelatedPeopleRequest
    {
        public PersonEntity person = null;
        public PersonEntity relatedPerson = null;
        public PersonEntityCollection relatedPeople = new
        PersonEntityCollection();
    }
}
```

It is extremely easy to retrieve related people. We will need to do a call to People with graphClient.Users[Id].People.Request().GetAsync();.

This call will return the top ten related people and groups. To make sure that we only get people returned, we will add a filter in the call by using graphClient.Users[Id]. People.Request().Filter(filter).GetAsync(); where filter = "personType/class eq 'Person' and personType/subclass eq 'OrganizationUser'";.

The person data returned is not as complete as the previous call for getting a person. In this example, we are retrieving the photo of the person. That process takes time, since we are executing a separate call every time when we have a new related person. Therefore, we have a method containing two callback methods. The first one is called for each related person retrieved. This will fill the property relatedPerson of the RelatedPeopleRequest. The second callback will return when all related people are found. That will fill the property relatedPeople of the RelatedPeopleRequest.

Add the following code in the class PeopleService:

```
namespace Office365DataHub.Services
{
    public class PeopleService : Singleton<PeopleService>
    {
        public delegate void OnGetRelatedPersonCompleted(RelatedPeopleReque
        st request);
```

```
public delegate void OnGetRelatedPeopleCompleted(RelatedPeopleReque
st request);

public void GetRelatedPeople(RelatedPeopleRequest request,
OnGetRelatedPersonCompleted onGetRelatedPersonCompleted,
OnGetRelatedPeopleCompleted onGetRelatedPeopleCompleted)
{
    System.Threading.Tasks.Task.Run(
        () => GetRelatedPeopleASync(request,
        onGetRelatedPersonCompleted, onGetRelatedPeopleCompleted) );
}

public async Task GetRelatedPeopleASync(RelatedPeopleRequest
request, OnGetRelatedPersonCompleted onGetRelatedPersonCompleted,
OnGetRelatedPeopleCompleted onGetRelatedPeopleCompleted)
{
    List<Person> persons = new List<Person>();

    var graphClient = AuthenticationHelper.Instance.
    GetAuthenticatedClient();

    string filter = "personType/class eq 'Person' and personType/
    subclass eq 'OrganizationUser'";

    if (graphClient != null)
    {
        if (request.person.Id == "")
        {
            IUserPeopleCollectionPage people = await graphClient.
            Me.People.Request().Filter(filter).GetAsync();
            persons.AddRange(people);
        }
        else
        {
            try
            {
```

```
            IUserPeopleCollectionPage people = await
            graphClient.Users[request.person.Id].People.
            Request().Filter(filter).GetAsync();
            persons.AddRange(people);
        }
        catch (Exception)
        {
        }
    }

}

foreach (Person person in persons)
{
    switch (person.PersonType.Class)
    {
        case "Person":
            PhotoDetail detail = await GetPhotoAsync(person.Id);

            PersonEntity data = new PersonEntity()
            {
                FullName = person.DisplayName,
                Surname = person.Surname,
                GivenName = person.GivenName,
                JobTitle = person.JobTitle,
                Department = person.Department,
                OfficeLocation = person.OfficeLocation,
                PhoneNumber = person.Phones.Any() ? person.
                Phones.First().Number : "",
                EmailAddress = person.ScoredEmailAddresses.
                Any() ? person.ScoredEmailAddresses.First().
                Address : "",
                Id = person.Id,
                PhotoDetail = detail
            };

            request.relatedPerson = data;
            onGetRelatedPersonCompleted(request);
```

```
                        request.relatedPeople.Add(data);
                        break;

                    case "Group":
                        break;
                }
            }

            request.relatedPerson = null;
            onGetRelatedPeopleCompleted(request);
        }

    }
}
```

Get a Team

Another interesting part of Office 365 is Teams. We need to create a data entity for a Team. Create a new file TeamEntity.cs in the folder Entities. Copy the following code into the new file TeamEntity.cs:

```
namespace Office365DataHub.Entities
{
    public class TeamEntity : BaseEntity
    {
        public string DisplayName = "";
        public string Description = "";
        public bool? IsArchived = false;
    }

    public class TeamEntityCollection : List<TeamEntity>
    {
    }
}
```

We are going through several methods to get the members of a Team. The first method is to retrieve Team information based on the ID. To retrieve information about the Team, we reach out to the Groups collection. Each Team is represented by a Group, which contains the base information. Getting the information requires us to execute the call graphClient.Groups[teamId].Request().GetAsync();.

Copy the following code, which describes the TeamService class, into a new file called TeamService.cs in the folder Services.

```
using Microsoft.Graph;
using Office365DataHub.Entities;
using System;
using System.Threading.Tasks;
using Office365DataHub.Data;

namespace Office365DataHub.Services
{
    public class TeamService : Singleton<TeamService>
    {
        public delegate void OnGetTeamCompleted(TeamEntity team);

        public void GetTeam(string teamId, OnGetTeamCompleted
        onGetTeamCompleted)
        {
            System.Threading.Tasks.Task.Run(
                () => GetTeamAsync(teamId, onGetTeamCompleted) );
        }

        public async Task GetTeamAsync(string teamId, OnGetTeamCompleted
        onGetTeamCompleted)
        {
            GraphServiceClient graphClient = AuthenticationHelper.Instance.
            GetAuthenticatedClient();

            if (graphClient != null)
            {
                var group = await graphClient.Groups[teamId].Request().
                GetAsync();

                var team = new TeamEntity
                {
                    Id = group.Id,
```

```
                    DisplayName = group.DisplayName,
                    Description = group.Description,
                    IsArchived = group.IsArchived

            };

            onGetTeamCompleted(team);
        }
      }
    }
}
```

Get Joined Teams

The previous method requires you to know the ID of the Team. Microsoft Graph is always built from a user perspective. It would be more logical to retrieve Teams that you have joined as a user.

Create the following class TeamDataRequest in a new file called TeamDataRequest.cs in the folder Data. This class is used when the call is made and returned in the callback of the method.

```
using Office365DataHub.Entities;

namespace Office365DataHub.Data
{
    public class TeamDataRequest
    {
        public TeamEntityCollection teams = new TeamEntityCollection();
        public PersonEntity person = null;
    }
}
```

It is easy to retrieve the joined teams of a user. Execute the code graphClient.
Users[Id].JoinedTeams.Request().GetAsync();. Copy the following code in the
existing TeamService.cs file:

```
namespace Office365DataHub.Services
{
    public class TeamService : Singleton<TeamService>
    {
        public delegate void OnGetTeamsCompleted(TeamDataRequest request);

        public void GetJoinedTeams(TeamDataRequest request,
        OnGetTeamsCompleted onGetTeamsCompleted)
        {
            System.Threading.Tasks.Task.Run(
                () => GetJoinedTeamsAsync(request, onGetTeamsCompleted) );
        }

        public async Task GetJoinedTeamsAsync(TeamDataRequest request,
        OnGetTeamsCompleted onGetTeamsCompleted)
        {
            GraphServiceClient graphClient = AuthenticationHelper.Instance.
            GetAuthenticatedClient();

            if (graphClient != null)
            {
                TeamEntityCollection teamList = new TeamEntityCollection();

                var teams = await graphClient.Users[request.person.Id].
                JoinedTeams.Request().GetAsync();

                foreach (var team in teams)
                {
                    request.teams.Add(new TeamEntity
                    {
                        Id = team.Id,
                        DisplayName = team.PrimaryChannel != null ? team.
                        PrimaryChannel.DisplayName : "Undefined",
```

```
                        Description = team.PrimaryChannel != null ? team.
                        PrimaryChannel.Description : "",
                        IsArchived = team.IsArchived

                    });
                }

                onGetTeamsCompleted(request);
            }
        }
    }
}
```

Getting Team Members

Members of a Team can be retrieved through the Group object in the Microsoft Graph. We require an enumeration, which defines the role of a team member. Create a new file called TeamMemberRole in the folder Data. Add the following code:

```
namespace Office365DataHub.Data
{
    public enum TeamMemberRole
    {
        Member,
        Owner
    }
}
```

We use a data class called TeamMemberRequest, which takes care of having the original person and team included in the returned data. Copy the following code into a new file called TeamMemberRequest.cs:

```
namespace Office365DataHub.Data
{
    public class TeamMemberRequest
    {
        public PersonEntity person = null;
        public TeamEntity team = null;
```

```
    public TeamMemberRole role = TeamMemberRole.Member;

  }
}
```

The following code shows how to retrieve the team members from a Team site. We need to create an instance of the TeamMembersDataRequest and set the person and team property. That instance of the class is used to call the method. The method uses graphClient.Groups[request.team.Id].Members.Request().GetAsync(); to retrieve all the members. The returned collection is iterated to retrieve each person separately, using graphClient.Users[teamMember.Id].Request().GetAsync();.

Copy the following code in the existing file TeamService.cs:

```
namespace Office365DataHub.Services
{
    public class TeamService : Singleton<TeamService>
    {
        public delegate void OnGetTeamMembersCompleted(TeamMembersDataReque
        st request);

        public void GetTeamMembers(TeamMembersDataRequest request,
        OnGetTeamMembersCompleted onGetTeamMembersCompleted)
        {
            System.Threading.Tasks.Task.Run(
                () => GetTeamMembersAsync(request,
                onGetTeamMembersCompleted) );
        }

        public async Task GetTeamMembersAsync(TeamMembersDataRequest
        request, OnGetTeamMembersCompleted onGetTeamMembersCompleted)
        {
            GraphServiceClient graphClient = AuthenticationHelper.Instance.
            GetAuthenticatedClient();

            if (graphClient != null)
            {
                PersonEntityCollection persons = new
                PersonEntityCollection();
```

```
var teamMembers = await graphClient.Groups[request.team.
Id].Members.Request().GetAsync();

foreach (var teamMember in teamMembers)
{
    User user = await graphClient.Users[teamMember.Id].
    Request().GetAsync();

    request.members.Add(new PersonEntity
    {
        FullName = user.DisplayName,
        Surname = user.Surname,
        GivenName = user.GivenName,
        JobTitle = user.JobTitle,
        Department = user.Department,
        OfficeLocation = user.OfficeLocation,
        PhoneNumber = user.MobilePhone,
        EmailAddress = user.Mail,
        Id = user.Id,
        PhotoDetail = await PeopleService.Instance.
        GetPhotoAsync(user.Id)
    });
}

onGetTeamMembersCompleted(request);
        }
      }
    }
}
```

Adding a Team Member

In the previous examples, we have been accessing a variety of different API calls
to retrieve information around a person, people, and teams from Office 365. What
if we want to make changes to Office 365? That is possible too. In the following
example, we see how to add a new member to a team. We use the same data object
TeamMembersDataRequest to execute the call. We need to fill in the person, team and

role properties. The person will be added to the team in the role of role. This data object will be returned in the callback of the method. The TeamMembersDataRequest object contains a ServiceException property. If an exception occurs, it is reported back in this property. This requires having the following code placed in a new file called ServiceException.cs:

```
namespace Office365DataHub
{
    public class ServiceException
    {
        public ServiceException()
        {
            Error = ServiceError.NoError;
            Exception = null;
        }

        public Exception Exception { get; set; }

        public ServiceError Error { get; set; }
    }
}
```

The class contains a ServiceError property describing the error message and an Exception property containing the occurring exception. The ServiceError is a separate enumeration, which can be found as follows:

```
namespace Office365DataHub
{
    public enum ServiceError
    {
        NoError = 0,
        UserAlreadyExists = 1,
        UnknownError = 100
    }
}
```

Adding a team member requires two additional steps. The first step is getting the User object based on the person with the call User user = await graphClient. Users[request.person.Id].Request().GetAsync();. The second step is adding the user as a member or owner. The Group object contains two corresponding properties Members and Owners. Adding the user as a member requires the following code:

```
graphClient.Groups[request.team.Id].Members.References.Request().
AddAsync(user);
```

Adding the user as an owner requires the following code:

```
graphClient.Groups[request.team.Id].Owners.References.Request().
AddAsync(user);
```

The complete code can be found in the following and needs to be copied in the existing file TeamService.cs:

```
namespace Office365DataHub.Services
{
    public class TeamService : Singleton<TeamService>
    {
OnGetTeamMembersCompleted(TeamMembersDataRequest request);
        public delegate void OnAddTeamMemberCompleted(TeamMemberRequest
        request);

        public void AddTeamMember(TeamMemberRequest request,
        OnAddTeamMemberCompleted onAddTeamMemberCompleted)
        {
            System.Threading.Tasks.Task.Run(
                () => AddTeamMemberAsync(request, onAddTeamMemberCompleted) );
        }

        public async Task AddTeamMemberAsync(TeamMemberRequest request,
        OnAddTeamMemberCompleted onAddTeamMemberCompleted)
        {
            GraphServiceClient graphClient = AuthenticationHelper.Instance.
            GetAuthenticatedClient();

            if (graphClient != null)
```

```
    {
        User user = await graphClient.Users[request.person.Id].
        Request().GetAsync();

        try
        {
            switch(request.role)
            {
                case TeamMemberRole.Owner:
                    await graphClient.Groups[request.team.Id].
                    Owners.References.Request().AddAsync(user);
                    break;

                default:
                    await graphClient.Groups[request.team.Id].
                    Members.References.Request().AddAsync(user);
                    break;
            }
        }
        catch (Exception ex)
        {
            request.expection = new ServiceException
            {
                Error = ServiceError.UserAlreadyExists,
                Exception = ex
            };
        }
    }

    onAddTeamMemberCompleted(request);
        }
    }
}
```

Test Our Application

Since Unity version 2019.x, the output of a solution is based on IL2CPP, as explained in previous chapters. Any change in assets and scripting requires us to go through the whole process of creating a solution and deploying it to the Microsoft HoloLens 2. We are not able to test our functionality inside Unity, since the Office365Hub DLL contains functionality that is not allowed in Unity. Therefore, we can use the Office365DataHubTestApp project to speed up the process of testing our functionality.

The following examples, which can be added to the MainPage class of the Office365DataHubTestApp project, show how to retrieve all members of each Team that the current user has joined. It starts with initializing the connection and calls the PeopleService.Instance.GetCurrentUser method to retrieve the current user.

```
public MainPage()
{
    this.InitializeComponent();

    AuthenticationHelper.Instance.UseBetaAPI = false;
    AuthenticationHelper.Instance.UserLogon = true;
    AuthenticationHelper.Instance.RedirectUri = "<your redirect uri";

    AuthenticationHelper.Instance.Authentication.ClientId = "<your client id>";
    AuthenticationHelper.Instance.Authentication.Scopes = new string[] {
        "User.Read", "User.Read.All", "People.Read", "People.Read.All",
        "Group.Read.All" };

    PeopleService.Instance.GetCurrentUser(OnGetCurrentUser);
}
```

The method will return immediately, since the call is asynchronous. If the user was not yet logged on, the call will cause the user to log on, as is shown in Figure 9-6. This same dialog will appear when you run the application on your Microsoft HoloLens 2 device.

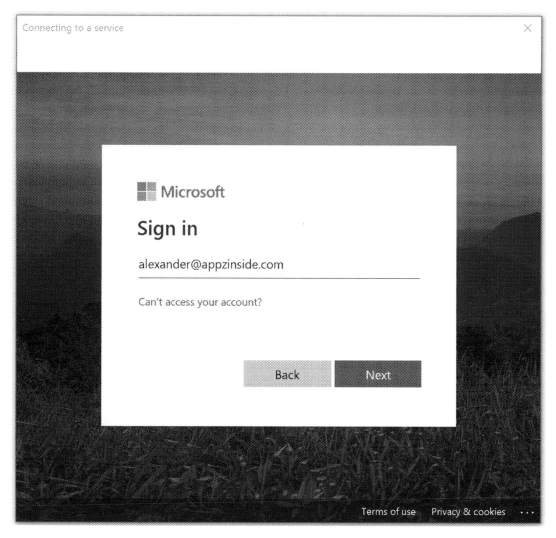

Figure 9-6. *Login dialog when authentication is required by the first method call*

The user is required the first time to give consent for the delegated permissions. The callback `OnGetCurrentUser` is called as soon as the method has finished.

A `TeamDataRequest` data object is built up inside the callback `OnGetCurrentUser` using the returned current user. That object is used to retrieve all the teams the current user has joined.

```
public void OnGetCurrentUser(PersonEntity person)
{
    // get joined teams
    TeamDataRequest request = new TeamDataRequest();
```

```
    request.person = person;
    TeamService.Instance.GetJoinedTeams(request, OnGetTeams);
}
```

The callback OnGetTeams of the method is called as soon as the joined teams are retrieved. The same data object TeamDataRequest is returned and also contains a collection of found teams.

```
public void OnGetTeams(TeamDataRequest request)
{
    foreach (TeamEntity team in request.teams)
    {
        TeamMembersDataRequest membersRequest = new
        TeamMembersDataRequest();
        membersRequest.team = team;
        TeamService.Instance.GetTeamMembers(membersRequest, OnGetTeamMembers);
        Debug.WriteLine(string.Format("Team:{0}, {1}", team.DisplayName,
        team.Id));
    }
}
```

In the callback OnGetTeams, we loop through each of the teams. In the loop we request for each of the teams the members by again calling a method that uses the TeamMembersDataRequest data object. We also write the name of the team via Debug to the console of the test application.

Since the call to retrieve the team members will return immediately, you can imagine that with a lot of teams several calls to team members are running in separate threads.

```
public void OnGetTeamMembers(TeamMembersDataRequest request)
{
    foreach (PersonEntity person in request.members)
    {
        Debug.WriteLine(string.Format("{0}:{1}", person.FullName, person.Id));
    }
}
```

Each finished call to team members will call the callback OnGetTeamMembers where we loop through the team members to output them in the console.

CHAPTER 10

Model Implementation

The previous chapter explained how to extend the libraries to retrieve data from Office 365 through the Microsoft Graph. This chapter goes into detail about how to connect that data to the force-directed graph code and run it on a Microsoft HoloLens 2 device.

Include the Libraries

We already added both libraries, *ImmersiveOffice365Hub* and *ImmersiveOffice365Stub*, to the Unity project in the folders WSA and WSA/Plugins. *ImmersiveOffice365Stub* contains only the definitions of the same classes and methods defined in *ImmersiveOffice365Hub*. Any newly added class and/or method in the hub is required to have a definition without any code in the stub.

Make sure that *ImmersiveOffice365Hub* and *ImmersiveOffice365Stub* both are compiled against Any CPU or x86.

The functionality in the *ImmersiveOffice365Hub* library is extended by accessing Office 365 data through the Microsoft Graph API. Therefor we need to add several packaged through the NuGet packages system. When the *ImmersiveOffice365Hub* library is compiled from Unity, those packages will be missing. This causes two major challenges.

The first challenge is to include the packages in the same Unity project. The packages are nothing more than the dynamic linked libraries (DLLs). We need to copy these libraries into the same Plugins/WSA folder.

Libraries can easily be found under the following path:

```
C:\Users\[Username]\.nuget\packages\[Name of the package]\[version]\lib\
netstandard2.0\[name of the DLL]
```

You will need to fill in your username, the name of the package, and the name of the DLL you are looking for. Always select the netstandard version.

© Alexander Meijers 2020
A. Meijers, *Immersive Office 365*, https://doi.org/10.1007/978-1-4842-5845-3_10

The solution found in GitHub, also contains an *ImmersiveOffice365HubTestApp* project. This is a project that allows you to test the different methods in the *ImmersiveOffice365Hub* project. When the test application is built for x86, all required assemblies with the correct version are found in that projects output folder `bin/x86/debug` or `bin/x86/release`.

We are using the following main libraries from the packages.

- Microsoft.Identity.Client.dll

- Microsoft.Graph.dll

But including these main libraries from those packages will not be enough. These libraries have dependencies on other libraries. The dependency libraries depend on the use of the classes and methods from the main libraries. Based on our requirements, we need the following additional libraries:

- **Microsoft.Graph.Core.dll** – Several classes are used by the Microsoft Graph API, like `Microsoft.Graph.DerivedTypeConverter`.

- **Newtonsoft.Json.dll** – JSON is used to serialize and deserialize the results from calls through the Microsoft Graph API.

Make sure you copy all the main and additional libraries to the `Plugins/WSA` folder under Assets, as can be seen in Figure 10-1.

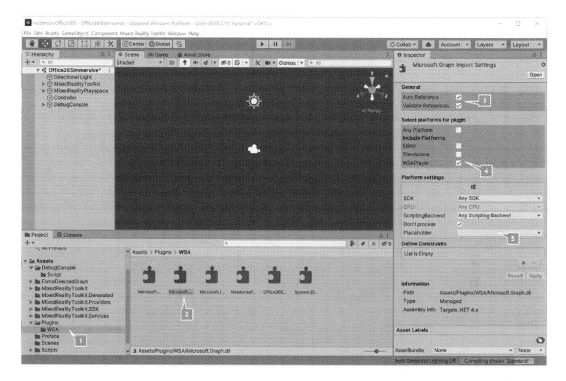

Figure 10-1. *Adding all main and additional libraries to the plugins folder*

Drag the libraries into the Plugins/WSA folder. We need to configure each of them when Unity has processed the import. We need to set the *Auto Reference* and *Validate Reference* to true by checking both checkboxes. Make sure that only the *WSAPlayer* platform is selected. This will include the code only for the generated Microsoft HoloLens 2 project. And finally, uncheck the *Don't process* checkbox to prevent Unity from serializing the classes. Press the *Apply* button to process the changes for Unity.

The second challenge is making sure that the code of the libraries is included in the outcome of the project. That sounds weird, but I will explain it. As explained earlier, deploying a Unity project results in a Visual Studio project using IL2CPP. The problem with that is that each part of the script files is converted to native code running in your project. What happens with your libraries? The libraries are included as assets into your project and loaded during the startup of the application. Unity creates native code files that can be compared with stub files to access the functionality in each library.

Since Unity nowadays compiles to IL2CPP, which generates native code, it has several ways to optimize the performance of your application. One of those optimizations is stripping of code to a certain level. Stripping code means removing code that is not used by the application from any call. And that will cause issues because Unity is not able to view which functions are called within the libraries and will therefor unfairly remove code that is required.

When Unity is optimizing code by stripping, it can only recognize functions being used by the scripting code in the project. References from libraries to other libraries are not seen. While the compiler will finish successfully, running the app on your device will generate errors due to missing classes, methods, and properties.

The level can be adjusted through *Project Settings* ➤ *Player* ➤ *Other settings* ➤ *Optimization* using the property *Managed Stripping* level. This can be seen in Figure 10-2.

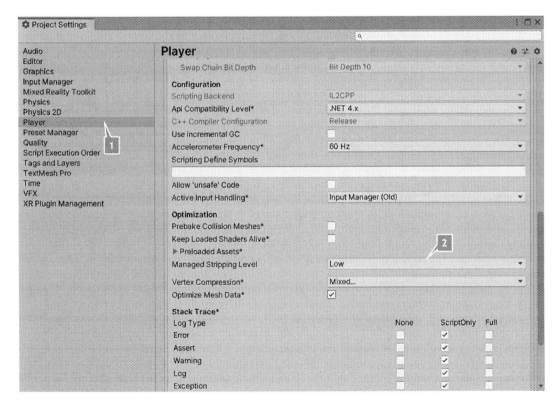

Figure 10-2. *Changing the managed stripping level of the application*

Unfortunately, we have only the options Low, Medium, and High for this property. If we didn't strip the code, you would get an incredible amount of generated native code. That is not what we want. There is another solution. This solution requires adding a link. xml file to the Assets folder. It can be placed anywhere in the Assets folder.

```xml
<linker>
  <!--
  exclude assemblies from being stripped
  -->
  <assembly fullname="Microsoft.Graph.Core" preserve="all"/>
  <assembly fullname="Microsoft.Identity.Client" preserve="all"/>
  <assembly fullname="Newtonsoft.Json" preserve="all"/>
  <assembly fullname="Microsoft.Graph" preserve="all"/>

  <assembly fullname="System.Core">
    <type fullname="System.Linq.Expressions.Interpreter.LightLambda"
preserve="all" />
  </assembly>
</linker>
```

This file describes which assemblies, namespaces, classes, and even methods need to be included in the build without using the stripping optimization. In our file we have added definitions for all the libraries we require. This makes sure that all code is included in the build. The *Microsoft.Graph* library uses a lambda to return results of calls to Office 365. To prevent the LightLambda class being excluded through optimization, it is added as a type of the assembly System.Core.

At the time of writing this book, the following assembly versions were used:

- **Microsoft.Graph.dll** – Version 3.8.0.0

- **Microsoft.Graph.Core.dll** – Version 1.20.1.0

- **Microsoft.Identity.Client.dll** – Version 4.16.1.0

- **Microsoft.Diagnostics.DiagnosticsSource.dll** – Version 4.700.19.46214

- **Newtonsoft.Json.dll** – Version 9.0.1.19813

Visual Studio 2019 version 16.6.4 and Microsoft Windows 10 OS Build 19041.388 were used.

Data Queue

The data queue is an important part of getting the entities into our 3D model. Data is retrieved in a separate thread created in the *ImmersiveOffice365Hub* assembly. *GameObjects* are only allowed to be created on the Unity thread, hence a data queue.

The data queue is like an intermediate system transporting entities and their relationships to other entities from Microsoft Graph into the Unity scene. Add a new folder Model under Assets/Apps/Scripts. Create a script called DataQueue.cs in the folder Model. Copy the following code in the file:

```
using Office365DataHub.Entities;
using System.Collections.Generic;

public class DataQueueItem
{
    public BaseEntity Root;
    public BaseEntity Refering;
}
```

We start with a DataQueueItem class. This class contains two entity references, since our 3D model is all about relationships. The relationship is represented between a Root entity and its relation to the Referring entity. Copy the following code into the same file just under the DataQueueItem class:

```
public class DataQueue: List<DataQueueItem>
{
    public bool GetFromQueue(out BaseEntity root, out BaseEntity refering)
    {
        if (this.Count > 0)
        {
            root = this[0].Root;
            refering = this[0].Refering;

            this.RemoveAt(0);

            return true;
        }
    }
}
```

```
        root = null;
        refering = null;

        return false;
    }
}
```

The second class, called DataQueue, is derived from a List collection based on the DataQueueItem class. It contains a method GetFromQueue that returns the first DataQueueItem on the stack. Copy the method AddToQueue into the class DataQueue as follows:

```
public class DataQueue: List<DataQueueItem>
{
    public void AddToQueue(BaseEntity root, BaseEntity refering)
    {
        Add(new DataQueueItem() { Root = root, Refering = refering });
    }
}
```

The second method, called AddToQueue, allows us to put a new DataQueue item on the stack. The new item is always added at the end.

Data Model

The first step is using the build functionality to retrieve data from Office 365, available from the *ImmersiveOffice365Hub* library. A separate class DataModel is created for retrieving the entities and putting them into the queue. Create a new script file called DataModel in the Assets/App/Scripts/Model folder. Copy the following code into the DataModel file:

```
using Office365DataHub.Data;
using Office365DataHub.Services;
using Office365DataHub.Entities;
public class DataModel : IDataModel
{
    private DataQueue queue = new DataQueue();
```

```
    public DataQueue Queue
    {
        get
        {
            return queue;
        }
    }
}
```

The class contains an instance of the DataQueue class, which incorporates the queue for our model. The second property is used to retrieve the queue. This is necessary to allow the GraphController class to access the queue. Add the following method to the DataModel class:

```
private void InitializeConnection()
{
    AuthenticationHelper.Instance.UseBetaAPI = false;
    AuthenticationHelper.Instance.UserLogon = true;
    AuthenticationHelper.Instance.RedirectUri = "<A redirect URL as
    specified in your app registration>";

    AuthenticationHelper.Instance.Authentication = new Office365DataHub.
    Authentication
    {
        ClientId = "<the client id of your app registration>",
        Scopes = new string[] {
          "User.Read",
                "User.Read.All",
                "People.Read",
                "People.Read.All" },
    };
}
```

The class contains several methods. The first method is called InitalizeConnection. In this method, we will initialize the AuthenticationHelper with the values from the App registration in Microsoft Azure done in the previous chapter. Since we didn't set any of the scopes in the App registration, we need to do this in code. In the preceding example you will see that we ask for permissions to access users and people. People access is needed for getting related people from a specific user.

The next method creates sample data, which is used when testing in the Unity editor. The method CreateSampleData shows how easy it is to create entities and their relationships. In this case I am using the names of my family and friends.

```
private void CreateSampleData()
{
    PersonEntity p1 = new PersonEntity { Id = "1", FullName = "Alexander" };
    PersonEntity p2 = new PersonEntity { Id = "2", FullName = "Colin" };
    PersonEntity p3 = new PersonEntity { Id = "3", FullName = "Owen" };
    PersonEntity p4 = new PersonEntity { Id = "4", FullName = "Tessa" };
    PersonEntity p5 = new PersonEntity { Id = "5", FullName = "Terry" };
    PersonEntity p6 = new PersonEntity { Id = "6", FullName = "Micheal" };
    PersonEntity p7 = new PersonEntity { Id = "7", FullName = "Jordy" };

    Queue.AddToQueue(null, p1);
    Queue.AddToQueue(p1, p2);
    Queue.AddToQueue(p1, p3);
    Queue.AddToQueue(p1, p4);
    Queue.AddToQueue(p3, p4);
    Queue.AddToQueue(p2, p3);
    Queue.AddToQueue(p1, p5);
    Queue.AddToQueue(p5, p6);
    Queue.AddToQueue(p6, p7);
}
```

The relationships are defined by putting them into the Queue. The first one has the Root entity set to null. This will only create the Referred entity without a relationship to another entity, and is used for the first entity put into the 3D model.

The next method is called LoadData. This method determines, by using a precompiler directive UNITY_EDITOR, if the app is started in the editor or on a device. The CreateSampleData is called when the app runs in the editor. Copy the following method into the DataModel class:

```
public void LoadData()
{
    InitializeConnection();
```

```
#if UNITY_EDITOR
    CreateSampleData();
#else
            Office365DataHub.Services.PeopleService.Instance.GetCurrentUser
            (OnGetPersonCompleted);
#endif
}
```

The GetCurrentUser method is called when the app is running on the device. The first call will call the AuthenticationHelper class to authenticate against Microsoft Azure Active Directory. This will show a popup dialog asking for credentials, and is explained later in this chapter. The call to GetCurrentUser requires a delegation or callback method. This method is called OnGetPersonCompleted. The method checks the returned PersonRequest object for the exception.Error to check if there are any errors. Errors are handled accordingly and can be shown through, for example, a dialog or through a debug window. Copy the following method in the DataModel class:

```
public void OnGetPersonCompleted(PersonRequest request)
{
    if (request.expection.Error != Office365DataHub.ServiceError.NoError)
    {
        DebugInformation.Instance.Log(request.expection.Exception.
        Message);
        DebugInformation.Instance.Log(request.expection.Exception.
        StackTrace);
        DebugInformation.Instance.Log(request.expection.Exception.
        InnerException.Message);
    }

    Queue.AddToQueue(null, request.person);

    RelatedPeopleRequest relrequest = new RelatedPeopleRequest
    {
        person = request.person
    };
```

```
Office365DataHub.Services.PeopleService.Instance.
GetRelatedPeople(relrequest, OnGetRelatedPersonCompleted,
OnGetRelatedPeopleCompleted);
}
```

The returned current user is added to the queue using the AddToQueue method. Subsequently a call to GetRelatedPeople based on the current user is executed. That method uses two delegates or callbacks to return the related people data. In this example, only the OnGetRelatedPersonCompleted method is used to add entities on the queue. Copy the following method in the DataModel class:

```
public void OnGetRelatedPersonCompleted(RelatedPeopleRequest request)
{
    Queue.AddToQueue(request.person, request.relatedPerson);
}

public void OnGetRelatedPeopleCompleted(RelatedPeopleRequest request)
{
}
```

Relationships between entities are added by AddToQueue with both entities.

Extend the GraphController

Since we moved all the code for getting entities into separate classes like DataModel and DataQueue, we need to do extend the GraphController class using these classes. A reference to a DataModel instance is added to the GraphController class, which will be used to initialize, load, and access the entities. Add the properties model and nodes to the GraphController class as follows:

```
public class GraphController : MonoBehaviour
{
    private DataModel model = new DataModel();

    private Dictionary<string, Node> nodes = new Dictionary<string, Node>();
}
```

We also require a dictionary to store all created nodes and edges based on their identification. This allows us to quickly identify if a node or edge is already created. A node represents an entity, while an edge represents the relationship between two nodes. Add the following code to the Start method of the GraphController class:

```
void Start()
{
    Initialize();

    model.LoadData();
}
```

The Start method only requires calling the LoadData method of the DataModel property. This will initialize the connection and start the process of getting the current user and the related people. Add the following code to the Update method in the GraphController class:

```
void Update()
{
    HandleQueue(model.Queue);

    graphRenderer.Draw(NodeUpdate);
}
```

The Update method does two things. It retrieves and handles the next first item in the queue by calling the HandleQueue method with DataQueue object in the DataModel class. Second, it calls the graph renderer to draw the force-directed graph model based on the created nodes and edges. Add the following method to the GraphController class:

```
public void HandleQueue(DataQueue queue)
{
    BaseEntity root;
    BaseEntity refering;
    GameObject go;

    if (queue.GetFromQueue(out root, out refering))
    {
        Node rootNode = nodes.ContainsKey(root.Id) ? nodes[root.Id] : null;
```

```
        Node referingNode = refering != null ? nodes.ContainsKey(refering.
        Id) ? nodes[refering.Id] : null : null;

        if (root != null && rootNode == null)
        {
            go = CreateNode(root.Id);
            NodeInformation nodeInfo = go.GetComponent<NodeInformation>();
            nodes[nodeInfo.node.ID] = nodeInfo.node;
            rootNode = nodeInfo.node;
            nodeInfo.entity = root;
        }

        if (refering != null && referingNode == null)
        {
            go = CreateNode(refering.Id);
            NodeInformation nodeInfo = go.GetComponent<NodeInformation>();
            nodes[nodeInfo.node.ID] = nodeInfo.node;
            referingNode = nodeInfo.node;
            nodeInfo.entity = refering;
        }

        if (rootNode != null && referingNode != null)
        {
            go = CreateEdge(rootNode, referingNode);
            EdgeInformation edgeInfo = go.GetComponent<EdgeInformation>();
        }
    }
}
```

The HandleQueue method creates the actual *GameObjects* based on the NodePrefab and the EdgePrefab. This method executes based on several rules, which are described as follows:

- The method checks if there is an item in the queue.

- Both root and referring nodes are checked if they already exist.

- A node and corresponding *GameObject* are created for the root if not yet present. The root is set and stored in the created nodes list.

- A node and corresponding *GameObject* are created for the referring if not yet present. The referring is set and stored in the created nodes list.

- An edge and corresponding *GameObject* are created when both root and referring are available.

Extend the Node

The current node prefab only contains a GameObject, which represents the node as a cube. We want to extend the prefab in such a way that shows the full name of the person. Open the prefab by double-clicking it. This will show the prefab and its contents as in Figure 10-3.

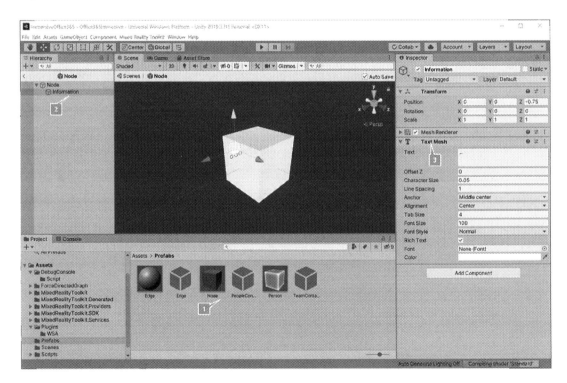

Figure 10-3. *Extending the node with a TextMesh*

Create an empty GameObject as a child object under the node by right-clicking the Node GameObject and select *Create Empty*. Make sure that it is placed in front of the cube by setting the *Position* to (0, 0, -0,75) in the Transform component.

Add a `TextMesh` component to that new child `GameObject`. Set the following values to configure the text:

- **Character Size** = *0.05*

- **Font Size** = 100

- **Anchor** = *Middle center*

- **Alignment** = *Center*

Keep in mind that the text is not occluded by other objects and will therefore seemly appearing through the cubes if you look from another site. We have left out occlusion to simplify the model. Update the script in the `NodeInformation` class by replacing it with the following code:

```
using EpForceDirectedGraph.cs;
using Office365DataHub.Entities;
using System;
using System.Collections;
using System.Collections.Generic;
using UnityEngine;

public class NodeInformation : MonoBehaviour
{
    public Node node = null;
    public BaseEntity entity = null;

    private TextMesh textMesh = null;

    private void Start()
    {
        textMesh = gameObject.GetComponentInChildren<TextMesh>();
    }

    private void Update()
    {
        if (textMesh != null && node != null)
        {
            PersonEntity person = entity as PersonEntity;
            if (person != null)
```

```
        {
            textMesh.text = person.FullName;
        }
    }
  }
}
```

In the Start method, we retrieve the TextMesh component. We need to use the GetComponentInChildren to retrieve it, since the TextMesh is one level deeper.

We need to add the Update method. The text is set to the FullName of the person when the TextMesh is found and the entity property is correctly set. The entity property is set by the HandleQueue that was described earlier.

Result in HoloLens

The final step is getting it all to work on a Microsoft HoloLens 2 device. The first step is building a Visual Studio solution via Unity. Open the *Build Settings* dialog via *File ➤ Build Settings*. You will notice that I have selected ARM64 in the settings, as shown in Figure 10-4. But it does not matter which target architecture you choose. The solution will be built again in Visual Studio.

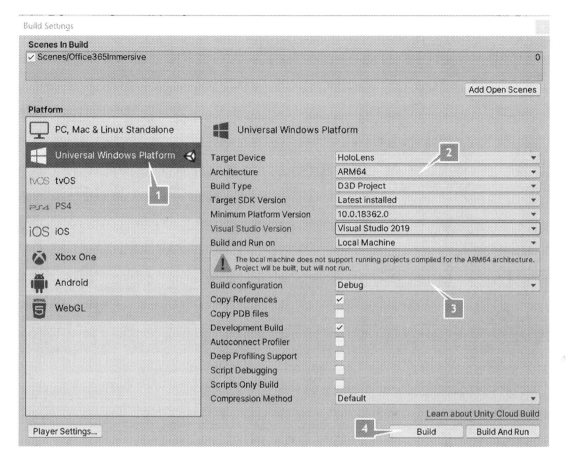

Figure 10-4. *Build a Visual Studio solution using the Build settings dialog*

Using the right target, architecture, Target SDK, and platform version inside Unity will give you more confidence that the solution compiles without any errors when building the solution in Visual Studio.

Press the Build button to start the build. This will create a Visual Studio solution with native CPP code.

Build the solution against ARM64 in Visual Studio and deploy it to your Microsoft HoloLens 2 device. Use the x64 build if you are using the HoloLens 2 emulator.

Start the application on your device or emulator. The application will request you as a user to authenticate against Microsoft Azure Active Directory. It requires a username and password of a work or school account, as is shown in Figure 10-5.

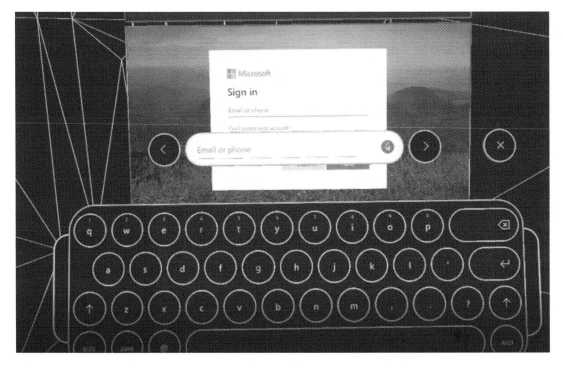

Figure 10-5. *Authenticate against Microsoft Azure Active Directory*

The application requires several permissions to access certain parts of the Microsoft Graph. In our example, we need to have access to users and related people. For that, we define the following Scopes property in the DataModel class:

```
Scopes = new string[] {
"User.Read",
"User.Read.All",
"People.Read",
"People.Read.All" };
```

The application will request the user to give consent to those permissions, as you can see in Figure 10-6. These permissions are more readable than the ones we defined in the Scopes property. To use the application, the user needs to give consent. It is also important to understand that the user needs to have those permissions in the first place.

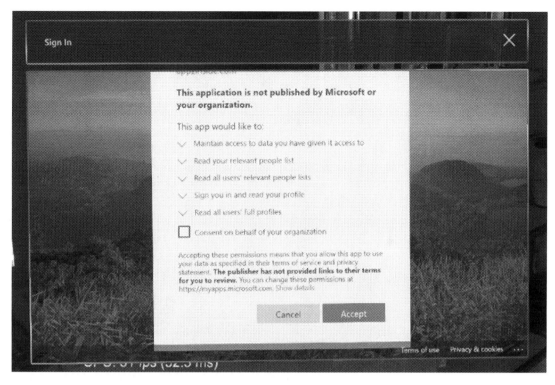

Figure 10-6. *Give the application consent as a user*

If the user has an administrative role, the user can consent on behalf of their organization. This will prevent other users from being presented with the same consent question.

The application will now access the Office 365 data via the Microsoft Graph API on behalf of the logged-on user. The information is stored in the DataQueue via the DataModel class. The GraphController will update itself based on the items stored in the DataQueue. This will build the 3D model, as shown in Figure 10-7.

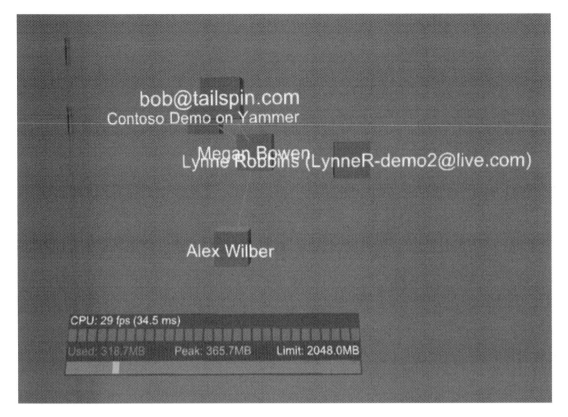

Figure 10-7. *The application gets data from Office 365 and builds the 3D model*

The next chapter will expand the application by primarily focusing on interacting with the model based on gestures.

CHAPTER 11

Interact with the Model

We have learned a lot in the previous chapters when it comes to building Microsoft HoloLens 2 applications that can retrieve content from the Office 365 platform via the Microsoft Graph into a 3D model, based on the authenticated and authorized user. But there is not yet any interaction possible with the model. We discussed some different gestures and interactions in Chapter 6, and the ability to move a person from one collection to another. This final chapter shows how you can pick people from the force redirect graph model into one of the collections to form teams, and have menus in place to make this a proper application running on a Microsoft HoloLens 2.

Hand Menu

We start by implementing the hand menu. The hand menu allows us to pop up a menu using several different types of controls and buttons to handle different actions in our application. This allows us to easily access different global functions of our application that are not necessarily bound to the context the user is in.

In Figure 11-1 you can see an overview of the end result, based on all the steps we need to take to get a hand menu implemented in our application:

1. Create an empty *GameObject* called *HandMenu* by right-clicking the scene and select Create empty.

2. Select the *HandMenu* GameObject.

© Alexander Meijers 2020
A. Meijers, *Immersive Office 365*, https://doi.org/10.1007/978-1-4842-5845-3_11

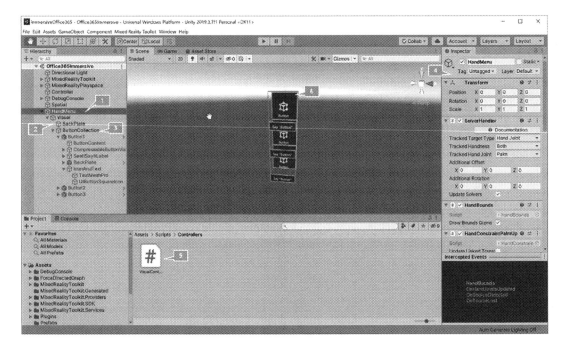

Figure 11-1. *An overview of the end results and the different parts t are used*

We need to add two components to this *GameObject* via the Add Component button in the Inspector window:

1. Add the component *SolverHandler.* A solver component facilitates the position and orientation of an object based on different algorithms. The *SolverHandler* references and updates the object to track it against, for example, the main camera, the ray, or the hands. We will track the hands by changing the property *Tracked Target Type* to *Hand Joint.*

2. Add the component *HandConstraintPalmUp,* which is also based on a solver. We do not need to change any settings. We will be adding some events later.

The next step creates the actual menu shown next to the hand and is placed under a child *GameObject* called *Visual.* We start with the background. Create a Quad *GameObject* under *Visual* with the name *BackPlate.* Change the material to *HolographicBackPlate.* Use the following settings for the transform component:

- **Position** (0.0, 0.0, 0.01)
- **Scale** (0.0032, 0.096, 0.02)

278

Create another empty *GameObject* under *Visual* and call that *ButtonCollection*. Add the *GridObjectCollection* component. This will arrange all the underlaying buttons in the right position. The default settings are OK for our menu.

We will add three buttons. Buttons will be created based on the *PressableButtonHoloLens2.prefab* defined in the MRTK v2. Each button is added by dragging the *PressableButtonHoloLens2.prefab* as a child under the *ButtonCollection*. You can find the prefab by searching for the name in the search field above the project assets. As soon as you drag the first button into the hierarchy, a *TMP Importer* popup will appear that requests you to install the *TMP Essentials*. This is caused due to the buttons using *TextMeshPro*. The *TMP importer* dialog is shown in Figure 11-2.

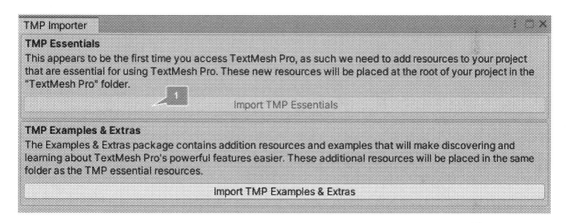

Figure 11-2. *TMP Importer dialog*

You will notice that the buttons are not lining up directly. You will find an *Update Collection* button in the *GridObjectCollection*. Pressing the button will rearrange all the buttons that are defined under the *ButtonCollection GameObject*. You need to press the button again when adding additional buttons. Keep in mind that the *BackPlate* does not resize automatically. That is something you have to do yourself. For now, the *BackPlate* has the correct size for three buttons. As soon as you have another button count, you will need to change the size of the *Backplate* via the Transform component of the *BackPlate*.

If we don't do anything, the menu appears and stays visible as soon as we hold our hand up. We want to add behavior that shows the menu when holding up our hand and hides the menu when the hand goes into another position. We need to implement two actions based on events. Go to the *HandConstraintPalmUp* component under the *HandMenu* GameObject. You will notice an *On First Hand Detected()* property. Adding a new event is done through the plus button. For each event, you will need to specify when it is available, which object it corresponds to, and what function with optional parameters need to be called.

Add the following actions to the events.

Event	When	Object	Function
On First Hand Detected	Runtime only	Visual	GameObject.SetActive with checkbox checked
On Last Hand Lost	Runtime only	Visual	GameObject.SetActive with checkbox unchecked

The object *Visual* needs to be dragged onto the object field in the event. The result of adding both actions is shown in Figure 11-3.

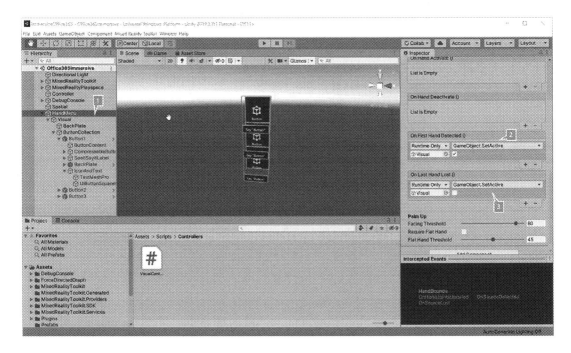

Figure 11-3. *Actions placed on the event of the HandMenu*

We implement two of the three buttons to execute actions in our application. The first action is toggling the 3D Models' visibility. This requires us to create a class called VisualController. This class will have a public method called ToggleActive() and will show or hide the *GameObject* to which it is attached. Because the functionality is placed in a separate component, it allows us to reuse it on any *GameObject* in our scene.

Create a new script file called VisualController in the folder Assets/App/Scripts/Controllers. Add the following code to the script:

```
using UnityEngine;

public class VisualController : MonoBehaviour
{
    public void ToggleActive()
    {
        gameObject.SetActive(!isActiveAndEnabled);
    }
}
```

Add the *VisualController* component to the *GraphController* GameObject by selecting the *GraphController* GameObject, and use the Add Component button in the Inspector window.

Calling ToggleActive() will show or hide the 3D model generated by the *GraphController*. Add an action to an event on the first button. Select *Button1* GameObject. Look for the *Button Released()* property and use the plus button to add a new event. Use the following settings to set the event.

Event	When	Object	Function
Button Released	Runtime only	Controller	VisualController. ToggleActive

The object *Controller* needs to be dragged onto the object field in the event. The result of adding the action is shown in Figure 11-4.

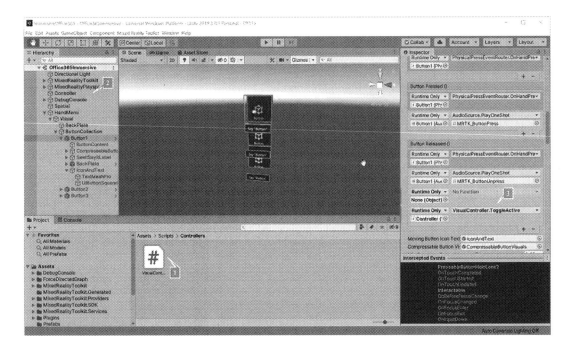

Figure 11-4. *Adding an action to the Button Pressed event of the first button*

The second button will reload the content for the 3D model. We need to create a new method Reload() on the GraphController class, since this is specific to the GraphController. The code is shown as follows:

```
public void Reload()
{
    gameObject.SetActive(true);

    nodes.Clear();

    foreach (Transform child in gameObject.transform)
    {
        GameObject.Destroy(child.gameObject);
    }

    Initialize();

    model.LoadData();
}
```

Add an action to an event on the third button. Select *Button3* GameObject. Look for the *Button Released()* property and use the plus button to add a new event. Use the following settings.

Event	When	Object	Function
Button Released	Runtime only	Controller	GraphController.Reload

The object *Controller* needs to be dragged onto the object field in the event.

We can define two major interactions: interaction with the model itself and interaction between models. Interactions with the model itself incorporate moving it around and rotating the model. Other examples are a context menu displaying different actions on the model.

Draggable Container

The draggable container is a concept that allows us to move and rotate a model. The MRTK delivers a set of components that we can use to give the draggable container these features. But enabling the features requires some area that we can touch. We cannot use the entire model. Doing that would prevent us from selecting the objects in the model. Therefore, we will add a header to the draggable container. This header has a background and text. Touching the header will allow us to control the features of moving and rotating.

Create an empty *GameObject* in the root of the scene and call it DraggableContainer. Add an empty *GameObject* named *Header*, a child. Create a Quad *GameObject* named *BackPlate* as a child of *Header. The BackPlate* is used to create a visible background for our header. Set the properties of the transform of the *BackPlate* GameObject to the following values:

- **Position** (0.0, 0.0, 0.001)

- **Scale** (0.32, 0.08, 1)

Change the material of the mesh renderer to HolographicBackPlate.

Create an empty *GameObject* named *Title* as child of *Header*. Add a *TextMeshPro – Text* component and set the following values:

- **Text** – Draggable container

- **Font Size** – 0.16

- **Alignment** – Center horizontally and vertically

The next step is building in the features of moving and rotation. Add a *Box Collider* component to the *Header*. Set the following values:

- **Size** – (0.08, 0.02, 0.01)

This box collider allows us to hit the header of the draggable container.

Add a *BoundingBox* component to the *Header*. This component has the features built in for rotation and shows a fancy wireframe around the header when we come into its proximity. Set the following values:

- **Target Object** – Drag the *DraggableContainer* into this field.

- **Bounds Override** – Drag the *Box Collider* component from this *Header* in here.

- **Activation** – Activate By Proximity and Pointer. This allows us to activate the bounding box when our hands get close to the header, as when we use a far pointer.

- **Box Material** – BoundingBox

- **Box Grabbed Material** – BoudingBoxGrabbed

- **Handle Material** – BoundingBoxHandleWhite

- **Handle Grabbed Material** – BoundingBoxHandleBlueGrabbed

- **Show Scale Handles** – unchecked

- **Show Rotation Handle for X** – unchecked

- **Show Rotation Handle for Z** – unchecked

Add the *NearInteractionGrabbable* component to the *Header*. This will allow us to do near gestures on the *Header*.

And finally, add the *ManipulationHandler* to the *Header*. This allows us to define which object we are manipulating and how it can be manipulated. Set the following values:

- **Host Transform** – Drag the *DraggableContainer* into this field.

- **Manipulation Type** – One hand only. We require only one hand, since we are not allowed to resize the object.

- **Constrain on Rotation** – Y-axis only

The final part is adding two actions on the manipulation events in the *ManipulationHandler* component. These events will make sure the wireframe around the header will be in sync during movement of the model.

Event	When	Object	Function
On Manipulation Started	Runtime only	Header (Bounding Box)	BoundingBox. HighlightWires
On Manipulation Ended	Runtime only	Header (Bounding Box)	BoundingBox. UnhighlightWires

Now drag the *DraggableContainer* and all its elements into the `Assets/App/Prefabs` folder. This will automatically create a prefab of the *DraggableContainer*. Remove the *DraggableContainer* GameObject from the scene.

Draggable Model

Let's make our model with the related people draggable by using our new *DraggableContainer* prefab. Create in the root of the scene an empty GameObject called *Containers*.

Drag the *DraggableContainer* prefab onto the *Containers* GameObject. This will create a child GameObject based on the prefab. Rename the child GameObject to *DraggableModel*. The header needs to be more in the front, since the model creates itself in three dimensions. Set the position in the *Transform* of the *Header* to (`0.0, 0.35, 0.0`).

Now drag the *Controller* GameObject, which is in the root of the scene, under this *DraggableModel* as a child *GameObject*. And that is it!

Draggable Containers

We want to have the same behavior for containers. In this case we want to build the draggable containers dynamically. This allows us to create these containers by pressing the second button on the hand menu. That requires us to create a script called ContainerController with a method called CreateContainer. Create a new script file called ContainerController under the folder Assets/App/Scripts/Controllers. Add the following code to the file:

```
using Microsoft.MixedReality.Toolkit.Utilities;
using TMPro;
using UnityEngine;

public class ContainerController : MonoBehaviour
{
    public GameObject Root = null;

    public GameObject DraggableContainerPrefab = null;

    public GameObject ContainerPrefab = null;

    public string ContainerTitle = "";

    public void CreateContainer()
    {
        // create draggablecontainer
        GameObject draggable = GameObject.Instantiate(DraggableContainerPr
        efab);
        draggable.transform.parent = Root.transform;

        // create container
        GameObject container = GameObject.Instantiate(ContainerPrefab);
        container.transform.parent = draggable.transform;

        // set title
        Transform title = draggable.transform.Find("Header/Title");
        title.GetComponent<TextMeshPro>().text = ContainerTitle;

        // set position and rotation according to camera
        draggable.transform.position = Camera.main.transform.position;
```

```
        draggable.transform.rotation = Quaternion.Euler(0, Camera.main.
        transform.eulerAngles.y, 0);
        draggable.transform.Translate(Vector3.forward * 2, Space.Self);
    }
}
```

The class contains several public properties allowing us to set the prefabs for the draggable container and the container holding the persons. It also contains a reference to the *GameObject* that will be the root for all created containers. Container creation is easy. We instantiate a *DraggableContainer* object and set its parent in the root reference. A container is instantiated under the *DraggableContainer*. The title of the header is set to ContainerTitle. In the last step, we set the draggable container two meters in front of the user wearing the device. It is important that the container only rotates around the Y-axis.

The position of the draggable container is set to the position of the user by setting it to the main camera.

```
draggable.transform.position = Camera.main.transform.position;
```

The draggable container is rotated only over the Y-axis based on the Y angle of the main camera.

```
draggable.transform.rotation = Quaternion.Euler(0, Camera.main.transform.
eulerAngles.y, 0);
```

Then the draggable container is set in front of the device.

```
draggable.transform.Translate(Vector3.forward * 2, Space.Self);
```

Create in the scene a location where containers are created by adding an empty *GameObject* named *Containers* at the highest level of the hierarchy, as shown in Figure 11-5.

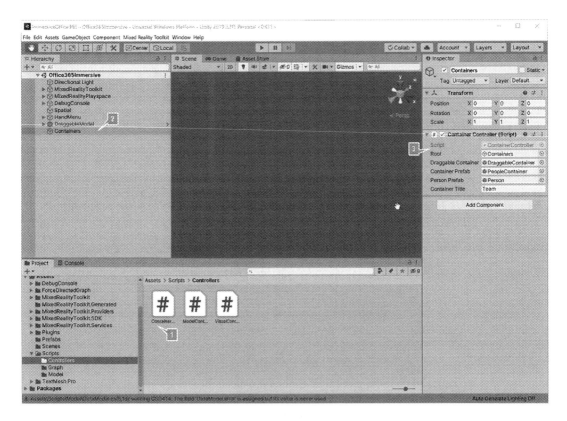

Figure 11-5. *A location is set where new containers are created*

Add the *ContainerController* component to the *Containers*. Drag the Containers into the Root property. Drag the *DraggableContainer* prefab into the *Draggable Container* property. Drag the *PeopleContainer* prefab into the Container Prefab property. Set the container title to *Team*.

Select the *Button2* GameObject under the hand menu, as shown in Figure 11-6.

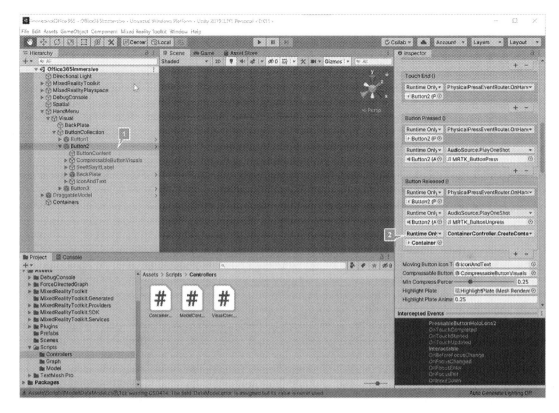

Figure 11-6. *Adding an action to the button released event for creating a new container under Containers*

The final part is adding an action on the button released event. Use the plus button under the event property to add a new event with the following settings.

Event	When	Object	Function
Button Released	Runtime only	Containers	ContainerControl. CreateContainer()

Whenever the second button is hit, a new container is created in front of the user. Each container can be moved and rotated in the room.

Move People Between Containers

We want to be able to move people between containers and the model. The containers make use of the *Person* prefab. This *Person* prefab has to move between containers by dragging with your hands or using far gestures. This behavior is implemented in the `ObjectDataBehavior` class.

Our model is based on the `GraphController` class, which uses at the moment the *Node* prefab. We need to change this to the *Person* prefab by dragging the *Person* Prefab onto the *Node prefab* property (Figure 11-7).

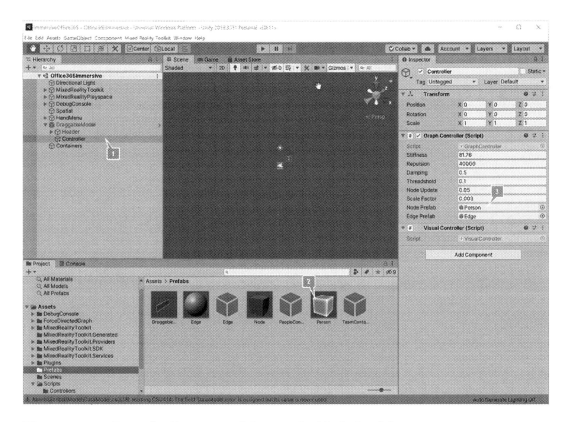

Figure 11-7. *Drag the Person prefab onto the Node Prefab property*

We need to update the `ObjectDataBehavior` class to get everything to work. It starts with adding a property called `IsPartOfGraphController`, which will store true if the Person object is part of the model and not of a collection.

```
private bool isPartOfGraphController = false;
```

Moving people between different collections is removing them from the source collection and adding them to the destination collection. The model is a special collection of content returned from the Microsoft Graph. We don't want items to move out of the model. Therefore, a method `Duplicate()` is added. This method duplicates the *Person* based on the *Person* in the model.

```
private GameObject Duplicate()
{
    return GameObject.Instantiate(gameObject);
}
```

There are two important methods that require attention. One is called `OnPointerDown` and the other is `OnPointerUp`. There are several things happening in the `OnPointerDown`. We check if the *Person* is part of a model or a collection. The *Person* is duplicated and assigned to the object to move property `objectToMove` when it is part of a model. Add the following method to the `ObjectDataBehavior` class:

```
public void OnPointerDown(MixedRealityPointerEventData eventData)
{
    objectToMove = gameObject;

    // store the collection
    initialCollection = objectToMove.transform.parent;

    // check if part of the model
    isPartOfGraphController = initialCollection.
    GetComponent<GraphController>() != null ? true : false;

    if (isPartOfGraphController)
    {
        objectToMove = Duplicate();
    }

    // detach from the collection
    objectToMove.transform.parent = null;
}
```

The last change is in the `OnPointerUp` method. The code retrieves all collections based on the *GridObjectCollection* component. Then the distance between the *Person* and each found collection is measured. The collection found that is closest and closer

291

than 1 meter, is assigned as the collection to which the *Person* will be added. The Person object is returned to its initial collection when no nearby collection was found. The *Person*, the duplicate, is deleted when it came from a model.

A part of the method assigns the *Person* to the destination collection. If the destination collection is found and the *Person* is part of the model, a duplicate is generated and added to the destination collection. Otherwise, the *Person* is moved to the destination collection. Add the following method to the ObjectDataBehavior class:

```
public void OnPointerUp(MixedRealityPointerEventData eventData)
{
    GridObjectCollection[] collections = initialCollection.parent.parent.
    GetComponentsInChildren<GridObjectCollection>();

    // find closest collection
    float distance = 1f;
    GameObject closestCollection = null;

    foreach(GridObjectCollection collection in collections)
    {
        GameObject go = collection.gameObject;

        float dist = Vector3.Distance(go.transform.position, objectToMove.
        transform.position);
        if (dist < distance)
        {
            distance = dist;
            closestCollection = go;
        }
    }

    // update the parent to the closest collection
    if (closestCollection != null)
    {
        // set the closest collection as parent
        objectToMove.transform.parent = closestCollection.transform;

        // update the closest collection
```

```
    GridObjectCollection goc = closestCollection.GetComponent<GridObjec
    tCollection>();
    goc.UpdateCollection();

    if (!isPartOfGraphController)
    {
        // update the initial collection when no model
        GridObjectCollection gocInitial = initialCollection.GetComponen
        t<GridObjectCollection>();
        gocInitial.UpdateCollection();
    }

}
else
{
    if (isPartOfGraphController)
    {
        // remove duplicated item since no closest collection was found
        GameObject.Destroy(objectToMove);
    }
    else
    {
        // set back to the initial collection
        objectToMove.transform.parent = initialCollection;

        // update the initial collection
        GridObjectCollection gocInitial = initialCollection.GetComponen
        t<GridObjectCollection>();
        gocInitial.UpdateCollection();
    }
}
}
```

The preceding code requires us to move the model to the same *GameObject*
Containers as where the other collections are created. The result is shown in Figure 11-8.

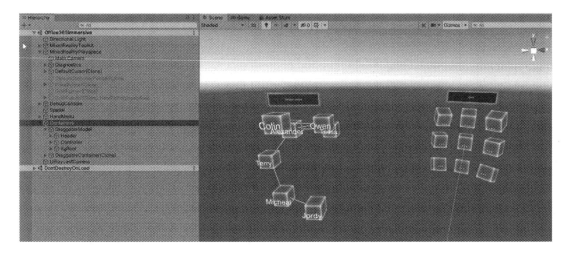

Figure 11-8. *Collections and model in the same Containers GameObject*

This allows us to move *Person* objects from one collection to another or duplicate a
Person from the model to a collection.

Remove a Person from a Collection

The last step is removing a person added to a collection. It would be nice to have some
sort of context menu that appears at the *Person* object to remove it. The *AppBar* is a great
menu that has some default buttons implemented like Show, Hide, Remove, and Close,
and attaches itself to the object. But creating a separate *AppBar* per *Person* would be
create too much overhead on the system and cause performance issues. It is better to
have a single context menu per collection, which only appears when you come into the
proximity with your index finger:

1. Search for *AppBar.prefab* in the search field of the *Assets* windows.

2. Drag the prefab into the highest level of the hierarchy and rename
   it to *ContextMenu*.

3. Uncheck the *Use Adjust* and *Use Hide* properties.

4. Now drag the *ContextMenu* into the prefabs folder. This will automatically transform it into a prefab. But because *ContextMenu* is based on an existing prefab, a popup dialog will appear requesting how to handle this new prefab. Select *Prefab Variant* as shown in Figure 11-9.

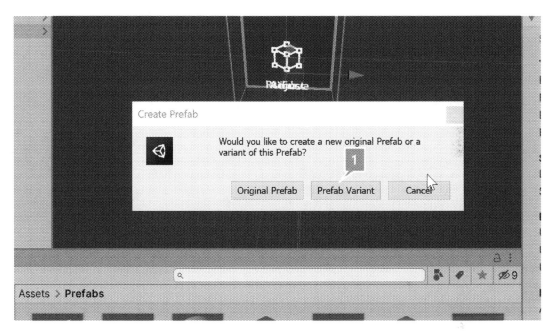

Figure 11-9. *A dialog requesting what type of prefab you want to create*

This option will create a new prefab based as a variant on the original prefab. Changes to the original prefab will be automatically updated into this new prefab. The complete process of these steps is shown in Figure 11-10.

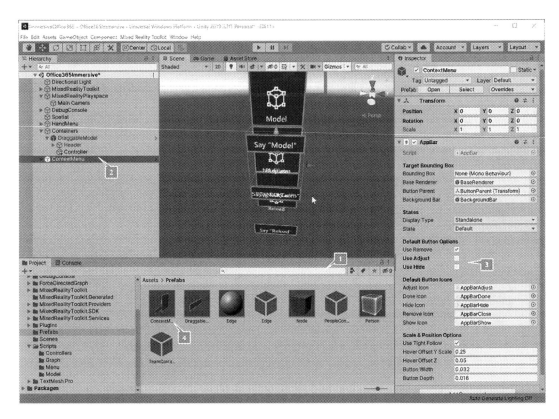

Figure 11-10. *Create the ContextMenu prefab based on the AppBar prefab*

Create a new folder `Assets/App/Scripts/Menu`. Create a new script called `ContextMenu` in this folder. This script will take care of showing and hiding the menu at the designated Person object which is closest and implements the removal of the Person. We have a public property called `ContextMenuPrefab`, which should contain a reference to the *ContextMenu* prefab which we created earlier. The second property `ActivationDistance` determines when the context menu is shown. Copy the following code into the `ContextMenu` file:

```
using Microsoft.MixedReality.Toolkit.Input;
using Microsoft.MixedReality.Toolkit.UI;
using Microsoft.MixedReality.Toolkit.Utilities;
using UnityEngine;

public class ContextMenu : MonoBehaviour
{
    public GameObject ContextMenuPrefab = null;
```

```
    public float ActivationDistance = 0.4f;
    private GameObject contextMenu = null;
    private AppBar contextMenuBar = null;
}
```

We need to store some global variables in the class. The first instantiates a *GameObject* based on the ContextMenuPrefab. The second one stores the actual *AppBar* component. Add the following method to the ContextMenu class:

```
void Start()
{
    contextMenu = GameObject.Instantiate(ContextMenuPrefab);
    contextMenuBar = contextMenu.GetComponent<AppBar>();
    contextMenu.SetActive(false);
}
```

The Update method tries to get the current pose of the tip of the index finger of one or both hands. We need to execute several steps if we get the pose. We start with getting the *BoundingBox* components of all the *Persons* in the collection. Then we need to check if one of them is the closest and within the range of the activation distance. The context menu is made active and bound to the one that is the closest. Bounding the *AppBar* is by setting its *BoundingBox* to the Target property. Add the following method to the ContextMenu class:

```
void Update()
{
    MixedRealityPose pose;

    // determine if any of the index tip fingers are tracked
    if (HandJointUtils.TryGetJointPose(TrackedHandJoint.IndexTip,
    Handedness.Any, out pose))
    {
        BoundingBox[] collection = gameObject.GetComponentsInChildren<Bound
        ingBox>();

        // find closest collection
        float distance = ActivationDistance;

        BoundingBox activeBox = null;
```

```
    foreach (BoundingBox item in collection)
    {
        float dist = Vector3.Distance(item.gameObject.transform.
        position, pose.Position);

        if (dist < distance)
        {
            distance = dist;
            activeBox = item;
        }
    }

    if (activeBox != null)
    {
        contextMenu.SetActive(true);
        contextMenuBar.Target = activeBox;
    }
    else
    {
        contextMenu.SetActive(false);
    }
}
else
{
    contextMenu.SetActive(false);
    gameObject.GetComponent<GridObjectCollection>().UpdateCollection();
}
}
}
```

The context menu is hidden when the hand is not visible anymore and not detected by the TryGetJointPose method. There is a reason why we update the collection when the hand is not visible anymore. If we were to update the collection from the remove command, we could accidentally hit the next Person object and remove more.

We need to implement the remove action. It requires creating a listener on the remove button. There are several ways of doing this. But for now we'll use the Find method, since we know the exact path to the remove button GameObject. Add the following code at the end in the Start method of the ContextMenu class:

```
void Start()
{
    ...

    // add listener to remove button
    Transform buttonRemove = contextMenu.transform.Find("BaseRenderer/
    ButtonParent/Remove");
    PressableButtonHoloLens2 button = buttonRemove.GetComponent<Pressable
    ButtonHoloLens2>();
    button.ButtonPressed.AddListener(Remove);
}
```

Retrieve the `PressableButtonHoloLens2` class and add a listener through the `ButtonPressed.AddListener()` method. The listener method is called `Remove()`. It looks for the *GameObject* object based on the target set to the *AppBar* and destroys it. Add the following method to the `ContextMenu` class:

```
public void Remove()
{
    GameObject.Destroy(contextMenuBar.Target.gameObject);
}
```

In the last step, we need to add this `ContextMenu` script to the *PeopleContainer* prefab, as shown in Figure 11-11. Double-click the *PeopleContainer* prefab and add the script via de *Add Component* button in the inspector.

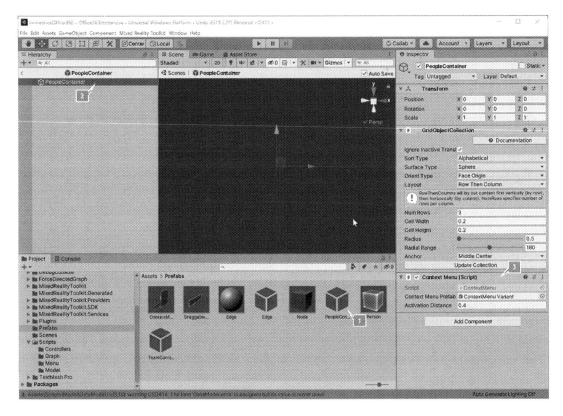

Figure 11-11. *Adding the Context Menu script to the PeopleContainer prefab*

Make sure you drag the *ContextMenu variant.prefab* into the *Context Menu Prefab* property. You can leave the *Activation Distance* property set to 0.4.

Build your Visual Studio solution via the Build Settings menu in Unity. Build the Visual Studio solution and deploy it to the HoloLens 2 emulator or a Microsoft HoloLens 2.

Start the application. Enter the credentials of your Office 365 tenant when the login screen appears. The application will start accessing the Office 365 tenant through the Microsoft Graph and retrieves related people, as shown in Figure 11-12.

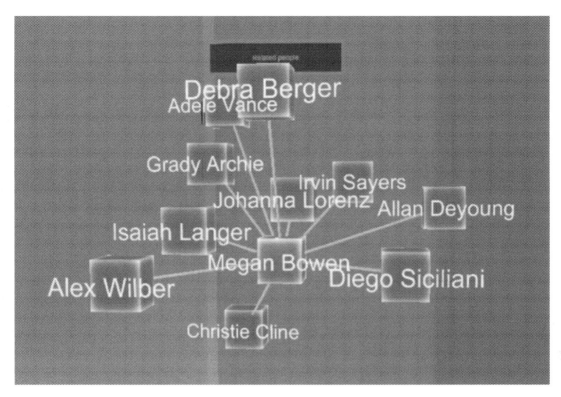

Figure 11-12. *Related people for Megan Bowen are shown in a force-directed graph model*

Use the hand palm menu to add a new Team model in your space. You can drag both the force-directed graph model and the Team model around by grabbing the title field with one of your hands. Grab one or more persons from the force-directed graph model and move them toward the Team model. As soon as you let them go within the range of the Team model, the persons are added, as shown in Figure 11-13.

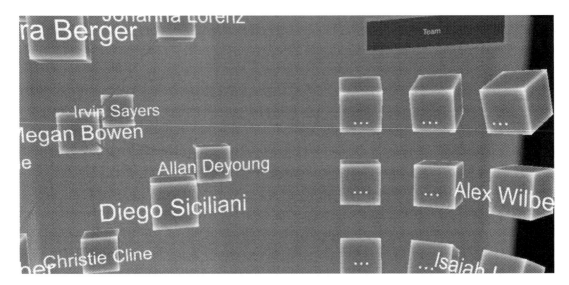

Figure 11-13. *Different people dragged from the force-directed graph into a visual team*

This final chapter has helped you build some interesting interactions with your model and collections. It allowed you to move people between the collections and the model itself. It also showed you how to interact with them each in a different way—using a hand menu for global actions, a context menu for context-specific actions, and hand gestures for moving objects around between collections.

Conclusion

Hopefully, this book has helped you as a .NET developer to understand from an Office 365 perspective how to implement an immersive application using Microsoft HoloLens 2 in combination with the Office 365 platform using the Microsoft Graph. As a mixed reality developer, this book will bring you closer to the other great parts of the Microsoft stack. It has hopefully helped you to realize the possibilities with building immersive applications using the Office 365 platform, which will give you more capabilities.

Index

A

AppBar, 294
Application architecture, 223, 224
Asset Store, 90
Augmented reality, 3
Authentication
    code, 231
    DelegateAuthenticationProvider, 234
    GraphServiceClient object, 233
    high-level permissions, 232
    login screen, user, 231
    PublicClientApplicatioBuilder class, 231
    UseBetaAPI, 229
    UserLogon property, 229
    variables, 230

B

Build Window, 90
ButtonPressed.AddListener() method, 299
Button Released() property, 281

C

Camera component, 108, 109
Collider components, 101, 102
Content retrieval
    batch processing, 43, 44, 46
    Graph Explorer, 47, 48
    insights, 58–60

Microsoft Graph API, 41, 42
Microsoft Graph client library, 49, 50
people entity, 56, 57
teams, 52–55
throttling, 43
user, 51, 52
Coroutines, 122
    code, 124
    IEnumerator object, 123
    postpone, 124
    stop, 124
    yield return null, 123

D

Data model
    AuthenticationHelper class, 266
    CreateSampleData, 265
    GraphController class, 264
    OnGetRelatedPersonCompleted
        method, 267
    referred entity, 265
    script file, 263
Data queue
    AddToQueue, 263
    DataQueueItem class, 262, 263
    ImmersiveOffice365Hub assembly, 262
Data visualization
    awareness phase, 198, 199
    back-end systems, 198

H

I, J, K